Wallace

Also by Jim Gorant

The Lost Dogs

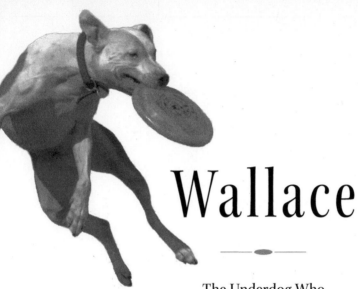

Wallace

The Underdog Who

Conquered a Sport,

Saved a Marriage, and

Championed Pit Bulls—

One Flying Disc at a Time

Jim Gorant

GOTHAM
BOOKS

GOTHAM BOOKS
Published by Penguin Group (USA) Inc.
375 Hudson Street, New York, New York 10014, U.S.A.
Penguin Group (Canada), 90 Eglinton Avenue East, Suite 700, Toronto, Ontario M4P 2Y3, Canada (a
division of Pearson Penguin Canada Inc.); Penguin Books Ltd, 80 Strand, London WC2R 0RL, En-
gland; Penguin Ireland, 25 St Stephen's Green, Dublin 2, Ireland (a division of Penguin Books Ltd);
Penguin Group (Australia), 250 Camberwell Road, Camberwell, Victoria 3124, Australia (a division of
Pearson Australia Group Pty Ltd); Penguin Books India Pvt Ltd, 11 Community Centre, Panchsheel
Park, New Delhi–110 017, India; Penguin Group (NZ), 67 Apollo Drive, Rosedale, Auckland 0632, New
Zealand (a division of Pearson New Zealand Ltd); Penguin Books (South Africa) (Pty) Ltd, 24 Sturdee
Avenue, Rosebank, Johannesburg 2196, South Africa

Penguin Books Ltd, Registered Offices: 80 Strand, London WC2R 0RL, England

Published by Gotham Books, a member of Penguin Group (USA) Inc.

First printing, September 2012
1   3   5   7   9   10   8   6   4   2

LIBRARY OF CONGRESS CATALOGING-IN-PUBLICATION DATA
has been applied for.

ISBN 978-1-592-40731-6

Printed in the United States of America
Designed by Nancy Resnick

While the author has made every effort to provide accurate telephone numbers, Internet addresses, and
other contact information at the time of publication, neither the publisher nor the author assumes any
responsibility for errors or for changes that occur after publication. Further, the publisher does not have
any control over and does not assume any responsibility for author or third-party websites or their con-
tent. The names and identifying details of some individuals have been changed to protect their privacy.

For my father,
George Gorant

Chapter 1

Meetings

———— ●️ ————

I'm gonna love you.

Clara Setzer

1

They arrived shortly after noon, with gear, a cooler, and a six-pack in tow. They planned to sail out to one of the islands in the lake and spend the afternoon fishing and soaking up the sun, then sail back. Roberts led the way since he was, in a sense, the host. He lived in a little yellow house on the outskirts of the Twin Cities, about an hour away. Graham had come up from Chicago to visit. The boat belonged to a third friend, but he had given them permission to use it.

The day was warm and clear, reaching a high of about seventy-five degrees, although the wind blew fifteen to twenty miles per hour with gusts into the midtwenties. The men knew how to operate the boat, but neither of them had sailed much. They had no idea that the breeze was too strong for the little flat-bottomed skiff bobbing on the water before them. They knew only that they had long looked forward to the excursion, and they were determined to make it happen.

They loaded up the boat and set off. The ride out had its moments, not scary so much as exhilarating, as the boat yawed to one side and water sprayed off the top of the waves. They reached the island in no time, dropped the sail, and rowed into a small public dock. Along the shore they caught sunnies and perch but the bass and walleye they were after could not be persuaded to bite. They ate the sandwiches they had brought. They drank the beer. The afternoon went quickly, and by the time they shoved off for home the sky was overcast and the light fading fast.

To their relief, the wind had abated slightly, but it was still blowing in the midteens with surprising gusts that felt even stronger because the temperature had dropped into the midfifties. They were dressed warmly and each knew how to swim, but the black lake water that splashed up felt even colder than the air.

The wind swirled and gusted, messing with them, alternately knocking them off course and slowing them down. They found some steadiness tracing the path of the shoreline, but eventually they had to clear a point of land and cross a patch of open water. The breeze pushed them hard toward the opposite shore, when suddenly the little boat shook. The sail wavered. The gunwale rose. The boat tipped, dumping both men in the water.

The coldness shocked them and grabbed their bodies, while the weight of their soaked clothing dragged them down. Graham stripped off his shirt and pulled for the surface. When he broke into night air he saw Roberts already swimming toward the shore. He began to swim, too. The coldness sucked the energy from him, and his arms soon grew weary. He lost track of where he was. His body went numb. When he pulled up his head the world blurred before him. He splashed and kicked but went nowhere. He felt himself sinking, giving up, when suddenly there were voices, hands on his body.

A homeowner who had been out walking his dog had heard the commotion and come running. He pulled Graham from the water. Graham gasped and sputtered and looked around, but there was no sign of Roberts. No one had seen him, and the lake sat dark and silent. He told the police everything he knew. Sometime around midnight the cops dragged the sailboat back to shore. At four A.M. they gave up the search, confirming what Graham had known in his heart for hours. His friend was dead.

Miles away, the little yellow house sat at the end of the block, nearly silent. There were no people inside, but the place was not empty. There were always dogs. So many dogs, coming and going. Sometimes chained in the yard, where they barked for hours during the afternoon or late into the night. The neighbors wondered about the dogs. They wondered about Roberts.

Now the man was gone, and inside the house two adult dogs sat in crates in the living room while in the garage six puppies chewed on the blankets and cardboard boxes spread on the floor. They were maybe six weeks old, brown-and-white bundles of energy with pink noses, droopy skin, and paws too big for their bodies. Full of curiosity and mischief, they played and ran, but their yips and barks had a different tone to them now. They carried an echo of hunger, a hint of desperation. No one had come to bring them food tonight or clean up after them. Could anyone hear them? Did anyone know they were there?

2

Andrew Yori got up off the couch and looked around the small dorm room that served as an on-duty office for resident assistants. There was not much else to the place—a small table with a computer on top and a few office chairs clustered around it. On the wall opposite the couch a TV sat on a stand. Andrew stretched and walked out.

It was September of 1998 and Andrew was in his first year as an RA at Saint Mary's University of Minnesota, and he was still figuring out the routine. Once a week he would be condemned to the office from seven until eleven p.m., his only break the hourly patrols through the halls of the four-story building and the one connected to it, making sure peace reigned.

At least, he thought as he started his rounds, the office was on an all-female floor. The possibility of meeting someone made it a little more appealing. Although it wasn't like he had time for much else in his life. He already played for the Saint Mary's University of Minnesota soccer team, sang and played trumpet in the choir, helped found and played on the school's club volleyball team, and majored in biology, which required him to take seventeen or eighteen credits a semester.

Also, this was his senior year, and he'd decided that it was time to get serious. He'd never been much of a partyer—during his first two years he'd drank maybe six beers total—but as a junior he'd shared a suite with a fellow soccer player and two other friends. He turned twenty-one during the year and found himself going out to bars. He dated, too. He had boyish good looks, with a strong jaw and soft hazel eyes, and little trouble attracting women. The relationships were casual, passing—*frivolous* might have been an overstatement but not by much.

This year he was stepping back from all of that. He wanted to finish strong, and he felt that as an RA he had to set an example. His plan included no more dating just for the sake of it. If he went out with someone this year it would have to be a serious girlfriend. *Serious,* that word again.

He reached the end of the hall and started up the stairs. When he entered the fourth-floor lounge he saw a guy he knew, another RA named Jason. They exchanged hellos. "This is my girlfriend, Clara," Jason said, pointing to the woman sitting next to him. "Clara, this is Roo."

Andrew waved. He saw the confused look in her eyes. "It's Andrew," he said, "but most people call me Roo." They all chatted for a minute before he ducked back out of the room. It was a serious year, but she was seriously cute—tall and fit with long brown hair and a bright smile. She also had a serious boyfriend. *Lucky guy,* thought Roo.

He ran into her again a few days later—it rarely took long to cross paths with someone at Saint Mary's, which had less than fourteen hundred undergrads. The encounter took place during his next RA shift. A group of the women who lived on the floor had gathered at the end of the hall, talking and hanging out. As Roo returned from his rounds he stopped to join the conversation. Clara was among them. She lived a few doors down from the RA office.

After that he saw her at the gym. When Roo had arrived at Saint Mary's he was short and skinny, five foot six and about 115 pounds. He had skills, but he found himself getting pushed around on the soccer pitch, so he had embarked on a hard-core workout program. Over the years he'd added strength and muscle, thanks to almost-daily sessions at the weight room, and had grown to five foot nine.

Clara stood five foot eight herself and she was a jock, too. She played on the women's basketball team as a freshman and would do so again during this, her sophomore year. She also ran cross-country, eventually giving up basketball to focus on track, becoming a standout performer in the heptathlon. She spent her share of time in the gym, too. They had experienced a glimmer of recognition upon that first introduction in the lounge, and they realized it came from having seen each other in the gym the previous year. But now they had been officially introduced and had an excuse to trade hellos at the gym before going on with their exercise.

Over the following weeks they continued to bump into each other, not only at the end-of-the-hallway bull sessions during Roo's RA shift and at the gym but after soccer games, too. As part of her work-study job, Clara manned the scorer's table at home matches. After the games the players and their families would often linger on the field talking. Clara would often hang around, too, and it was another opportunity for the two to interact.

"Hey," he said to her on the pitch after one particularly tough win.

"Good game," she replied.

"Actually," he said, "I messed up a few times there in the second half. Coach kinda let me have it."

"Oh, I wouldn't really know."

"Not a soccer fan?" he asked, kicking at the ground a little.

"I don't get soccer," she said. "It's boring. Sorry."

Roo laughed. "Well," he said, "if I wasn't playing I might feel that way, too."

Pretty quickly the brief chats transformed into longer conversations. It was early October when Roo was sitting in the RA office watching TV and Clara materialized in the doorway. "Hey," he said, wondering what she needed. Without saying anything back, she walked across the room, sat on the couch, and started watching along with him. After the initial surprise wore off, Roo reveled in this development. They had become, without question, friends. He wondered if they would ever become more than that.

Their Thursday-night TV sessions evolved into regular meetings, a chance to hang out together and talk. During commercials Roo learned about Clara's life growing up in three different towns in Minnesota. She heard about his eventful childhood in northern Illinois. They bonded over a shared love of root beer. Sometimes they talked about big things—life, religion, the future.

She came and went. Stopped in for a few minutes, then left. Came back for a half hour, then went again. Sometimes she was alone. Other times friends came with her. It was life in a dorm, full of open doors, scattered interests, and fungible schedules. She didn't seem to be able to stay away, and Roo looked forward to her arrivals.

Outside the little office the swing revival raged. Horn-filled bebop music and the accompanying hops and jives, dances from the thirties, forties, and fifties, had become cool again. A friend of Roo's started a swing club, and he recruited Roo to come to the first meeting. When he showed up, he found Clara, sans Jason. She'd been recruited by the same friend. Although she hadn't needed much convincing—her last name was Setzer, and she was a distant relative of Brian Setzer, the leader of the Brian Setzer Orchestra, one of the bands that sparked the trend, and she was determined to join the craze. Since they were each there unaccompanied, they jitterbugged and juked together.

Swing wasn't the only thing, though. Clara wanted to brush up on ballroom, too. A local studio offered lessons, but Jason wasn't any more inclined to take part, so Clara asked Roo if he would join her. Why not? They were good friends now and after the swing class she knew he could move. The pair spent six weeks waltzing and fox-trotting their way through the Minnesota winter.

As much as he tried not to, Roo developed feelings for Clara. He liked that, like him, she was into sports and music; she sang in the choir and for fun in the hallways with another girl who lived on the floor. That was another thing he liked about her—she was friends with everyone. She hung out with the jocks she knew from playing sports, but also the rocker girl who was never without her guitar and an Indigo Girls tune, the theater buffs, the girly girls. She had even quickly warmed to Roo's friend Beaker, a skinny math major with thick glasses, a refrigerator full of Coke that he pounded all day and night, and negligible social skills. For Roo's money, she was one of the best-looking girls on campus, but she didn't have an ego and didn't buy into anyone else's. And she liked to get involved, join a team, learn to dance, perform in the school's semiannual talent show.

Most of all, he liked the way they got along. They shared a vibe, a connection, and it was that feeling more than anything that made him think she might be attracted to him as well. They kept up their Thursday-night TV sessions. They continued to grow more relaxed and comfortable with each other. Clara even confided in Roo her reservations about Jason.

One night they sat on the floor in the hall, leaning against opposite walls. "I don't know," Clara was saying. "Sometimes I feel like

Jason and I aren't interested in the same things." Roo nodded. "He doesn't want to do any of the stuff I do. It feels like he just wants me around while he's out drinking with his friends." Roo nodded some more. "You know, I was sick in the hospital last summer and he came by for like fifteen minutes. My old high school boyfriend was there for half the day, but he came for fifteen minutes? Does that seem right to you?"

"Well, umm . . ." Roo hesitated. He desperately wanted Clara to dump Jason, but he didn't want it to appear that he'd had anything to do with the split. "Who knows what he had going on that day," he said finally. "If you've got other commitments, fifteen minutes can be more difficult than half a day. Jason's a decent guy." He hoped he'd seemed convincing. If she was going to put a bullet in her relationship he wasn't going to help pull the trigger.

As it turned out, he didn't need to. In early December, Clara and Jason broke up. Roo was secretly delighted. He considered moving in immediately, but he wanted to be with her for the right reasons, not because she was lonely and unsure of herself after a split.

He waited. But not too long. He didn't want her to go home over the holidays and find someone new. One day shortly before break, he found himself back in the RA office, on the couch, watching TV. With Clara.

Over the previous two weeks he'd paced his dorm room trying to figure how and when to make his move. He'd worked over scenarios, tried out words and phrases, and dreamed up conversational segues that might lead to the topic he wanted to discuss. He conspired to bring a casualness to the proceedings while at the same time making his feelings known. He pictured where she might be sitting and how he would stand.

Their relationship had been on a steady climb for four months. He knew all the time together, the dancing, the conversations, were signals sent and received. He knew this was his moment.

As they sat on the couch, he squirmed. He could not make any of the scenarios work, couldn't somehow force the topic to emerge organically. Finally, he gave in and simply launched into his approach. "Hey," he said, voice quavering. "I know we're great friends, and I wouldn't want to ruin that, but I think this is going really well and I wondered if you'd want to be more than friends?"

Clara turned to him. What was that look on her face? Relief? Happiness? She smiled a closemouthed smile. Then, very sweetly, she said, "No."

3

Officer Dan Grohln stepped out of the car and stood before the little yellow house. After more than twenty years in animal control he'd seen a lot, and whatever he'd missed he'd heard about from others. Dead animals, raids of fighting operations with severely injured dogs, abandonment, hoarding cases with dozens of cats living in squalor. He loved the job, working with animals and helping them find homes, but the scenes of abuse and deprivation could be hard to stomach. He had no idea what he'd find today.

The department had received a call from a neighbor, who reported near-constant barking coming from the house. The neighbor claimed that the homeowner had recently died, and the dogs must have been left unattended. A quick records search had showed the neighbor was right; the homeowner had died in an accident five days earlier.

As Grohln approached the house he could tell by the tall grass and stuffed mailbox that no one had been around—no neighbors or relatives had come to tend to the place. The door was locked, so he and his partner swung around back. They tried the door, and when it too was locked they forced it open and entered.

In the living room they found two crates, each containing a pit bull. Both male. Both intact. The dogs were thrilled to see the officers, wagging, barking, whining, and bouncing off the walls of the crates. Grohln and his partner petted the dogs through the grating but left them inside for the moment. While his partner went off to find food and water, Grohln heard a barrage of high yelps coming from behind a door on the side of the house.

As he approached he braced himself. This was where it could get Darwinian. A litter of puppies locked up without food for five or six days could end with the stronger ones turning on the weaker in an effort to survive. He opened the door and five brown-and-white pit bull puppies flew at his legs, jumping and yelping, crawling all over one another to get at him, tails wagging, legs flying, tongues flopping in an almost deranged burst of excitement.

Grohln bent to pet them as he scanned the room. There were torn-up bits of cardboard everywhere and the pups were dirty, smeared with their own waste, but everything else seemed in order. Except for one thing. A sixth puppy stood off to the side, wagging and happy but much calmer than the rest. Grohln moved over to inspect him, and the pup seemed fine. But there was something. Grohln picked the dog up and looked at him. His eyes were brown, but part of the right eye—from, say, three to six on the face of a clock—was blue.

———

Brad Mirren was happy to see Dan Grohln. Mirren was a young police officer in a neighboring town but the two men did not know each other through work; Grohln had gone to high school with Mirren's father. A day earlier, Mirren had received a call from Grohln telling him to stop by the pound.

For the past few months Mirren had been a regular visitor. Mirren had an older dog, a pit bull named DJ, and he was looking to adopt a puppy. He wanted a dog he could train to compete in ring games, competitions among dogs trained for law enforcement activities, and DJ was too old. He sought a youngster that was smart and driven that he could mold into a great competitor.

Grohln showed Mirren the six pit bull pups, which ran around in a small room off the main kennel. As the pups scampered around their feet and jumped up on their shins, Grohln explained the situation. According to local law the city had to hold dogs from abandonment cases for five days in case the family of the original owner came to claim them. On the second day the puppies were at the pound, two guys had shown up claiming to be relatives of the original owner. They wanted all the dogs from the house. Officer Grohln had taken their names and contact information and said he'd get back to them.

The more Grohln had thought about the scene at the yellow house, the more things didn't quite add up. Why two intact males? Why six very young pups with no sign of the mother? The owner had been a guy nearing thirty with almost no employment history and a few minor arrests.

Grohln had no direct evidence that the guy was a dogfighter—no training equipment or paraphernalia, none of the dogs had injuries or scars; in fact all were well kept and healthy—but something didn't feel right. It appeared that the guy was breeding pit bulls and selling them to anyone who wanted them for whatever purpose. At worst, the guy bred them specifically for fighting.

Then this pair showed up. They were telling the truth; they were distantly related to the dead man. But something was not quite right about them. Grohln had made some calls. Nothing could be proven, but local word pegged them as dogfighters. Grohln didn't want to give these two guys the dogs.

He went to his superior officer and made the case that since these men weren't immediate relatives of the owner, the city didn't have an obligation to turn over the dogs. He was persuasive enough that his boss didn't shoot down the idea. Still, he didn't think he had the authority to make a final decision. Slowly, the question rose up the chain of command.

Grohln stayed busy while he waited. He didn't want the puppies going to just anyone. He wanted people he could trust not to resell them or use them for ill purposes. And he wanted them to keep quiet about where the dogs had come from. He began recruiting trustworthy adopters. By the third day he had four of the six committed to other officers or city employees. Only two remained, one female and the male with the partially blue eye. That's when he called Mirren.

As Grohln finished his story he looked at Mirren. "So are you in?"

"Yeah," Mirren said.

"You want the male or the female?"

"Definitely the male," Mirren said.

Grohln had spent a fair bit of time with the puppies—stopping by to feed them and play with them—and he'd come to know them pretty well. Again and again he'd been impressed by the one pup with the partially blue eye. He seemed calmer than the rest, cooler and more laid-back. He lingered around the periphery but took everything in. He found that pup among the group and pointed him out to Mirren. "That's him," Grohln said.

Mirren stared into the frenzy that raged around their feet. All of the pups seemed great, strong and healthy with plenty of drive, but Mirren blocked out all the other activity and focused on the dog Grohln had pointed out. Mirren noticed that the dog stood off to the side. His partially blue eye stood out because his entire head and the front of his body were white. A large brown patch curved in over his right hindquarter and his back. His face and neck were creased with folds of skin, like rolls of fat on a baby's thighs. Those same flaps of extra flesh hung down his snout too, making his face look a little pushed in.

Mirren watched the puppy, wondering if it was the right one for him. Was he too calm? Did his disinterestedness indicate a lack of intelligence or a future as a couch potato? But as Mirren observed the pup his feelings changed. The little guy was alert and interested, he just wasn't running around like a squirrel in a nut processing plant. This made him seem cooler, more serious, ready to get down to business.

Four days later Mirren returned. The question about what to do with the dogs had risen all the way to the city attorney, who'd ultimately agreed with Grohln: Only immediate relatives were entitled to claim the dogs. The decision came as a great relief, since no one wanted to think about the alternative. The two guys had never returned but even if they did, Grohln now had the authority to deny their request. Still, he knew the dogs had street value, and he was afraid someone might come looking for them.

After Mirren completed the paperwork, Grohln asked him to keep the dog's origins a secret. No one could know where the puppy came from.

"Kind of like doggie witness protection," Mirren said.

"Sort of," Grohln replied.

Mirren walked out with the little dog under his arm. It was the second time it had been saved in ten days.

4

Something had changed with Clara. Roo could see it. Following her breakup with Jason she had spent the winter burning through a few shallow relationships. But as the weather began to break, she was once again single, and he found her drawing close. They had never stopped spending time together, watching TV in the office, chatting in the hall, going to the gym. And their chemistry persisted, too.

Earlier in the winter Clara's mother and sister had come to visit. She had taken them on a tour of the campus and when they ventured into the gym, there was Roo. The four of them had stood talking for a bit before the tour moved on. As soon as they were out of Roo's earshot Clara's mother and sister both asked if there was something going on between the two. The women had picked up on the vibe in that two-minute encounter.

Roo didn't know about the conversation, but he could certainly tell that Clara was acting differently toward him. She seemed to be putting on a full-scale charm offensive, unleashing a steady stream of big smiles, hair flips, and enchanted laughter.

He had taken the initial rejection in stride. He was bummed at the thought that he and she were never going to happen, but he valued her friendship enough to bury his feelings and forge on. But now he was confused. The signals Clara sent came through loud and clear, but he wasn't sure he could trust them. And even if he could, he didn't know if he was willing to risk another attempt. He didn't think the friendship could survive a second rejection.

Faced with such a dilemma he made the obvious choice: Do nothing.

Still, he thought about it. He sounded it out with Beaker, who grew so tired of hearing about Clara that he took action. Roo had been working part-time for a network marketing outfit that required him to consistently acquire new contacts. He'd fallen behind, and Beaker threw out a challenge: If Roo didn't hit his number of new contacts the following week, he would have to ask Clara out again. Roo lost.

The next night he found himself back in the RA office having a flashback—it was just like the first time he'd asked her out. He'd spent his day pacing, trying to summon the courage and figure out the right words. As the night went on Clara came and went from the room. Roo went on rounds and chatted in the halls.

Finally, it was getting toward the end of his shift, when he would have to leave the floor. Clara came in and sat down. Roo took a deep breath. "So," he said, "what's going on here? I mean, I like you and am getting some signals from you, but . . . where do we stand?"

Clara looked away for a minute, then turned back to him. "I like you, too." Roo exhaled. He was psyched. They agreed that they would need to go on an actual first date. Then it was time for Roo to leave. He shut the lights and locked up the office. He and Clara walked to the end of the hall. As he said good-bye he leaned forward and gave her a hug. Their cheeks brushed and slowly they turned their faces toward each other. Their lips met.

Clara leaned back and looked at him. "I feel like I just kissed my best friend," she said.

————

Roo went all-out for the first date. He assigned Beaker to serve as a driver for the night (the result of another bet, although this time Roo won). His friend showed up in a full suit and a chauffeur's cap, a fresh shine on his dark green 1995 Pontiac Grand Am.

He sped the new couple across the Mississippi River to a romantic restaurant on the Wisconsin side. Afterward he delivered them to Garvin Heights, a rocky overhang on the bluffs that rise above the Mississippi with panoramic views of the river. Roo and Clara made their way to a large flat rock along the ridge and took in the sights. The water glinted in the late-day sun, and the lakes and hills and fields twisted off into the distance. Roo produced a guitar and sang Clara a song that he had written just for her.

The last two months of school were something of a honeymoon for the pair, but when May came Roo graduated and moved back to his parents' house in Illinois while Clara went home to Red Wing, Minnesota. They saw each other as much as they could over the summer, but the future remained uncertain.

Roo had once intended to go to dental school, but the day of the entrance exams had coincided with a big soccer game. He blew off the exam. It was indicative of a larger decision: He wanted to make a run at professional soccer. The head coach at Saint Mary's had played professionally, and he thought Roo had a shot to make it if he worked on his game and built himself up. He offered Roo a job as the assistant coach in residence. It was a near-perfect scenario. It meant Roo would be living on campus again, making a little money and working on his game. Best of all he and Clara would be together.

The couple enjoyed campus life. As assistant coach Roo scored a room that was a little nicer than the average dorm room. It had a couch and small kitchenette. They huddled there together, watching TV, ordering pizza, and simply hanging out. They worked out together almost every day, they went to a lot of movies, and two or three times he cooked her spaghetti, using his mother's secret recipe. On occasion he played the guitar and sang to her. They continued to take dance classes together and twice a year the school hosted a talent show, in which they performed.

The previous summer's parting had been difficult, and this year's was even harder. The experience was a new one for Roo; with any previous girlfriend the intensity of feeling had long since dissipated by this point in the relationship. They hugged for what seemed like forever and promised to see each other as often as possible. It would be easier this year since Roo was spending the summer in Rochester, Minnesota, about forty-five minutes away from Red Wing.

In the fall Roo returned for a second year of coaching. And a second year of hanging out with Clara, who was now a senior. Knee surgery had stunted Roo's run at pro soccer and as he and Clara sat on the couch in his room watching TV, he wondered what else the future might hold.

———

"Clara?" Roo called as he walked into the house. It was winter, so he peeled off his heavy jacket to reveal the tan chinos and button-down that had become his standard work outfit. Back in spring, while Clara was still in school, Roo had heard that the Mayo Clinic, also in Rochester, was hiring. He'd dusted off his biology degree and sent in a résumé.

By the time Clara graduated, Mayo had hired him, and he went to work as a lab technologist, processing blood tests and performing genetic screens for a variety of conditions. Roo found that he enjoyed the work and liked the people. Even more, he liked the impact the job had on his bank account.

Within a few months he began looking for a house in town. Clara would come down from Red Wing on the weekends and help him search. The understanding was that once he found a place, they would move in together. In the fall Clara, who had earned a degree in studio art, began training as a massage therapist. Soon after, Roo bought a house in Eyota, a small town just outside Rochester, and the couple moved in.

The place was an all-stone structure built in 1916, with stately wood pillars inside and hardwood floors. It was cool, but it was also a fixer-upper marred with ancient wallpaper, cracked and hole-riddled walls, and crumbling stone. Roo worked at Mayo and Clara went to class, and when they were home they played Mr. and Mrs. Fixit. Roo's parents made trips up from Illinois to help. In the evenings they hooked up with old friends from college or collapsed on the couch, watching their favorite show, *Survivor*.

Now Clara came down from upstairs. "What's up?" she said. They kissed.

"Interesting thing happened at work today," he said. "Brian is having a new house built, and he's going to have to move into an apartment for a few months while they finish it. But the apartment complex won't let him bring his dog, and he asked if anyone would be willing to take her. I thought maybe we could try it."

"What's her name?" Clara asked.

"Jazz."

"What kind of dog is she?"

"A black Lab."

"And it's just for a few months, right?"

"Right."

"So if we don't like it, we're not committed."

"It seemed like a perfect chance to me," Roo said. "Plus it's always nice to do the boss a favor."

Jazz arrived a few days later, and Clara and Roo fell in love. She was perfectly house-trained, perfectly friendly, obedient, fun, and she didn't chew things when you left her alone. Roo appreciated her morning wake-up calls—as soon as the sun came up and Roo began to stir, Jazz would body-slam the bed, throwing herself into the side of the mattress like a hockey player crashing into the walls of a rink, until she was sure everyone was fully awake. Then she'd haul herself up onto the bed.

Within a few weeks of Jazz's arrival, they knew they definitely wanted a dog of their own. And since this one was a black Lab, they figured they'd get one of those. All dogs of the same breed behaved the same way, right?

Then the plan hit a roadblock. Clara had become friendly with a guy she met at the gym. She was spending more and more time with him. Roo noticed. He said nothing, but he noticed.

One night Clara went out with the guy and his friends. At about the time she was supposed to come home she called to say that she'd had one drink so she was waiting to drive home but that she would be there soon. Roo was disturbed that she hadn't asked him to come pick her up or join them.

Roo's fears got the best of him. He knew the password to her e-mail. He felt creepy logging into her account, but he couldn't stop himself. He found a series of messages from the guy, and as he read them he felt both anger and relief. The notes made it clear that nothing had happened between Clara and the guy but also acknowledged that a strong attraction existed between the two. When she arrived home, he confronted her. "What's going on?" he said. She denied there was anything between them, and he mentioned the e-mails. She started to cry and ran for the door. Roo cut her off.

"No," he said. "You're going to sit and listen. I've been working my ass off to provide for us, fixing our house and being loyal to you. If that doesn't mean anything to you or if you'd rather be with someone else, tell me now, because I don't have to do all this." He went on, but not for long. The whole thing couldn't have lasted five minutes and he wasn't even sure what he was saying after a while. Clara said nothing. Finally, still crying, she got up and ran out of the house. Roo went up to bed, and before he fell asleep he shed a few tears of his own.

When Clara returned a few hours later she retreated to the couch. The next morning she packed up some stuff and went to her parents' house.

5

Officer Brad Mirren had a second job, common for cops in their first few years on the beat, when they are last in line for overtime and lucrative outside gigs guarding construction sites and providing security for public events. Mirren's side gig was at a local hotel, where he worked as a security guard. For most of those shifts he holed up in a suite of back offices. Although he wasn't there full-time, Mirren was one of the most popular employees in the office. That was because he brought along the white-and-brown pit bull pup he'd adopted every time he went in. He had a crate for the dog, but the little guy spent most of the day on the loose, and a steady stream of hotel employees stopped by to play with him.

Mirren had taken to calling the dog Chuck, and the two were inseparable. Mirren took Chuck to work, he took him for rides in the car, took him when he went for walks, when he did chores in the yard, and when he went to the store. He also took Chuck to area parks, where he let the dog experiment with rope bridges and climbing ladders and other obstacles.

Mirren wanted to make sure that Chuck was well socialized— comfortable with a wide range of people, places, and experiences— so that he would be friendly and relaxed out in public. He also liked to keep the dog by his side because he enjoyed having the pup around, although part of the motivation was a sort of homeland defense strategy on Mirren's part. Chuck hated being in a crate, but the few times Mirren had left him home unrestrained the dog had done serious damage. The most egregious incident was an attack on the couch pillows.

Mirren, though angry, felt a touch of appreciation for the crime. Chuck hadn't gone after one pillow and torn it to shreds; instead he did small but irreparable damage to each of them, chewing the corners off and tearing the seams. The former approach—the more typical one—would have allowed Mirren to simply replace a single pillow. This way he had to trash the entire set.

Mirren began to realize there wasn't much that was typical about this dog. Whatever had caused him to be so calm and focused in the shelter no longer held sway. Chuck was a nonstop ball of energy. Always on the go, always in pursuit of the next thing.

As a result, Mirren spent a lot of time out behind his house with Chuck. The yard was connected to his neighbor's, so that Chuck could run free over the full range. When he did he often encountered another small, energetic creature: the five-year-old girl who lived next door. She and Chuck became great friends. They spent hours together in the yard. The girl loved the dog, but she didn't like the name. In her mind he didn't look like a Chuck. He looked like a Ranger. And so the dog unofficially became Ranger, although Mirren contended that his full official name was Ranger T. Chuck.

Mirren liked *Ranger* because the name had a law-enforcement overtone, and he still planned to train the dog to compete in police games. By the time the pup received his new name Mirren had already begun the work.

Known as *Schutzhund* or ring sports, these games include competitions in a variety of categories: street protection, tracking, disarming, suspect apprehension. The games are scenario based, which means the dog is put in a situation where a crime is acted out and he must react. A panel of judges scores his performance.

The first step in training a dog to compete in any of these events is to build his prey drive—his instinct to chase and catch small, fast-moving objects. If a trainer can teach a dog to go after a tug toy like there's nothing else in the world that matters, to chase it the way a politician goes after money, eventually he can transfer the reaction to other targets, such as an arm.

Mirren began the work with a flirt pole, a stick with a feather or a strip of leather or fur, something that's eye-catching and fun to chew, attached to it by a string. It's the tool of choice for building prey drive. Mirren would hold the stick so that the chewy part dangled near Ranger. When it caught the dog's attention, Mirren made the toy skitter away, as a fleeing rabbit or squirrel might. Sometimes, for a change of pace, Mirren would tie a toy to the end of a long rope and then spin the rope over his head so the toy whipped around in a circle just above the ground.

As soon as Mirren brought the furry target out, the little dog would charge forward and dive into a play bow, with both front legs extended forward and his butt in the air, tail swishing. He'd bark and lunge at the strip of fur. As it danced away he'd watch, seeming astonished that he had not captured it. Then he'd jump up and chase it. As Ranger groped and swatted at the retreating fluff he'd tumble and fall, then regain his feet, cock his head, and eye Mirren with a quizzical look, as if he was playing to some unseen camera.

The fun and games would last for a while but before long Ranger would reach a state of frothy engagement. He loved a good game, but he also wanted that chewy thing. His movements became more urgent and his body language less playful. When Mirren finally let Ranger catch the target, the dog would pounce on it, growling and shaking it from side to side as he held it in his teeth. Mirren showered Ranger with praise and treats, and the mood once again turned light. The dog learned quickly that this game was not only fun, but it got him the kind of rewards he cherished most of all.

From his earliest days with Officer Mirren, Ranger spent three or four sessions a week playing these games. Combined with his natural puppy enthusiasm and playfulness, these romps became some of the dog's favorite times. As the months passed Ranger grew quickly and his prey drive did, too.

6

Clara had sobbed through the worst few days of her life. Her relationship with the other guy had been nothing, really. It felt fun and innocent. She had enjoyed the attention, the flirtation, and the excitement of the moment. In her mind it had been a harmless diversion. Until she saw the look on Roo's face that night. Suddenly it hit her that what she was doing caused harm to the person she cared most about in the world.

Their conversation that night was a blur—but one fact came through loud and clear: Roo had broken up with her. She left not because she'd stopped loving him or didn't want to be with him, but because she thought she was no longer welcome in their home. Still, she couldn't make herself accept that. She invited Roo out to her parents' for the weekend.

Roo wasn't sure whether to accept the invitation. He was hurt and angry, but on the inside he also understood what was happening. They were at the two-year point of their relationship. They were still very young—twenty-four and twenty-two—and it had been a long time since the kiss in the hallway and the serenade on the bluffs, since the dance lessons and the workout sessions and the talent-show collaborations. With Roo working five days a week in the lab and Clara in class, their lives had settled into a not unhappy but predictable routine, like a grinding stone inching forward on a wheel. There were moments when he too wondered if he should see what else was out there. An unasked question sat in the silence of the house: Is this it?

Roo decided to go, but he remained uncertain. He arrived at Clara's parents' house stern faced and grave. She sensed his reticence but refused to be brought down by it. "It was nothing," she told him. "I guess I just liked the attention, but it didn't mean anything to me. It's not what I want. I love you. I love our life now, and I love what I see our life becoming in the future. I'm so sorry."

Roo said nothing. "It'll never happen again," she promised. He came around slowly. As the weekend went along he began to talk more. His body language eased. He laughed a little. When Sunday came they returned to Eyota together.

Clara was relieved, but she knew this was a truce more than a victory, and a tenuous truce at that. She could see that Roo harbored uncertainty. He was watching, waiting, easing back in.

They still had Jazz, but the time was coming when they would have to return her. Clara suggested that they start looking for a dog of their own. Roo countered that he wasn't ready. She knew what that meant: He wasn't ready to fully recommit to the relationship, to their future.

She stayed patient. Time passed and their life returned to what it had been before. They worked on the house, went out with their friends, checked in on *Survivor*. Clara even sent a few audition tapes to the show. Every now and then Clara would ask, "Ready yet?" and Roo would say, "Not yet."

Eventually, they started to visit shelters, just to see what was out there. They were thrilled to find that the facilities were overrun with black Labs, or at least Lab mixes, which is what they were looking for after getting to attached to Jazz. Sometimes on the visits they'd play with one of the dogs, and at those times Clara could feel that invisible wall, that microscopic membrane that had arisen between them, start to fall.

They would both get caught up in the joy and when Roo seemed happiest, most absorbed, she would say, "Ready yet?" And Roo's face would go dark again.

"Not yet," he'd say, and soon thereafter the dog would be on his way back to the pen.

Clara did not despair at these moments. She could feel Roo coming back to her. She knew it was only a matter of time before their future got back on track. Finally, in August of 2002, they set out for Paws & Claws Humane Society, a "no kill" facility in Rochester that they'd visited several times before.

They met a five-month-old black Lab–German shepherd mix named Angus who looked more like an animated plush toy than an actual dog. His head was so large that he looked as though at any given moment he might tip forward, and his paws were so big that he moved like a person wearing scuba fins. As he ran and chased around the room he regularly stumbled and fell, and when he approached Roo and Clara with a play bow, then turned and ran, he clearly expected them to play chase. When he looked back to find them still sitting on the couch, laughing, he looked first shocked and then almost hurt.

They met another Lab mix named Ajax. He'd been at the facility for about eighteen months because he had some behavioral issues that made him difficult to place. He sniffed at Roo and Clara for a few moments and lay down at their feet. The shelter attendant's eyebrows went up. Ajax held a ball in his mouth and as he sat there he let it drop on the floor. Without thinking anything of it, Roo snatched the ball off the floor. Ajax's eyes followed Roo, and the volunteer's jaw went down.

Clara and Roo played with Ajax as the attendant explained that the dog's problem was not aggressiveness toward other dogs but toward people. This surprised the couple: They didn't see any sign of bad behavior. It surprised the volunteer, too—Ajax wasn't displaying the agitation he typically did around strangers.

A short while later, Roo and Clara walked out of the shelter. It was a bright afternoon and they had been looking for dogs—in a sense examining their own future—for several months. As they reached the car, Roo looked at Clara and said, "I'm ready."

A smile creased her face, and though she remained quiet on the outside, inside she screamed, *Yes!*

She had her guy, and she had her dog. Or at least she thought she did.

7

Most of the wrinkles were gone. Those folds of extra skin that had made Ranger such an appealing puppy had stretched out as he grew. He still had those big rolls that formed on his forehead when he seemed puzzled or unsure of himself—they made him look like he was really thinking deeply—but he was two years old and full-size, almost fifty-five pounds of bone and muscle with a giant cinder-block head. Almost overnight it seemed he went from a clumsy pup that tripped over his own paws to a big strong dog.

He remained a puppy at heart, though. His energy was boundless. He wanted nothing more than to run and chew and chase all day long. The more he could do—the more places he could visit, people he could see, and games he could play—the happier he was. Those traits were fed by his police game training. He'd grown to love the flirt pole and some of the other games Officer Mirren played with him. About the only thing that exceeded his prey drive was his work capacity, his willingness—in fact, desire—to do whatever was asked of him over and over again to the point of exhaustion.

These developments in Ranger's personality, temperament, and physical prowess indicated great things for his future in ring games but they made life tough for Mirren. He couldn't leave Ranger at home. He felt bad confining the high-energy dog to a crate; the few times he tried, the dog whined and barked and threw himself into the gate over and over. He also couldn't let Ranger roam free because Ranger and DJ would not tolerate each other. It hadn't been a problem while Ranger was small and nonthreatening. Back then DJ could simply cuff Ranger aside like the pesky kid brother he was. Now, though, DJ saw Ranger as a rival, a physical equal, and he did not like it. It didn't help that Ranger's endless desire to play and chase moved him to harass DJ—following DJ around, nudging him, nipping at him, provoking him. Mirren could not leave the two dogs alone.

At the same time it had become harder to take Ranger along with him. In the car Ranger was distracting, if not downright dangerous. He climbed all over the seats, pushed the buttons with his nose, bonked the rearview mirror with his anvil head, and tried to climb in Mirren's lap. At the hotel he was big and a little unruly and although Mirren had a crate for him there, Ranger no more liked that one than the one he had at home.

Slowly, painfully, Mirren came to a realization. One of his dogs had to go. DJ had been with him for six years and they'd been through a lot together. He would never be a ring sports star like Ranger had the potential to become, but that wasn't the most important thing to Mirren. He valued loyalty and friendship and seniority. If any dog went, it would have to be Ranger.

Ranger's past and status as an unofficial "witness protection" dog meant that Mirren couldn't simply hand him off. He didn't want to take Ranger back to the local pound, because that facility euthanized dogs for which it could not find homes.

A friend told him about a no-kill shelter in Rochester that was well run and very successful in placing animals. Mirren checked the place out. He liked what he saw. In his heart he knew that keeping the dog would not be fair to Ranger. Turning Ranger over gave him the best chance to find a happy life.

Finally, he called the shelter and said that he'd found a stray dog that he wanted to turn in. Two days later Paws & Claws called back and informed him that they'd accept the stray. Mirren walked through the door with Ranger, filled out some paperwork, and walked out. As he left he took a final look back. The dog was being led away on a leash but swung its head around to look back at Mirren one last time.

8

Clara walked into the main building of Paws & Claws and dropped her stuff on the little desk in her cubicle. She'd heard there was a new dog at the shelter and she wanted to go check him out. It was late July of 2004, and almost two years had passed since she and Roo had first visited the shelter to adopt a dog of their own. They left that day sure they had found a future pet, but with different opinions about which dog they should take home.

Roo preferred Angus. He was a black Lab, which was what they had wanted at the start. He was still a pup, so they could train him themselves and, hopefully, influence his behavior. He was goofy and lovable. Most of all, he would be a much easier dog.

Clara was drawn to Ajax. She felt like they could help him; the dog had reacted so well to them. And if not them, who would take him? He'd been at the shelter for so long and had such a hard time with people that management had begun to wonder if the dog was better off being put down. Paws & Claws was a no-kill facility but in rare cases, when an animal was sick or had a behavior issue, they would euthanize.

They spent a few days debating the topic, creating pro and con lists and combing through all the options. Finally, they made a decision: They would take both dogs. The people at the shelter reacted to this news like parents whose eighteen-year-old has just told them she's going to join the Peace Corps and build bridges in Afghanistan—they smiled and nodded but inside they were concerned. Paws & Claws had tested the dogs together and knew that they got along, but would a young couple with minimal dog-owning experience be able to handle two at once, one with behavior issues and the other a non-housebroken puppy?

The management made a suggestion: Why didn't Clara and Roo take Ajax for a week and the shelter would hold on to Angus in the interim. If after the time at home with Ajax, the couple still wanted a second dog, they could come back for Angus.

Roo and Clara agreed. They brought Ajax home that day, and when Roo went across the street to run an errand, the dog sat at the door watching him through the window. As Roo disappeared into the building, Ajax sagged to the floor. When Roo reappeared Ajax hopped up and greeted him at the door with a wagging tail and perked-up ears. They knew then they had picked the right dog. The attendants at Paws & Claws begged to differ: They said that Ajax had picked *them*. One week later Clara and Roo returned to the shelter and adopted Angus.

And as much as it made them happy, it also made them feel bad about all the dogs they knew were still back at Paws & Claws in need of attention and a home of their own. They adopted their dogs in August, and by the end of November both were volunteering at Paws & Claws.

Before long it turned into an actual job for Clara. She cleaned kennels, washed blankets, met with potential adopters, walked and played with dogs, and wrote up notes on their state of being. She got paid to be there roughly thirty-two hours a week, but she often spent up to forty hours on the job. After he got out of work at the lab, Roo would walk over and help out, too.

Over the next eighteen months, the two learned an incredible amount about dogs. Roo took an online dog-training course and became an accomplished trainer. Along the way the couple had moved into a new house in Rochester and he'd even taken on a string of foster dogs. There was Griffin, who'd been rescued from a meth house; Doogie, who never stopped barking; Stella, who was recovering from heartworms; and Murphy, who puked in the car on the ride home.

But for all the time Roo and Clara logged at Paws & Claws, somehow neither of them was there when a man dropped off a white-and-brown pit bull named Ranger. They'd heard about the dog though, and both were anxious to meet him.

Now Clara made her way through the kennels to the quarantine room, where the new dogs were kept for a few days. She peered over the top of the wall and into the pen. The dog was already standing, and he turned toward her. Their eyes met, and Clara swore she caught something in the way he looked at her. Perhaps it was the gleam in his eyes or the way the right one had a small arc of blue within the larger circle of brown. Maybe it was something else altogether. "Oooh," she said, "you're naughty." Then she smiled and added, "I'm gonna love you."

Chapter 2

Going Home

Well, I guess we're it.

Roo Yori

1

Maybe it was an omen.

Every new arrival at Paws & Claws gets a fresh name, so on Ranger's second day at the shelter Adam Lattimer and Sue Stanek puzzled over what to call him. Adam was a Paws & Claws employee who bred and trained dogs on the side, and he served as the shelter's general dog expert and pit bull enthusiast in particular. Stanek had been a longtime, core volunteer who had at one time served on the shelter's board of directors. The shelter had a tradition of naming dogs after staffers and volunteers, so Sue suggested *Adam* as a name for the newest resident. Adam laughed: He knew that as a matter of policy all dogs admitted to the shelter were soon neutered.

"Well," he said, "I don't think I want a dog out there that has my name and no balls." Besides, Adam preferred a little more mischief in his dog names. He'd dubbed one of the shelter's pit bulls Friendly, so that when people inevitably and continually asked, "Is he friendly?" Adam could say yes without hesitation.

Sue nodded. They stood in silence for a few moments looking at Ranger. "Scottie Pippen is my all-time favorite basketball player. How about Pippen?"

"Pippen?" Adam said. "He played for the Bulls. We can't name this dog after someone from Chicago."

"Well, my favorite player on the Pistons is Rasheed Wallace. How about Rasheed?" They tossed it around a bit. They liked it, but it didn't really seem to fit the dog. They decided against it. Still, that left Wallace. They liked that, too. It was cool, dignified, and it seemed to mesh with the dog's sensibility. So Ranger T. Chuck officially became Wallace.

His name wasn't the only thing changing. Now that he was at Paws & Claws his life underwent a serious overhaul, too. There were no more rides in the car or romps in the yard with the little girl next door. There were no more trips to the hotel office, where a parade of women would coo at him in high-pitched voices. Instead he had a four-foot-by-six-foot pen, with cinder-block walls on either side topped by chain-link fencing and closed off with a chain-link gate. The pen was one of about twenty in the shelter, and they all faced one another across a small walkway, so the dogs could not only hear and smell one another but see one another as well.

Wallace had never had great manners. He was a ball of energy in constant search of attention. In these new surroundings, everything set him off. He bounced off the walls. He pitched up on the gate with his big front paws. When approached he jumped up and barked as if he were trying to knock someone over with the sound. He leapt up on attendants who tried to take him out for walks or to play. He nipped at them. He whined. He growled.

He didn't do much better with the other dogs. Some, for whatever reason, he simply went after. But even the dogs he wasn't inclined to assault he pestered and harassed relentlessly, as he had DJ. He jumped on them, nipped at them, pushed and rammed them with his head, chased them, and constantly tried to circle behind them.

As the first weeks passed, the situation became worse. Wallace could no longer use up all his energy. He paced and jumped in his pen and ran in the yard when he got a chance, but it wasn't enough. He had been placed in the first pen next to the door that led in and out of the kennel, so every time someone came or went, or another dog would trot past on his way out for a walk, Wallace could see them. Every time someone walked past the other side of the door or stood talking, Wallace could hear them. The near-constant stimulation sent him into the stratosphere.

He developed a weird habit of peeing in his food bowl as soon as he was done eating. He was mouthy when he arrived and the tendency only grew. When attendants fed him or walked him or took him in the yard, as soon as their attention wasn't fully on him, he bit softly at them. He grabbed pant legs and shirttails in his mouth and tugged. In his pen he barked for what felt like hours on end. He began fence fighting, trying to attack passing dogs through the chain-link gate, a fairly common occurrence in kennels but never a welcome one.

At the same time Roo and Clara could see that he was smart. He learned games quickly and enjoyed playing them. Clara had been able to cure his habit of peeing in the bowl without much trouble, and although it was sort of disturbing, it showed that he had a personality. They liked that, too. He wasn't a snuggler, but sometimes he would walk up beside someone and press his head and neck against their legs. They knew there was a good dog in there somewhere.

By early September Wallace had become a regular topic of debate on a message board set up for volunteers who worked at Paws & Claws. One conversation on September 6 showed the combination of fear, confusion, and desire to help that had spread through the shelter. Clara wrote:

> Wallace does get quite aggressive with me, too. I'm still trying to figure him out. I've found so far that I have to hold him down to the ground by his collar and yell, "NO!" Then I wait quietly until he calms down a little bit. . . . Wallace has come the closest to scaring me at this job, but it makes me want to figure him out even more. What is freaking me out is that Wallace seems to get gradually

worse during his time at Paws & Claws. Please don't anybody be afraid of him because he needs us right now. He's definitely NOT beyond help.

Another volunteer responded:

Clara! I'm so glad I'm not the only one, because that will make me much more confident in working with him. He definitely does need work. I agree about the getting worse. I've interacted with him three times: he did nothing the first time, slight aggression/jumping/mouthing the second time that stopped immediately, and the third time is when he grabbed my hand.

A third joined:

I am having the same problems as you are it seems. I think when Wallace starts rolling around in the grass, it's a sign of things to come because he gets himself all excited and then wants to play. I always start getting a little frightened when I see this begin to happen. I am trying to work on being brave with Wallace, partly because I don't want to just give up on him. . . . When he starts going nuts, I've tried distracting him with treats and it only seems to work some of the time. I use my voice and body language too, but I haven't been able to find anything that will work consistently.

Talk moved from the message board to the hallways and back rooms of Paws & Claws. It started slowly, with whispered asides, and grew from there, evolving into a conundrum: What are we going to do about Wallace? No one could imagine how the shelter would find an adopter for him, and some began to wonder if euthanasia might be the best option.

Back when they were picking a name for him no one had considered the symbolic possibilities. Rasheed Wallace, the NBAer, was a talented player known for having a bad attitude. Over a fifteen-year career he was whistled for 304 technical fouls (given for arguing, rough play, and general bad behavior), the most ever for a player. He also held the single-season record for technical fouls, going through one eighty-game stretch in which he accumulated forty-one.

Maybe it was the wrong name for a dog with a borderline personality. Or maybe it was perfect.

2

It took more than a month for Roo to take action.

Within the shelter each dog had a classification that indicated its temperament. Green dogs could be handled by anyone. Purple dogs could be handled only by staffers and certain volunteers. Red dogs were off-limits to any but a select group of staffers—and Roo.

Over the year and a half he'd spent volunteering, Roo had built up enough experience and earned enough trust that he was allowed to work with the hardest cases. He now spent almost all of his time with the "red" dogs, "walking the dogs that no one else wants to walk," as he often summed it up. Wallace was a red dog, so it was little surprise that he and Roo wound up together.

Roo consulted with Adam. They spent some time with Wallace,

trying to figure out the dog's problem and how they might be able to deal with it. Clara was a big help. She had spent a lot of time with Wallace and provided valuable reconnaissance.

During their sessions in the yard she learned that Wallace was motivated by toys. She didn't know about the dog's training with Officer Mirren, but she soon figured out that Wallace loved to chase. Nothing made him happier than running down a good squeaky ball. But good luck getting it back from him.

Normally, when she played catch with a dog that didn't want to give the ball back, she'd make a trade: a treat for the ball. The first time she ran into this problem with Wallace she attempted to broker a deal. He wasn't going for it. She could keep her treat, thanks; he was sticking with the ball.

She went to the toy box and pulled out another ball. She squeezed it a few times, and it let out a high squeal. Wallace was interested. He came over. Clara held the ball out to him. He sniffed at it, eyed it up, but never let the first ball drop from his mouth. After a few seconds he clamped his jaws, sending up a loud squeak from the ball he already held, and trotted away.

Clara looked at the ball in her hand. She had to admit, it wasn't as appetizing as the one Wallace already had. She went back to the toy box and dug around a bit. Finally, she pulled out a squeaker that was similar in size and color to Wallace's. She gave it a few quick hard squeezes and out wheezed a sound that brought to mind a New Year's horn.

Wallace swung around. He liked what he saw. Clara wound up to throw the toy. Wallace dropped the ball in his mouth and shot across the yard after the new offering. When he picked up that one, Clara squeezed the first one again, and Wallace came back. He dropped the new one in front of her and prepared to chase the original. Now they were playing, and now she knew how to engage him.

"So that's it," she said. "It's gotta be a fair deal? One for one. You won't just chase after anything, will you? Well"—she threw the ball and watched as Wallace took off after it—"good for you."

And although they had fun together, she saw his bad-boy side, too. Numerous times when they were in the yard he jumped up on her and nipped at her hands and arms. Like most of the other volunteers, Clara attempted to use a combination of sound and body language to settle him. When two dogs are playing rough and one of them wants to quit or is getting more than he can handle, he turns his back to the aggressor and gives a sort of high-pitched yelp. This often puts an end to the game and gets the more dominant dog to back off.

Clara had tried it with various dogs over the months. When rough play broke out, she'd turn her back, cross her arms in front of her chest, and yelp. It worked. The dogs would either completely stop or at least take it down a notch. Not Wallace. Sometimes he'd back off, but other times it only made him more determined to get attention. He wouldn't stop, but she also knew that he never meant her any harm. He simply wanted her attention and interaction. He had no ill will but no self-control either.

With other dogs, he still showed aggression, but he had potential. Eventually he made friends with a few dogs at the shelter, and he played with them under close observation. Two puppies came to the shelter, Rock and Rocky, and one staffer brought them into the yard with Wallace. He romped happily with them and seemed pleased that their puppy energy matched his own tireless drive. At one point, Rocky actually humped Wallace, which can be an attempt to show dominance. Many dogs would have reacted violently to such an affront. Wallace was unbothered.

Adam and Roo took all that information into consideration, added their own observations, and decided that Wallace needed an outlet. He wasn't a bad dog; he was simply a high-drive working dog with a well-developed prey instinct and no direction for his abundant energy. His current existence, locked up inside a tiny kennel with lots of action happening around him, left him all revved up with nowhere to go. He needed a mission. He needed focus. He needed to burn some juice.

Adam had a plan.

———

Roo searched through his old stuff. After all those years as an athlete and gym rat, he had remained a fitness buff. He belonged to a gym but he also worked out at home sometimes and had a collection of weights and barbells. What he sought now was an old set of plastic, sand-filled weights. When he finally found them he threw them in the trunk of his car.

He already had some other equipment loaded in there. After measuring Wallace as if he were fitting him for a tuxedo, Roo had gone online and ordered a convoluted-looking harness. The contraption had two massive straps that went over the dog's shoulders and connected under his chest, then ran over his back and flanks. Behind his legs a short spreader bar kept the straps separated until they converged in a metal ring.

Roo had heard of canine weight pulling. The sport was growing, with no less than six governing bodies hosting dozens of events around the country. He knew the basics. A dog is hooked up to a wagon or sled and attempts to pull a load of weight over a short distance (usually twenty feet or less) in a certain amount of time (usually a minute or less). Typically, the wagon pullers compete on asphalt or concrete with a carpeted run, while the sled pullers perform on snow.

As weight is loaded onto the pull vehicle, the dogs that succeed in moving the vehicle the entire distance within the designated time advance to the next round, and more weight is added until a winner emerges. In the case of a tie, whichever dog completes the heaviest pull in the least amount of time wins. Within the competition dogs are split by gender and into as many as eight categories based on body weight. There are winners in each class and an overall winner determined by weight pulled as a percentage of body mass.

Roo had never participated in a weight pull before—he'd never even seen one—but he was curious about them, for a few reasons. He understood that pit bulls often excelled at the pursuit. It made sense; the breed was, generally speaking, strong, determined, and built low to the ground, all of which helped in weight pulling.

Some rescue and advocacy groups were starting to use weight pulls as a way to combat dogfighting. The idea was simple: If part of the appeal of dogfighting was testing your ability as a breeder and trainer and showing off your dog's strength, weight pulls offered another option. And they did so in a way that didn't lead to any animals getting hurt or people going to jail.

Weight pulls also helped combat another issue: negligence. Problem dogs are a common symptom of owners who don't spend enough time with them. They don't train them or walk them enough. Even worse, they leave the dogs untended or tied up in the yard all day, which can make them territorial and afraid of strangers. Preparing for a competition forces owners to work with their dogs and to get the animals more exercise.

Roo and Clara's work at Paws & Claws had begun to make them aware of the issues surrounding pit bulls. They hoped to one day help solve some of these problems, so the weight-pull movement interested them. For the moment, though, Roo simply wanted to help one particular dog—Wallace.

3

Roo and Adam brought Wallace outside. Adam had started something called the Northcentral Working Dog Club, through which he'd begun to organize and participate in weight pulls, so he gave Roo a few pointers on how to proceed. It was late in the afternoon, so there were very few cars in the parking lot, giving them plenty of room to work.

Roo slipped the harness over Wallace's head. The dog looked ridiculous, like some combination of the world's shortest trotting horse and a bandito from an old Western with two straps of bullets falling across his chest. This effect was exaggerated by Wallace's unrelenting, slobbering eagerness—he was thrilled at any chance to be outside. He was unbothered by these new entanglements at first, but when he tried to walk, the spreader bar hit him on the back of the legs. He twirled around to try to catch it, and he bit and gnawed at the harness. Roo worried. Would this experiment come to an end before it had even started?

After some tinkering, Roo added just enough weight—five pounds—to keep tension on the straps and prevent the spreader bar from hitting Wallace. He took the leash in one hand and a squeaky ball in the other, then gave a few squeezes and started walking. Wallace trotted after him, as if he were totally unencumbered.

Wallace wasn't an easy dog to walk, and Roo didn't see much difference with the weights attached. As always, Wallace pulled and weaved as the weights dragged and skittered and bounced behind him. He tried to dart after every squirrel and bird he saw. He sniffed everywhere. Roo never expected a miracle, but this would clearly take some time to have an impact.

Three or four times a week Roo took Wallace out behind the shelter onto a dirt path that ran next to a canal. He would hook Wallace into his harness, add some weight, squeeze the ball, and run, and Wallace would chase after him. When Roo reached the far end of the path he'd give Wallace the ball as a reward and let the dog chew on it for thirty seconds. Then Roo would pull a second ball out of his pocket, squeeze that, and sprint back in the other direction, Wallace hot on his heels.

Roo gradually increased the weight, from five pounds to ten to fifteen to twenty. Wallace hardly seemed to notice, but Roo knew that at the very least the exercise was good for the dog. A few weeks into this regimen, Roo's car needed a tire change. Roo had read that dragging tires was good practice for weight-pull dogs, so he asked to keep one of the old radials being taken off his car. He didn't know if Wallace was ready for a tire drag, but he decided to try.

He returned to the parking lot for the debut. Instead of the sprints, Roo started off at a walk. At first Wallace reacted as if nothing had changed. He set off after Roo, but as he crossed the lot and reached the small bridge that went over the canal, he slowed a bit. The tire created a lot more drag. Roo came back the next day and did it again, with similar results. He took a few days off, then did it again.

Roo could see a change. Wallace was less skittish and distracted. He didn't pull as much or romp. The tire created drag, and Wallace could feel it. He walked straighter, with his eyes in front of him. For the first time, Roo could actually walk alongside Wallace. Across the bridge sat a small park, and Roo would run Wallace up and down its bike path, each session lasting ten or fifteen minutes, until Wallace was wiped out. As Wallace's stamina built, Roo began stuffing the old plastic weights inside the tire to increase the challenge.

The volunteers at Paws & Claws reported that for the day or so after Roo took Wallace out on a weight pull, the dog behaved better. He was more focused, less manic. He didn't jump up as much, didn't nip and bite. Sometimes Roo couldn't get to the shelter for two or three days—he had to work late at the lab or had other after-work obligations. When that happened Wallace reverted to his old antics and everyone in the shelter suffered.

When he returned to the shelter after these absences Roo really felt the love around Paws & Claws. People were delighted to see him. "Wallace needs you," they would say. So he made the ten-block trek as often as he could, and he and Wallace fell into a comfortable routine. As soon as they hit the parking lot, Wallace, brimming with excitement, would begin to search for Roo's black Oldsmobile Intrigue. Once he spotted it, he'd charge over and pop up on his hind legs, leaning against the trunk with his front paws, waiting.

Roo enjoyed the sessions with Wallace just as much. He loved his job at Mayo and had plenty of friends there, but life in the lab was different. It was literally a sterile environment, flooded with fluorescent light and the unending hum of the air-conditioning. People in white coats shuffled from machine to machine. Roo filled his time running samples through centrifuges and processors, sequencing nucleotides, and running software analyses. He filled out reports while sitting on a chair in a windowless room where eight computers sat on a long table.

The first time Roo saw Wallace he thought the dog, with his crazy blue eye, looked cool. And as he'd gotten to know him he came to appreciate Wallace's exuberance. His spirit could not be dimmed—not by life in the shelter or by its worn cinder blocks and fluorescent lights—and Roo liked that. Of all the tough cases he'd taken on, this one felt different. As the weights grew heavier and the distance piled up behind them, man and dog bonded.

Clara, too, built a relationship with Wallace. She often played with him in the yard and walked him during the day. She led him to the same park across the bridge and sat with him in the grass, where she'd whisper to him and stroke his sides. He'd release a deep breath and let his eyes roll closed for a moment.

But only for a moment. Then he was up again and on the move. Clara would have to hop up and go along but she knew that for a short time at least she'd unwound the spring that coiled inside him.

She also worked on his manners. When playing, Wallace had a way of lunging at a toy that would lead him to get not only the object but part of the hand holding it. He wouldn't do any damage, but it was intimidating to those who didn't know him well. Roo and Clara knew that in order to give him something, they had to grab him by the collar and hold him back. But Clara had been teaching him to take a toy more gently. One day Roo received a call at work from Clara. "Wallace is taking the ball so nicely. He's not even touching my hand. I can play catch with him so easily!" To an outsider her excitement would have seemed a bit over the top, but Roo understood.

Likewise, Clara had been trying to get Wallace to sit before going through a door. Normally he would burst through with his usual unbridled spunk. Slowly, Clara got him to the point where he would sit, wait for a door to be opened, then walk through. He was fidgety and impatient while he waited, and he didn't always do it right, but he was making progress.

At night, in their little house, their lives coalesced around the happenings at Paws & Claws. They had become, as Clara joked to friends, dog nerds, and the topic dominated their conversations. Whatever past troubles they had been through were just that— past—and their bond was stronger than ever thanks to the shared sense of purpose the dogs and the shelter provided. Wallace emerged as a new and nearly endless subject of discussion. "He's a good dog," Clara would say as they sat to eat.

"Yep, yep," responded Roo with his signature phrase.

"They're afraid no one will want to adopt him," she said.

"Maybe not," Roo responded. "He needs people with a lot of experience."

"Someone will want him."

"I hope so."

They were rooting for Wallace. Which is why they were devastated when they heard about the incident.

4

Roo and Clara had gotten engaged the previous fall, back at Garvin Heights, on the bluff overlooking the Mississippi. Clara knew what was coming as soon as they pulled up. She had given him her grandmother's engagement ring months before—just in case. Now she couldn't wait to see it again. She didn't hear anything he said, she just kept thinking, *Come on, ask, ask!*

For Roo, the moment was one he had long anticipated. From the start he thought Clara could be *the* one for him. Any lingering doubts were long behind them, and his feelings for her only seemed to grow stronger. Her job at Paws & Claws was a symbol of everything he saw in her. She was compassionate and dedicated and not afraid to get involved. She connected with the people around her and through her good nature made everything around her better. As they stood on the bluff, Roo pulled out a ring, dropped to one knee: "You're the only woman I've ever truly loved. Will you marry me?"

In the aftermath, the couple rose to a new level of happiness. They spent more and more time together. They played with the dogs, they gathered with friends, they spent time at Paws & Claws trying to make a difference. But not everything in their lives remained similarly charmed. A few months after their engagement, Clara's mom, Sally, had gone into the hospital with stomach pain and had a large tumor removed from her abdomen. The mass was tested and determined to be leiomyosarcoma, a rare form of cancer.

The word "cancer" hit hard, and after Clara recovered from the shock she was full of questions. She sat with her mom asking what it all meant. Sally talked about the condition, the treatments, and the medical prospects in dry scientific terms. Roo asked for an update.

"From what my mom tells me," Clara told him, "the whole thing was this self-contained little blob. It wasn't attached to anything, and it wasn't in any of the organs. Since they removed the whole thing she should be fine, I think. She'll have follow-up tests every month, and if they don't find anything after like six months she's in the clear."

Beyond that Sally had little to say. She refused to entertain any talk of feelings or fears or potential long-term implications. She continued working and living her life the way she always had. There was no room for pity or pathos. Sally's approach felt a little odd or old-fashioned at times, but in truth Roo and Clara had a similar view: Do what could and should be done and don't dwell on the rest of it. It helped that the long-term prognosis seemed positive.

Sally was heavily involved in the wedding planning. It took her mind off her health, and for Clara, it felt so normal and productive that it made it easy for her to assume the best and move on. Roo and Clara floated back into their own lives, their particular concerns. They spruced up the house, they got involved with Wallace, they worked out.

Clara had casually mentioned to Roo that she'd put on some weight, and she wanted to lose it. She figured she had gained a little because she wasn't as active as she had been in college. But no matter what she tried she couldn't seem to drop the extra pounds. Roo could see it bummed her out a little, but she had too much going on to dwell on it, starting and ending with the wedding.

The ceremony took place on September 25, 2004, outdoors, with Angus and Ajax serving as ring bearers. The dogs wore tuxes and harnesses that held little pillows on their backs, and on the pillows sat the rings. Before the ceremony a friend held the pair out of sight. Roo stood at the makeshift altar with treats in his pocket and the moment before Clara came down the aisle, Roo gave a whistle and the dogs delivered the rings.

The reception was held on the property of an old farm that had been converted to a bed-and-breakfast. Following the ceremony, the group moved into a two-story circular barn, where they were greeted by a mashed potato bar and a steady stream of music. At one point, Clara changed into a red dress, and she and Roo danced a tango. Before the newlyweds knew it the DJ was packing up the speakers, their friends were heading for their cars, and they were standing with their families outside the little bed-and-breakfast, soaking up every minute of the perfect starlit night.

They had planned their honeymoon for December, closer to the holidays, so when the weekend was over and all the guests had gone home, they returned to their everyday lives. Back to the lab and the shelter, to Angus and Ajax and to Wallace, too.

Wallace had become a shared project, and they were happy to see he was making progress. He had a long way to go, though. Many of the people who worked at the shelter were still scared of him, and even if he managed to behave at times, he continued to be a ball of frantic energy who barked and jumped and nipped.

One day he unleashed a torrent of noise at a passing dog, who took up the challenge and charged at Wallace. They met at the gate to Wallace's kennel and Wallace caught the dog on the lip. Blood spurted on the floor.

It was a minor injury, but the story spread quickly and Wallace's rep, if it had improved at all, sank again. The whispering and the message-board banter grew louder. Roo redoubled his efforts, and Clara continued trying to instill some manners. It just wasn't enough.

About a week after the first incident there was another. A large Lab mix named Reggie lived in the kennel next to Wallace. The two dogs often barked at each other and pawed through the gate. On this day Reggie stood on his bed, raised up on his hind legs so his mouth was right near the top of the cinder-block wall dividing the two pens. He barked at Wallace, who tracked where the sound was coming from and assumed the same position.

The two dogs were inches away from each other, like bookends pushing in on either side of the thick cinder blocks. Chain-link fencing extended above the blocks, and as the dogs continued to bark they became more agitated. Finally, Reggie stuck his paw through the chain link. Wallace bit.

Reggie squealed.

The attendant on duty heard the sound and rushed in. She burst into Reggie's pen, grabbed his paw, and tried to free it, but she couldn't do anything to loosen Wallace's grip because he was on the other side of the fence. Reggie, in pain and afraid, lashed out, biting the woman on the arm. Now she yelped too, and with a final determined pull, wrested Reggie's paw from Wallace's mouth.

The attendant was bleeding. Reggie was bleeding. Wallace was apoplectic.

———

Clara arrived at Paws & Claws around noon, for her regular shift. As soon as she stepped through the door the receptionist said, "Did you hear about Wallace?"

"What?" Clara said.

"Well, he went after another dog and bit his foot. And when someone tried to break it up, he bit her, too."

Clara couldn't believe it. She ran back to the kennel. She burst through the door and almost knocked over Adam. "How?" she said. "Who?"

Adam told her what happened—really. That *Reggie* had stuck his paw through the fence and that Wallace had bitten it. That *Reggie* had bitten the attendant, not Wallace. And that although the damage to Reggie's paw was pretty bad, it would have been much less severe had someone pulled open Wallace's mouth instead of wrenching the limb out from the other side.

Clara felt a wave of relief, followed quickly by a spike of anger and a surge of sadness. It was clear how quickly everyone wanted to believe the worst about Wallace. She realized what this meant. Even if they could get everyone to hear the true story, the damage was done.

The questions about Wallace's future would only grow louder. Clara, Roo, and Adam felt as though they needed to get out in front of that question. They huddled together and devised a new plan for Wallace. First, they moved him. They had known all along that the highly stimulating atmosphere in the kennel amped him up. There was a small room in the main building where the shelter kept dogs in quarantine. The other dogs were moved, and that room became Wallace's new home.

Next, they limited his exposure. Only four people would interact with Wallace—Clara, Roo, Adam, and another staffer who had a positive history with Wallace and was committed to helping him. They felt fewer interactions would provide additional stability that might help calm him. Also, they didn't want something to happen because Wallace was mishandled or cared for by someone who didn't fully understand him.

Last, they would push to have him neutered. It was standard practice for all the dogs at the shelter, but the procedures were donated by local veterinarians and the organization only had access to roughly three a month. Dogs were prioritized based on which seemed the most adoptable, so Wallace remained pretty far down the ledger. The irony was that he likely would have benefitted the most, since many experts believe the operation, and the subsequent drop in hormones, tends to take the edge off a dog's personality. Wallace was all edge.

Unfortunately, news of Wallace's issues had reached the board, and some board members had begun asking around about him. The rumor mill spun. Word had it that the board was coming to view Wallace as a "dangerous dog." The talk of euthanasia turned serious.

This development represented a turning point for Clara and Roo. They had been on Wallace's side from the beginning. They were young and full of passion. When the first rumors of euthanasia circulated they didn't like them, but they understood. If Wallace was unadoptable—and everyone considered him pretty much so: He wasn't even on the adoptable-dogs list at the shelter—and incapable of functioning in a shelter environment, at some point it would be in not only the shelter's best interest but in Wallace's to end his suffering.

This was different. They were talking about putting Wallace down because he was a risk to both people and animals. To Clara and Roo—and Adam too—that simply was not true. Wallace was a brat, but he was also a high-intelligence, high-drive dog locked in an overstimulating setting with little to no outlet for his energy. That may have been reason to loathe him, but not to kill him.

Clara and Roo suspected something else was at play, a fact of Wallace's existence that he could do nothing about—his breed. Rochester's shelters had not yet been overrun with pit bulls, so the dogs remained a sort of unknown that existed more in myth and headline hyperbole than as actual canines. People had heard the tales of aggressiveness, of unprovoked attacks, and believed the hype. Even within the walls of Paws & Claws these half-truths persisted—as a private shelter P & C took in only the dogs it wanted to, so a limited number of pit bulls had come through the facility.

Clara and Roo felt that another dog in the shelter, a Lab mix named Roofus, was every bit as bratty and difficult as Wallace, but he seemed to receive a lot more understanding and patience. In one message-board posting Roo posed a question for the group: "What if Wallace acted the same, but looked like Roofus?"

It was weird to use the language of civil rights to discuss dogs, but for Clara and Roo no other word fit except *discrimination*. They could live with euthanasia for the right reasons, but bias and fear were not the right reasons. Saving Wallace became a mission.

5

The middle of October arrived. Clara had requested that Wallace get neutered and was told she'd have to get approval from the board. For Clara and most of the people who worked at Paws & Claws, the board remained something of a mystery. With few exceptions, the members were seldom around. The most accessible may have been Patti Evans. Clara and Roo knew her well, although she didn't confide much in them. Patti did speak regularly with Sue Stanek, the former board member who had given Wallace his name. Sue and Clara were good friends.

A daisy chain of communication formed. Patti would attend meetings and have conversations with other board members. She would share some of what she learned with Sue. Clara would pump Sue for information. Whatever nuggets she could dig up Clara would immediately tell Roo and Adam.

The process worked in reverse, too. Roo and Clara would discuss the issues surrounding Wallace and gather evidence in his defense. Clara would share it with Sue, who would tell it to Patti, who would argue the points among the board. They also had Adam. As the resident dog expert he talked directly to the board and spoke out in Wallace's favor.

In the past, those efforts would likely have been more than enough to erase any questions about Wallace, but things were changing at Paws & Claws. A woman named Marge Mourning had founded Paws & Claws Humane Society out of her house in 1976. She'd funded the operation by selling memberships and soliciting donations, and all the animals were eventually placed in foster homes. In 1988 she'd bought a house in the town of Salem Corners, where she built a kennel that could house up to thirty dogs. A year later she'd retired, turning the organization over to a board of directors made up largely of volunteers. In 2001, the dogs were moved to Rochester, where they remain.

The original mom-and-pop spirit of the place persisted until a few months before Wallace arrived. At the beginning of 2004, according to internal documents, P & C's "first strategic plan was created and implemented," and a "professional board with solid business experience" was put in place. Those professionals included an administrator at Mayo and a small-business owner, but no one who had run an animal shelter. In the years prior to Wallace's arrival almost all the board members had been hands-on volunteers in the shelter.

The new board hired the first nonvolunteer shelter manager, too. Amy Schoenwetter came on board several weeks before Wallace moved in. She did not have any experience running an animal facility, but she had been the manager of another nonprofit, a shelter for battered women. She had also grown up on a farm outside Rochester, surrounded by all sorts of animals, including a succession of Australian shepherds—midsize herding dogs that love to run and chase. She considered herself a dog lover, although she admitted to being scared of big dogs.

She didn't figure that would matter, though, because she had been brought in as a temporary fix while the board sought a permanent hire. And the job, as she understood it, was strictly managerial and administrative.

At least that was the theory, but an animal shelter has a way of sucking a person in elbow deep—if not deeper. Every pen had a bed and a blanket, and all those beds needed to be changed and the blankets washed. Schoenwetter found herself doing laundry, making beds, cleaning kennels, and walking dogs. She liked that part of the job fine, and although she was still a bit cautious around the bigger dogs, she realized that for the most part the large guys were just as nice as the little fellas.

Except for one.

Clara had looked in Wallace's eyes and seen mischief; Amy looked in those same eyes and saw menace. She avoided Wallace as much as possible, and when she had to walk past his pen she stayed as far to the opposite side of the passage as she could.

One day Clara walked into Amy's office with Wallace on a leash. Wallace raised up on his hind legs and put his paws on the desk. Amy canted backward in her chair. "Why are you so afraid of him?" Clara asked.

Amy thought for a minute and said, "I just don't like the way he looks at me."

To Roo and Clara's growing frustration, Amy seemed to pull as much weight with the board as Adam. The members consistently sought out her opinion on Wallace. That alarmed Roo.

One day, he'd been standing in the parking lot getting ready to take Wallace weight pulling. Wallace leaned against the trunk. Amy pulled in next to them, her dog, a white bichon frise, in the car with her. As Amy stepped out, her dog began to bark at Wallace as if it had seen an army of squirrels running by. Amy looked at Wallace and said, "I'm sorry, he's just scary." Roo looked at the little white ball of fluff going ballistic in the back of her car, running back and forth and barking. He looked at Wallace, sitting peacefully. He shook his head.

As far as Roo and Clara were concerned, Amy wasn't a dog person, and she had never run a shelter before. She had low credibility and an unreasonable fear of Wallace, but she had influence. And the board, it had become clear, was concerned about liability. If Wallace was adopted out and something went wrong, could the shelter be sued?

For Patti and many of the longtime volunteers, this was the pitfall of the "MBA types" taking over. The newbies worried more about the finances than the animals. For their part, the board members felt the staffers and volunteers—and even some of the holdover members like Patti—were too emotionally involved.

That might have been true of Clara, and she wasn't afraid to show it. Through every channel available to her, she continued to press for a neutering appointment for Wallace. Finally, she got an answer.

6

Clara and Wallace stood in the yard. Clara threw a ball, waited for Wallace to bring it back, and then threw another. After all her work he'd become more patient and much more gentle about taking things out of someone's hand—although he was by no means a delicate creature.

As they played, Wallace approached with a freshly retrieved ball in his mouth. For whatever reason, he didn't feel like waiting for Clara to throw the one in her hand. He released the ball in his mouth and lunged at the one she held. As he grabbed the ball, he grabbed a little of Clara's hand, too. She pulled back instinctively and yelled at him as he bolted off.

She looked at her hand. It hurt, but not too bad. She was not really bleeding, but in one spot, where the stab of pain had originated, a little red dot had formed. She looked closer. She ran her finger over the spot. It wasn't much but it was indisputably a small puncture wound.

The shelter's policy stated that any incident in which an animal breaks skin required an official bite report. Clara was alone in the yard. No one had seen what had happened or would ever know. She could simply put Wallace back in his pen, slap on some disinfectant and a Band-Aid, and that would be it.

The thought tempted her, but as Wallace had become more of a point of focus and disagreement around Paws & Claws the atmosphere had deteriorated. An undercurrent of animosity had developed as people took sides. Clara didn't want anyone to accuse her of hiding the truth or being anything but aboveboard.

She went back to her desk and filled out the report. Tears rolled down her face. She felt as though she might be signing Wallace's death warrant. He clearly hadn't meant to hurt her. As usual he was being a jerk, not a malcontent, but would anyone listen to that argument or would they simply see *Wallace* and *bite wound*?

She had reason to be pessimistic. After all of her efforts Wallace had been scheduled to be neutered on October 26. But when the day came, the appointment had been canceled. She'd heard conflicting reports—that the appointment had been given to another dog and that the vet had backed out because of a scheduling snafu. She didn't know whom to believe, but she suspected that the change had come from higher up. She couldn't help but feel that the board still wasn't sure if Wallace would be kept around much longer.

And the bad news continued. One of the volunteers had posted a summary of Wallace's situation on an Internet forum for shelter managers. The volunteer asked for advice. The majority of respondents suggested euthanasia.

It was another strike against Wallace, not only because of the verdict, but because members of the board felt the response increased the shelter's liability. If they set loose a dog that a panel of professionals had recommended putting down, they believed they'd be even more vulnerable to a lawsuit should something happen.

Patti had come to expect a call from Sue after such news leaked, but when she picked up her phone that day, it was Clara. "We can't let this happen," Clara pleaded. "We can't do nothing. Wallace needs us." Patti was moved by Clara's passion.

She returned to her fellow board members and argued that rather than trusting an anonymous group of Internet posters to analyze a dog they'd never met, Paws & Claws should hire its own expert to evaluate Wallace. The board agreed.

After some discussion Patti targeted a local woman named Natalie Faas-Gerber, a trainer who ran a pet-supply business and had done some work for Paws & Claws in the past. More important to Patti and Roo, she had a pit bull of her own, which meant she wouldn't be intimidated by—or prejudge—Wallace. Roo and Clara had used her for some obedience training when they first brought home Angus and Ajax and they both had a lot of respect for her knowledge and approach.

Team Wallace kept fighting. Adam had a weight-pull competition coming up in a few weeks. They knew that the type of people who attend a weight pull are the type that might adopt a dog like Wallace. Clara asked if they could enter Wallace in the weight pull. Amy would need to run it by the board, but hope glimmered.

Roo was ecstatic. Angus and Ajax would be competing in the pull, and Roo was certain Wallace could out-haul Angus, who was stronger than Ajax. He also felt it gave Wallace the best chance to find a home. Roo walked Wallace a little longer than usual that night and when they returned to the car, the dog panted with exhaustion. Roo leaned down and scratched him under the chin and behind the ears. Wallace stood still, looking at him, and Roo couldn't help but wonder how this one dog caused so much angst.

Momentum continued to build. Wallace had a new appointment to be neutered the following week. Clara volunteered to take
him herself. This time she would make sure that he made it to his
appointment.

Clara waited anxiously. She came in for a shift at the shelter. A
prospective adopter stopped by. Clara showed the man around, and
as they walked they spoke about what sort of dog he wanted. It
turned out he'd previously owned a bulldog, and a light went off in
Clara's head. Nice guy. Experience with bull breeds. Could it be?

Wallace wasn't officially up for adoption, so Clara again went to
Amy and asked permission to introduce them. Amy gave the okay.
Clara brought the man into the little room where Wallace stayed.
Man and dog hit it off. He stayed for a long time, and he and Clara
talked all about Wallace—the good and the bad, his needs and
quirks. The guy was interested but unwilling to commit on the spot.
He left his number and said he'd be in touch.

Clara was buoyant. Things had started to break Wallace's way.

7

Clara was up early. She fed and walked Angus and Ajax, piled
into her Pontiac Aztek, and set out for Paws & Claws. Wallace,
as always, was thrilled to see her. He wiggled with excitement when
she entered his private suite at the shelter, and when she opened the
pen to let him out he jumped up on her. After a quick walk she led
him to the car and opened the door. He bounced right in, perhaps
remembering his many rides with Officer Mirren.

She couldn't help but feel a little guilty. Wallace was so happy and eager to go on an adventure, but the poor guy had no idea what he was about to endure. Still, she wasn't going to kill his buzz, because she was equally excited. She knew the morning's business meant a new start for Wallace. He would, she hoped, chill out a little as a result of the procedure, which would improve his life at the shelter and his chances of finding a home. And it indicated a commitment on the part of the board to invest in his future, to give him a chance.

They walked into the vet's office and Wallace pulled and sniffed and tried to jump on the furniture, his tail sweeping the air like a helicopter blade and threatening to knock over any number of things—magazines, vases, tissue boxes. He turned his head with interest when Clara spoke his name to the woman at the reception desk. There was a momentary delay and Clara reached down to stroke his head, hoping to settle him a little.

"I'm sorry," said the woman. Clara froze, her hand coming to rest on Wallace's head. She straightened slowly and looked at the woman.

"What?" she said.

"Oh, I'm sorry," the woman repeated in her Minnesota accent, "but we don't seem to have an appointment for him."

"How can that be?" Clara responded, anxious. "It was all set. When I left work yesterday afternoon everything was set."

"Yeah," the woman said, looking at her appointment book. "Seems we received a call yesterday evening switching the appointment to another dog."

Clara put her hand to her mouth. She said nothing. She turned and headed for the door, gaining speed as she went. Reaching her car, she flung open the back door. Wallace hopped in and she slammed the door behind him. As she thrust herself into the front seat, she pulled out her phone and began dialing Roo as quickly as she could.

Suddenly the phone flew out of her hands. Wallace had jumped up from the backseat and trounced into her lap. She looked at him for a second and something inside her broke. She threw her arms around his neck and began to cry. This was not the resigned weep she had suffered through the day of the puncture wound. These were free-flowing tears accompanied by great heaving sobs.

————

After being turned away at the vet's office, Clara returned to Paws & Claws. She slipped Wallace back into his pen.

"What happened to Wallace's appointment?" she asked the receptionist later.

"They told me to switch it," the woman replied.

"Why?"

"They don't tell me those kind of things," she said. Clara had the sense that the woman knew more than she was saying.

"What does this mean for him?" Clara asked.

"Well, I don't know," the woman said.

Clara moved on with her day, but she was not happy and made sure everyone at the shelter knew. She told anyone who would listen what had happened and that she was worried about what it meant for Wallace's future. No one knew how to respond, and she left having gathered little besides awkward silences and blank shrugs.

The situation with Wallace was coming to a head and a collective uptick in the anxiety level came with it. Roo didn't like the situation either, and it showed when he came to take Wallace for his evening pulls. The weight-pull competition was now only about a week away and Roo wanted Wallace to be as impressive as possible. He had not yet been given permission from the board to enter Wallace, but he remained hopeful.

Adam had made a direct appeal to the board, arguing that this was Wallace's best chance to find a home, and that he and Roo and Clara would all be there to ensure that nothing went wrong. But the days kept sliding by with no word. Roo and Clara pressed for an answer. Finally two days before the event a decision came down: no.

Roo's post on the volunteers' message board began, "Well, I'm officially pissed off." It was followed by another that explained, "It would have been nice to get him into his element and around people that understand his breed to show that he's not as scary as everyone thinks he is."

Clara chimed in, too. "Most people in this organization have deemed him a liability in public. It seems that nobody will listen to me when I tell them his true personality. He has some problems, and I won't deny that, but I have worked very hard to get to know Wallace, and I understand why he does the things he does. I feel insulted that I am not allowed to handle him in public. Besides, this isn't any old public. The people at these pulls are mostly people that know this type of dog. . . . I understand why people have reservations about this dog, but I also understand that almost nobody is willing to learn otherwise."

Adam was mad, too. If the board didn't follow his lead on matters relating to the dogs, then what was he doing there? He felt undermined, underappreciated, and disrespected.

He quit.

The optimism that had blossomed in the previous weeks quickly faded. Many of the other volunteers expressed sympathy and understanding, but few rose up to support Wallace. Roo and Clara's fight grew lonelier, but they refused to give up.

They proposed finding a foster home for Wallace, with an experienced dog owner who would take him in and care for him until a permanent situation could be found. The board said no. Why? Liability.

They offered to foster Wallace themselves and to sign paperwork releasing Paws & Claws from any legal obligations. The board said no. Liability.

The only acceptable outcome, as far as the board saw it, would be for another shelter or rescue group to take Wallace, because the liability would then shift to the new organization. Roo and Clara and others made calls to as many such groups as they could find but none would take Wallace.

The board wasn't composed of bad or heartless people. On the contrary, they were caring sorts who volunteered their time, but they had been charged with the task of running Paws & Claws in a way that ensured its continued operation. As much as they may not have wanted to put an animal down, they weren't going to place the needs of one ahead of those of many. What good would it do if they saved one dog but bankrupted the place? They were simply doing their job as they saw it.

Adam, Roo, and Clara didn't see it the same way. As time passed it became clear that Wallace's future lay in the hands of the outside evaluator. Patti had finally succeeded in setting up the appointment with Natalie Faas-Gerber. Roo and Clara were nervous about how it would go—would Wallace be in one of his uncooperative moods?—but excited that Wallace would get a chance to show his true self.

Unfortunately, the evaluation could not have been scheduled for a worse date.

8

Wisconsin Dells is a resort town in the central part of the state, bisected by the Wisconsin River. It has spas, shopping, restaurants, golf, entertainment, wineries, and a casino, among other attractions, but it is best known as the self-proclaimed "water park capital of the world," thanks to an elaborate system of indoor and outdoor water slides. Roo and Clara thought it would be a fun place for a honeymoon because it would be decorated for the holidays but relatively empty as families with kids normally don't visit in early December. They were right. There were life-size gingerbread houses, decorated trees in every corner of every building, and carols echoed from the sound system. Best of all, the lines were relatively short.

Yet they spent most of their first day at the Dells holed up in their time-share unit (a wedding gift from a friend), glued to their cell phones. Wallace's evaluation was taking place that day, and it appeared to be a zero-sum game: If he did well the board would consider alternatives to help him, but if he showed troublesome signs it would almost certainly be the end for him. Clara and Roo were stressed. It killed them not to know what was happening.

The "friends of Wallace" phone tree shook with activity. Sue, the former board member, worked the lines to get information from Patti and other current board members. Clara hounded Sue. Adam, though he had quit, was still one of the small band of individuals who was willing and had been approved to care for Wallace, so he had agreed to come in three times a day to walk and feed the dog while the Yoris were away. Adam also talked to various board members, employees, and volunteers and heard his share of rumors.

The group networked and hustled to keep up with what may or may not have been happening. And after they had talked and wondered and plotted all they could, they continued to brainstorm ideas on how to save Wallace. Who could they find to take the dog that the board would actually approve? As the afternoon wore on, Clara talked and Roo paced.

Clara's phone rang. It was Sue. She'd heard from Patti, who had attended the evaluation. It had been Patti and Natalie in a room with Wallace. Natalie had performed a series of temperament tests—everything from putting her hands in the bowl while Wallace ate, to giving him a delicious treat like a piece of dried meat and then taking it away, to approaching him from behind. Wallace had seemed, in Patti's estimation, to do well. He wasn't perfect, but he

hadn't done anything as far as she could tell that would lead someone to determine that he was a "dangerous dog."

As Clara relayed this, Roo picked up his pace, back and forth,
back and forth across the little room. The key moment had occurred
when Wallace got excited and started jumping up on Natalie. She
had given a yelp, and Wallace reacted appropriately, backing off and
sitting down. In Roo's mind this carried a lot of weight. He knew
it was the kind of moment that could have gone either way, and he
was relieved that Wallace had done the right thing.

When Clara hung up, Roo let out a whoop and gave her a hug.
For the first time in weeks they felt like they could exhale.

They enjoyed the moment. Then Roo started pacing again, running through scenarios of what might come next. If Patti was correct, Wallace's chances had improved. Still, there remained the
problem of what to do with him: Certainly, a positive report would
justify sparing him and ease some of the board's liability fears, but
it wouldn't eliminate the risk of a lawsuit, and it wouldn't make
finding him a home any easier. Wallace would remain a long-term
shelter case with little hope of adoption. And if he continued to live
in the shelter chances were he'd continue to deteriorate.

———

When Clara and Roo woke the next morning they felt as though
their vacation had just begun. They planned a big day at the water
park, but their first move was a trip to Walmart to stock their rental
unit with snacks and goodies. As they shopped, Clara's phone rang,
and once again it was Sue. She had more news.

The evaluation had in fact been positive, although Natalie
thought Wallace would need an experienced handler to succeed
outside the shelter. Patti took the information and ran with it.

She and Adam had come up with a plan. The Northcentral Working Dog Club, Adam's weight-pulling organization, was technically
qualified to function as a rescue group. Patti had suggested that

Northcentral take Wallace on as a rescue, thereby assuming the liability. Northcentral could then hand the dog over to Clara and Roo as a foster.

It was a bit of a shell game, yes, but it was also perfectly legal. It involved some risk for Clara, Roo, and Adam, but they had all talked about Wallace's potential and this gave them the opportunity to put their asses where their assessments had been. As Roo listened in on the conversation he began to bounce down the aisles, picking things off the shelves and tossing them in the cart.

Patti wasn't done. She had pitched the idea to the board, and it had been approved. Wallace would be neutered the next day, and a day after that Clara and Roo could pick him up. Clara felt a wave of relief; Wallace was getting out of there. Roo virtually skipped through the store. And that afternoon they hit the water slides with abandon.

By evening they were back in their time-share. Out the back window a fountain sprayed in the middle of a small pond. Roo and Clara went out to the balcony, and as they sat in the cold December air, Roo began to throw bread to a flock of ducks that had gathered below the window. Clara's thoughts turned to what lay ahead. She worried that something could still go wrong. She also wondered if they could give Wallace what he needed, if they could provide the home, training, exercise, and focus that would calm him. Would he be as crazy in their house as he was at the shelter? Would there be problems between Wallace and their other dogs? Could they really find someone to adopt him? Would they end up on the wrong side of a lawsuit?

Roo had begun to pace again, and she knew he was thinking about the same things. They sat in silence for a few minutes, then Roo said, "Well, I guess we're it."

"I guess so," Clara said.

Chapter 3

Taking Flight

———— ● ————

I think Wallace might be awesome.

Roo Yori

1

It wasn't a Frisbee. That's a brand name that refers to a specific product. The generic name for that round saucerlike object made for playing catch is a flying disc or simply a disc. But this thing wasn't really a disc either. It was fabric, green with a thick weighted yellow tube around the perimeter, which is what made it fly. It had been picked off a shelf of dog toys weeks earlier, and it hadn't seen much action since, but as Roo ran out the door he stuffed the thing in his pocket.

Ajax waited in the car. Although he was nothing like Wallace, Ajax continued to have problems of his own, and his issues were definitely with people. He was okay around those he felt comfortable with—as Roo often said, once you were in the circle of trust you were fine—but he remained wary of strangers and had a habit of biting at the ankles of those he felt threatened by. For whatever reason, baseball hats triggered his aggression, too.

Roo and Clara continued to work on all these issues. They tried to keep Ajax engaged and at the same time expose him to a lot of different situations and people. They'd taken him for obedience training and on extensive outdoor excursions, and they'd entered both Ajax and Angus in weight pulls, although Angus seemed to have the real pulling potential. Ajax, they thought, might like to have some fun chasing discs around a field.

At the park they ran through their familiar routines. A long walk, a short romp, general frolicking. Then Roo pulled out the fabric disc. It was not the first time Ajax had seen it. Roo had tossed it to Ajax around the house and the two occasionally played tug-of-war with it. Roo let Ajax smell the disc and waved it in front of him to get the dog interested. He made a few short tosses that Ajax could catch without moving. Finally, Roo let the disc fly. Ajax took off after it.

And he kept right on running as the thing fluttered to the ground. He came back and sniffed at it, then picked the disc up and trotted back. Roo was not easily dissuaded. He met Ajax with an enthusiastic greeting and gave him a treat for returning with the disc. Ajax was psyched.

Roo flung the disc. Once again, Ajax bolted off, his eyes locked on the spinning circle. When it reached the apex of its flight and began to float back to earth, Ajax sped toward it and snagged it out of the air. Roo let out a whoop and thrust his arms up.

When Ajax returned with his prize, Roo hugged him and gave him another treat. Ajax jumped with excitement. Roo threw the disc again and Ajax went after it. He didn't make every catch, but he tried. Roo was exhilarated.

Dog and man had hit a high that day in the park, but that was as far as it would go. Before they could return to try again the Minnesota winter settled around them. And with the winter came something else: Wallace.

―――――

The Yoris lived on a corner lot on the west side of town, a pleasant suburban-feeling neighborhood from which Roo could make the three-mile ride into work on his bicycle when the weather allowed. Their split-level ranch had four bedrooms, two upstairs and two down. Angus and Ajax lived in one of the upstairs bedrooms. Thanks to his penchant for troublemaking (and pillow eating), Angus spent the night, and the daytime hours when Roo and Clara were out, in a crate. Ajax had the run of the place.

Roo and Clara had won the battle of Paws & Claws, but they soon realized it was only the opening skirmish in the War of Wallace. The next fight had just begun: integrating Wallace into a house that already had two large, strong-minded dogs.

Guest dogs—of which there had been several—got one of the downstairs rooms. Wallace kept up that tradition, although he did get a deluxe crate, a five-foot-by-five-foot castle that allowed him to chill in comfort.

On Wallace's first day in the house, Angus and Ajax came down to check him out. The pair sniffed at the newcomer warily. Wallace returned their lukewarm welcome. But that was as close as they got. Roo and Clara made sure to give each of the dogs as much out-of-crate time as possible each day, but they had to manage the shifts carefully. Angus and Ajax could be out together. But Wallace needed the house to himself, and when he left his crate, trouble followed.

True to form, Wallace was relentless. He needed constant engagement. If someone played with him he wanted to play long and hard. He never quit first. If ignored, he would jump and nip and nudge, and if that didn't work he'd go off in search of entertainment, a quest that often led him to a countertop or a dresser or the deepest recesses of a previously filled laundry basket.

The one saving grace was that he wanted whatever Roo or Clara had, so if they spotted him eyeing up a pillow with bad intent, all they had to do was pick up a rawhide and Wallace would come begging for it. And he'd be satisfied for a good five or ten minutes before he needed some new diversion. When he chewed a toy he didn't simply gnaw at it; he chewed it to pieces.

If Clara tried to simply sit and pet him, like she would back in the park, he'd mouth at her hands. Clara and Roo tried to remain patient. They knew it would take any dog some time to decompress after that many months in a shelter, and they also knew Wallace needed training. Still, they shared more than a few "What have we gotten ourselves into?" moments.

One of those came when they tried to buy homeowner's insurance. Some companies charged more for households containing a pit bull, and some flat-out refused coverage. Even Clara's parents expressed reservations. They had heard about Wallace's antics during the months he lived at Paws & Claws. Upon getting the news that Wallace would now be living with Roo and Clara, the Setzers had asked, "Are you sure you know what you're doing?" with more than a little wariness.

Roo and Clara knew from working at the shelter that the American pit bull terrier and the group of related breeds that were often lumped together and referred to as pit bulls had a poor image. But they had no idea how bad things were. As they tiptoed into the world of pit bulls, they read online accounts of people who had been cursed at and spit on while walking their dogs. They heard tell of those who had been hassled by police. They paged through stories about people in Denver, which has a zero-tolerance pit bull ban, who had seen their family pets, which had never caused a problem, seized and euthanized strictly because of their breed. One time Clara took Wallace for a walk, and they bumped into a neighbor. The woman stood petting Wallace as she chatted with Clara. After a few minutes of idle chatter, she asked about Wallace's breed.

"Oh, he's a pit bull," Clara said without thinking.

"Really," said the woman, pulling her hand away. "I don't like pit bulls."

Clara felt a little hurt, but she and Roo weren't going to let such things stop them. They knew pit bulls had a bad reputation—and Wallace in particular had issues—but they were going to do everything they could to prove that he could still make a good pet.

That included integrating him with the other dogs, if for no other reason than to allow them all more out-of-crate time. They figured out quickly that Ajax and Wallace would not mesh—no surprise there. But Angus and Wallace had potential. In brief tests, they seemed to tolerate each other.

One day Roo and Clara let Angus and Wallace roam free, keeping a close eye on them. At one point Angus, who was taller than Wallace and close to twenty pounds heavier, lay on the kitchen floor, dozing. Wallace came to the door. Angus's eyes opened and a low rumble emerged from deep within. Wallace stopped and stared.

2

Roo picked up his tools and headed for Wallace's room. He couldn't quite believe how dogs had come to dominate his life. When he wasn't walking or feeding them, he worked on weight pulling with them. Now he was taking his weekend to build a platform for Wallace's kennel. Actually a second platform. Wallace never peed in the house, unless he was in the kennel. Roo figured it was a throwback to shelter living, and as he and Clara struggled to break the dog of the habit, the carpet in Wallace's room became polluted with urine.

So a few weeks into Wallace's stay, Roo had pulled out all the carpet and built a platform with low wooden edging and lined it with linoleum. It worked for a while but eventually the urine worked its way under the linoleum, where it began to fester and smell. So Roo embarked on a new platform. The structure was similar but this one was sealed and lined with epoxy. At the same time Roo covered the floor with the sort of spongy, brightly colored tiles that are often used for a rec room. Clara and Roo began calling Wallace's abode the Pit Bull Playroom.

Besides the domestic efforts, Roo continued to volunteer at Paws & Claws, where Clara still worked. He enjoyed the full immersion. As a kid, he had always wanted a dog, and he'd begged his parents endlessly. His sister, who was five years older, wanted a cat. His parents never got behind either idea. Instead Roo received a parakeet, three lizards—named Larry, Mo, and Curly—some turtles, a lobster, and a crayfish. He enjoyed them all, but none of them was a dog.

Nothing changed until he got himself a gun. And a ten-gallon hat.

The summer after his senior year in high school, Roo took a job as a cowboy at Donley's Wild West Town, a cowboy-themed amusement park in Union, Illinois. The gig required him to dress up like a latter-day Lone Ranger, mosey around the "town," and take photos with the visitors. That wasn't good enough for Roo, though. He wanted to be part of the shootout that was staged several times a day. He pestered the head cowboy until he was finally given the role of the dopey deputy who gets flattened in a classic Old West dustup. Eventually, Roo became the lead bad guy, and as the choreography went, the last gunshot would knock Roo's character backward off a roof, at which point he'd land on a hidden platform. That wasn't good enough for Roo, either. He started doing forward falls off a two-by-four and landing on a mat obscured by a tan tarp and hidden by a few barrels.

One day, during a rehearsal a small dog appeared—a tan cairn terrier. Roo reached out and the little dog came to him. He found a piece of rope and tied it to the dog's collar, then walked around hoping to find the dog's owner. No luck. He tied the dog up, gave it some water, and went back to rehearsal.

Next to Donley's sat an RV park and campground and Roo figured the dog must have wandered over, so on his next break he went door-to-door searching for her family. Again, no luck. He went back to work, and after practice he spent the rest of the day trying to reunite the dog with whoever had lost it. Finally, out of options, he brought the dog home.

How would he tell his parents? He needed to think. He stepped out of the car and paced up and down the driveway. Finally, he took the dog and tied her to the banister that led to the front porch. He went in the house. His parents sat in the living room. "Mom, Dad," he said. He paused. They could see something was on his mind. Seconds ticked by. "You see," he said, "well, I have this . . ." He began to pace. "Well . . . um . . . There's this dog," he blurted.

Ron Yori cut his son off. "How big is it?" Roo turned and walked toward the front door. His dad followed. They stepped onto the porch, and as they did the dog popped its little head over the edge right between two spindles. Her ears perked, she tilted her head sideways. Ron exhaled audibly. "You can keep it in the basement tonight, but tomorrow you have to find the owners," he said.

They brought the dog into the basement. Roo gathered up some food and water and made a small bed out of an old blanket. Mr. Yori said, "Sit," and the dog sat. It didn't bark at all during the night, and when they went downstairs in the morning the dog had not had an accident. Those were all good signs, Roo figured.

Still, the day's plan called for Roo to take the dog back to work and check with the houses in the area. If he couldn't find the dog's home, he should take it to the shelter. Roo followed directions, again going door-to-door. The more times he heard, "No, that's not my dog," the farther and harder he pushed. He didn't know much about shelters, but he believed they held dogs for a few days and then put them down.

Eventually, though, Roo had to get to work and could search no more. At the same time he couldn't bring himself to take the dog to the shelter. As he thought about it he figured the dog had been running loose when he found her, so what was the harm if she were set loose again? At least on her own she would have a chance. Maybe she could find her way home or at least be found by someone who would take her in.

He pulled over to the side of the road and opened the door. The little dog looked at him quizzically. She didn't want to get out. He tried shooing her a little and pointing, but she didn't move. Finally, he had to pretend he was getting out on his side. When he did, the dog jumped out in anticipation of an adventure. Roo jumped back in the car, pulled the door shut, and drove away. As he did he looked in the rearview mirror. There she was, a little tan blob of fur chasing after the car. Roo knew he couldn't stop. It killed him, but this was the only answer and the best he could do.

He lasted about half a mile. "I can't," he said out loud, and swung the car around. As he approached the area where he had dropped the dog he searched the road, but there was no sign of her. There weren't many side streets, but as he passed each one he scanned down the block. As he glided past one of them he saw her, walking on the side of the road a few hundred yards down the street. She looked up as he went by. He pulled to the side and checked his mirror to make sure no cars were coming before he made a U-turn. What he saw surprised him.

The little dog came around the corner in a full sprint. She had recognized his car and come chasing after him. As the dog approached, Roo opened the door and she leapt in, excited and bouncing for a second before settling onto the passenger seat as if nothing had ever happened.

Roo went to work, but he was not allowed to bring the dog inside the park. So he tied her to a post near his car and brought her food and water throughout the day. He had no idea what he would do with the dog. He felt like the shelter was a death sentence, but home didn't seem like an option either. He asked around; none of his coworkers was interested in a new pet. On breaks, his spurs jangled as he paced.

Late in the day, the front office paged him. He had a phone call. It was his mom. "Do you still have the dog?" she said.

Roo hesitated. "Yep."

"Well," his mom said, "Dad thought it was a very nice dog. Why don't you bring it home, and we'll see what we can figure out."

The next day Mr. Yori ran an ad in the local paper seeking out anyone who might have lost a dog that fit the description. No one responded. As the days went by, the family started calling the dog Rigby and letting her out of the basement at night. After years of pleading, Roo finally had a dog. Four weeks later he left for college. Rigby lived in his old house for eight years. Both the dog and the parents seemed pretty happy with the arrangement.

Now Roo had taken in another abandoned dog, but this one couldn't rely on its cuteness and good manners to find a home. Roo would have to find another way.

3

Roo considered himself a reasonably good trainer by this point, but Wallace presented a challenge that would confound many dog experts: He wasn't motivated by food. How then could they train Wallace? On the Internet Roo had discovered a school of training that used play as a motivating force. For Wallace in particular this came down to his favorite pastime: tug.

So training Wallace, like everything else that involved Wallace, was going to be interesting. Roo had borrowed a DVD from a friend called *The Game*, which dealt with tug training. Following the program outlined on the disc, Roo and Clara began teaching Wallace how to live with people by regulating his play. When he did something right he got time with his favorite toys and a chance to play tug-of-war. When he misbehaved, he had his toys taken away until he showed appropriate manners.

Slowly, he learned "sit," "stay," "no," and most important, "out," which caused him to let go of whatever he had in his mouth and represented a pinnacle of self-control for Wallace. He became a little less of a menace around the house. He could still be unruly and excitable, but now he knew when he had misbehaved and he was much easier to bring back under control. He and Angus developed a working relationship. On the day Angus had growled at him in the kitchen, Wallace had backed out of the room and walked away. The instance more or less defined the relationship—a sort of tenuous détente. Sometimes Wallace would pester and challenge Angus, and Roo or Clara would have to step in, but for the most part peace reigned.

The improved behavior did little to dim Wallace's personality. One weekend Roo and Clara took Wallace to a clinic called "Coaching the Canine Athlete." At one point, each dog in the program was supposed to walk across an area filled with low obstacles. For the drill, the dogs were handled by one of the instructor's assistants. As luck had it, the assistant who wound up with Wallace was a small, pregnant woman. Roo wondered if the woman would be able to hold Wallace, but he also worried that Wallace would be distracted by one of the many other dogs around, especially a small fluffy one that sat in the lap of an older lady right by the starting line. To keep Wallace focused, Roo flashed a squeaky toy as Wallace's turn approached. Wallace got so excited he plowed right through the field of obstacles, knocking every one of them over and almost pulling the woman off her feet. Roo buried his face in his hands.

Back at home, Roo supplemented the training with plenty of activity. He and Wallace continued to pull the tire a few evenings a week, giving the dog the exercise and focus he needed. And at night the garage became Wallace's playpen: Roo installed a spring pole, which is a large spring that attaches to the ceiling, then leads to a rope that hangs just beyond the dog's reach and is tied to a chew toy. The dog jumps to grab the toy, and as he pulls at it the spring gives and pulls back. Basically, the dog plays tug-of-war with the ceiling.

Wallace loved it. Roo would turn him loose on the spring pole nearly every night. Wallace would grab the toy and pull, letting out long pulsating growls and dancing around the room on his hind feet. It became something of a ritual, and each night when Roo came home and Wallace was let out of his kennel, the dog would go to the door that led to the garage and sit waiting. One time, Roo opened the door, but the lightbulb had gone out. When he finally replaced it and the light came on, there was Wallace, up on his hind legs searching in the dark for the chew toy, which dangled an inch behind his head.

The setup was not without its flaws, though. Roo felt a little uneasy and secretive about the spring pole because the contraption was sometimes used by dogfighters to strengthen a dog's jaws and neck. That wasn't Roo's aim, but as Wallace dangled from the pole his feet would wear against the rough concrete floor, and one time they actually started to bleed from the wear and tear, leaving stains on the floor. One night, Roo had agreed to take care of the neighbors' dog while they were away, so he left Wallace in the garage while he ran over to feed the other pooch. As he crossed the yard on the way home he heard a strange sound—a horrible, near-feral growl. He looked around to see if some wild animal had wandered into the neighborhood. He didn't see anything, and he soon realized the sound was coming from his house. More specifically, his garage. He heard Wallace growl every night while he sat with him, but he never realized how the sound traveled. It was awful.

When he walked back inside, he realized the scene looked even worse than it sounded—a pit bull swinging from a spring pole, scary growling, blood on the floor. Someone was going to think *Roo* was a dogfighter. He couldn't take the spring pole away from

Wallace, but he had to make some changes. He attempted some minor soundproofing, put Astroturf on the floor, and acquired booties to protect Wallace's feet. Wallace hardly seemed to notice the new gear. As long as he got to play he would have worn ballet slippers and a tutu.

As Wallace's manners got better—not good, but better—Roo and Clara set to the task of finding him a home. They listed him on Petfinder, and they entered him in a weight-pull competition, as they had hoped to when he was at Paws & Claws. They still thought Wallace's best chance to find a home would be with someone who had experience with large strong breeds and a willingness to put him to work. The weight-pull crowd presented the right mix.

Since it was late January, the event would take place at an indoor facility. Roo and Clara knew there would be a lot of other dogs and not a lot of space. They weren't sure how Wallace would respond, so the day would be a test of not only his pulling prowess, but of his behavior and their handling abilities. Echoes of the board's liability fears bounced around their heads. They devised a simple plan: Keep Wallace in his crate, and when he needed downtime or if he seemed overexcited, put a sheet over the crate to cut down on the stimulation. Plus, Adam was running the event, so he would be there to help if needed.

As they had suspected, the place was jammed. Dogs barked constantly. People shouted to urge their dogs on. Squeak toys squealed, and the smell of everything from hot dogs to treats to other animals filled the air. But Roo and Clara had nothing to worry about—Wallace behaved like a champ all day. He'd already come a long way since Paws & Claws.

The harness was familiar, but it was the first time Wallace had ever been hooked up to a cart. Through the first few rounds he proceeded without hesitation. Roo stood at the end of the run squeezing a squeaky ball, and Wallace went right to him.

As the weight increased though, Wallace seemed uncertain how to react. Roo had never worked with anything heavier than the tire, and he'd never taught Wallace how to bear down and pull when the weight was more than he could simply trot off with. The first time this happened, when Wallace tried to start walking but couldn't, he didn't know what to do. He tried to go to Roo, but he didn't know how to get low and dig in. He went as far as he could on his own instincts, but he would need more training.

Still, his potential was obvious. Without really knowing what he was doing, he finished second in his weight class. Adam had nothing but compliments; they were all proud of how Wallace had handled himself in his first public outing. Best of all, Roo and Clara were approached by a guy who inquired about adopting Wallace. He was young, maybe in his early twenties, and Roo and Clara worried that he didn't have enough experience to handle Wallace. But it at least justified the strategy. People at these events would take notice. Maybe Wallace would find a home.

4

A change at the Yori house arrived in a small bundle, less than twelve pounds, swaddled in a blanket, and helpless. Mindy Lou was her name.

A few weeks earlier someone had brought Mindy into Paws & Claws, reporting that he'd seen her tossed from a moving car. A toy Aussie, Mindy Lou had multiple injuries, the worst of which, a fractured pelvis, required her to remain crate-bound for at least a month. Clara couldn't see the point of making Mindy stay in the cold, noisy shelter to recover. Instead, she brought the dog home and set her up in one of the downstairs rooms, where the surroundings were at least friendlier and more comfortable.

Clara couldn't help herself. She'd argued for Ajax because he needed them. She'd argued for Wallace because he needed anyone. She argued for Mindy because she was sweet and helpless. But there was something else too. Clara needed Mindy. She needed all of them.

Her relationship with dogs went back to her childhood. When Clara was five, she, her sister, and her mom began to beat the drum: They wanted a dog. Clara's dad wasn't so sure. The debate went back and forth, until finally they rescued a beagle-sheltie mix from the local shelter, and they named her Heidi.

Clara and her mother doted on Heidi and for years the pup lived a happy life. Then something happened. Clara grew up. She started playing sports and spending more time with her friends. Heidi fell by the wayside. Clara's parents decided to place the dog in another home with another family that could give her the attention she deserved. Clara didn't like the idea but she couldn't really argue.

But problems arose in the new home and Heidi's transfer didn't take. A year later, Heidi returned. Clara made a renewed effort to care for her, but besides the sports and friends she now had something else on her plate: boys.

Finally, on a summer day the year Clara turned fifteen, Heidi was tied up in the front yard, and when the paperboy arrived, Heidi bit him. Coming off the problems she'd had in her transfer home, the incident raised serious concerns about Heidi's stability, and after consulting with the family vet, Clara's parents decided they would have to put Heidi down. Clara hated the idea, and she fought, but in the end she didn't have much of an argument, because she had not done more to support the dog.

Roo's experience with Rigby had taught him the joy that came from rescuing a dog. How persistence and following his instincts had made life happier for everyone. Clara learned the same lesson in reverse. She knew the horrible feeling that came from taking responsibility for another creature's life and failing it. That reality hadn't hit her as hard as a callow teenager, but when she looked back on it now it haunted her.

Something else ate at her, too. Her mother's cancer had returned. The news burrowed underneath Roo and Clara. After the initial diagnosis, the disease had seemed beatable, but this second round felt ominous. "The doctors told her that they always knew this was a strong possibility," Clara said.

"I thought that once she hit six months she was in the clear," Roo said.

"Me too," Clara said. "That's what she made it sound like to me. I don't know if she misunderstood what they told her or if she was trying to protect me, but everything's different now."

"This sucks," Roo said. Sally remained upbeat and positive, even as she prepared for another surgery followed by chemotherapy. Roo and Clara both went online to research Sally's treatments, and they discussed what they found, but otherwise they didn't talk much about it.

Inside, though, Clara worried. More and more she'd found herself falling into little wells of sadness. The dogs helped. They made her feel better—when they weren't driving her nuts—and there were now four of them to do the job. Mindy had come home as a temporary acquisition, but Clara and Roo both had a sense she'd be staying. She had already taken control of the pack, barking out orders and shouting down the big boys around her. Except for one.

Wallace remained a handful. Besides his constant need for engagement, he could get hyper, running, jumping up on people and furniture, and pouncing on his toys like a kid going after a cupcake. Roo continued to work with the dog on basic commands and overall behavior, but they seemed to have hit a wall. He could learn to "sit" and "stay," but knowing those things didn't cool the fire that burned inside him. Their inability to gain control over him frustrated them, and on more than one occasion they said to each other, "Why can't he just be a normal dog?"

The spring pole provided a clue. Most nights, the sessions lasted about thirty minutes, although sometimes Roo would let Wallace go longer. Once, in some sort of endurance test, Wallace stayed on the pole for fifty minutes. When he finished he was so weary that he literally could not walk straight. He went back into the house and prepared to flop down onto the floor. *Wow,* Roo thought, *I finally exhausted him.*

But before Wallace touched down, he spotted a ball that sat across the room. He couldn't stand it. Wallace gathered himself and wobbled across the room to get the ball. Roo was astounded. He'd been calling Wallace a "high-drive" dog for months, but this was off the charts. It was almost scary. Wallace could not simply *be.* He always needed to be doing something, going somewhere, driving forward.

5

Roo logged on to an internal bulletin board where Mayo employees could post items. In the past Roo had bought a computer desk, a dining room set, and a lawn mower on it. Good deals. Nothing terribly interesting popped up for sale today, but one posting caught his eye: "Anyone interested in starting a disc-dog club? Call Josh."

Roo immediately thought of Ajax. They hadn't made any trips back to the park, but he and Clara had continued to throw Ajax a disc in the yard when the weather allowed. As far as Roo could tell, Ajax was pretty good. Clara had even bought him a disc made of Nylabone, a synthetic bone material. A disc-dog club could be the perfect thing for them.

A few days later he tried to recheck the number before dialing it. But when he went back on the bulletin board, the post had disappeared. Roo wondered what that meant. He was nervous. The guy's full name was Josh Grenell, and Roo had looked him up online, discovering that he'd placed fourteenth in the world finals. "Clara," Roo called out as he read, "he's a world qualifier." Roo hoped he and Ajax would be worthy. He dialed the number and asked for Josh.

"Hey," he said. "My name is Roo and I saw your posting about the disc club." He paused.

"Uhhh," the voice replied.

"Well, are you still doing it?"

"Yeah."

"Um, if you are, I'm interested in joining. I've got a dog here that I've played with, you know, just in the park and the yard, and I think he's pretty good."

"Uhhh."

"Well, if you want to do it, maybe we should meet up and I can show you what he can do," Roo offered.

"Yeah."

"Maybe you want to come here?"

"Sure."

Roo proceeded to give the man his address and arrange a time Saturday morning for him to swing by. He hung up the phone confused.

"How'd it go?" Clara said.

"Not sure," Roo answered. "The guy had either just woken up or he's really weird."

"Probably just woke up," said Clara.

"I hope so, because he's coming here on Saturday."

————

A gold Ford Focus rolled up in front of the Yoris' house, and a tall, lean man decked out in browns and olive greens approached the door, a baseball cap on his head and a few discs in hand. A woman walked beside him. Roo let them in and they introduced themselves as Josh and Jen; they were about the same ages as Roo and Clara. The two couples stared at each other across a ticking silence.

Finally, Roo asked Josh what he did at Mayo. "I'm a psychiatric-ward nurse," he said.

"Oh," Roo said.

"Yeah." Josh raised his eyebrows and pulled his mouth into a wide smile. "Some say I take my work home with me." Roo and Clara laughed a little uneasily. More silence.

"What kind of dog do you have?" Roo asked, moving on.

"An Australian cattle dog," Josh said. "His name is Wazee."

"How did you choose one of them?"

"Basically, I wanted a dog that wouldn't get run over by a car," Josh said. Roo and Clara waited, assuming an explanation would follow. More silence.

Finally Josh explained that he'd grown up with a grandmother who bred poodles, and over the years four or five of them had been hit by cars. His family also had a pack of hunting dogs, English springer spaniels, but when Josh was about four the dogs got out and killed close to a hundred of the neighbor's chickens. Josh's dad was forced to put many of the dogs down. He also grew up with two black Labs, Morgan and Casey, and although no tragedy had befallen them, Josh realized that Labs were the Peter Pan of dogs; they sort of never grew up.

So when Josh was looking to get a dog of his own he did a lot of research and found the Australian cattle dog, known for its stability and willingness to stay near its companion, even off leash. The breed is also known for its chasing prowess. Josh didn't know anything about canine disc but after Wazee chewed through a wall, Josh decided the dog needed a more constructive outlet.

That information had come out in fits and starts, with a lot of prodding, but Roo was happy to at least hear the man talk in complete sentences. Josh was proving more gregarious than he had been on the phone, but he was no one's idea of chatty. Jen made him seem like a talk-show host. Roo pressed on.

Over the last few years, Josh and Wazee had become regulars at a disc event in Wabasha, Minnesota, which was the only competition held in the state. Wazee and a dog named Bear took turns winning. In 2004, Josh and Wazee expanded their horizons. They traveled to Michigan to compete in a qualifier for the Skyhoundz World Championships. Despite the heavy wind, many of the competitors had attempted long throws, only to be foiled by the gusts. Josh focused on completing a higher number of short throws, and he took fourth, just good enough to advance to the next level. He then traveled to Atlanta for the world finals, where he finished fourteenth.

More important than the finish, though, was the experience. Atlanta had been a great time; Josh and Jen had met a lot of fun people and incredible dogs. The trip triggered their desire to immerse themselves more fully in the sport and the culture— leading Josh to post the notice about starting a disc-dog club. Mayo had made him take the post down because he wasn't actually selling anything. He'd considered reposting with an offer to sell discs as well but decided against it. Roo had been the only respondent.

Roo asked Josh what, exactly, the club would be, and it became clear that other than recruiting members, Josh didn't have much of a plan. Instead, he talked about the discs he had brought along; a Jawz model, which was a little heavy but durable and easy to throw. Clara and Roo brought out the Nylabone disc they had bought. Josh looked at it. "Whoever made that thing," he said, "doesn't like dogs."

Roo and Clara were a little embarrassed, but they were happy the gloves were off because they had some news they needed to share about Ajax. Their dog, they admitted, sometimes took issue with strangers. "Oh," Josh said as the four of them walked into the backyard. "What should I do about that?"

"Well," said Roo, "try not to move too much, especially your feet." Josh looked down. "Don't stare at him, either." Josh nodded. "And, um, take your hat off." Josh raised his eyebrows and looked up at the bill of his cap but did as requested. "Great," Roo said, and he disappeared into the house to get Ajax.

When the dog emerged, to everyone's relief he homed in on the bright orange discs Josh held and ignored the man himself. Josh explained that the way to test a dog's disc potential and to start training it was to execute rollers: Instead of tossing the disc in the air, he rolled it across the ground like a hubcap that had popped off a tire. Keeping it low ignited a dog's chase instinct and made it easier for the dog to grab the disc.

Ajax hesitated for an instant, then ran after the disc, plucked it off the ground, and trotted back. Roo liked what he saw. From some reading he'd done online he learned that sometimes a dog trained with a floppy disc would resist the feel of a plastic one in his mouth. It looked like Ajax didn't have that problem.

After maybe ten minutes of work, Josh declared the session both over and a success. They didn't make any firm plans about what would come next, but Josh let Roo have the discs he'd brought along and directed him to an online forum for disc dogs.

Roo took stock. The guy seemed to know what he was doing, and once you got past the social awkwardness he emerged as an interesting person, too. Any doubts Roo might have had were erased when the guy gave him the stack of discs.

"Hey," Roo said as the four of them walked back through the house. "You guys got a few minutes? You wanna see something wild?" They did.

Roo grabbed Wallace and brought him out to the garage. Everyone gathered around the door and watched as Wallace latched on to the spring pole. He was quite a sight. When he grabbed on to the chew toy he bobbed around like some life-size doggie yo-yo, or as if he were on an upside-down pogo stick, growling and shaking. Every now and then, the toy would slip from his mouth and, since it was spring-loaded, shoot up and slam into the ceiling.

As it bounced and swung around Wallace would leap into the air trying to recapture it. Sometimes he got it and went back to ping-ponging around the room. Other times he missed and soared through the air. His body would go diagonal to the ground with his feet facing the ceiling. And just when it looked like he'd come crashing down on his back, he'd arch his spine, roll to the side, and flip around to land on his feet.

Roo knew it was quite the spectacle, but when Josh and Jen reacted with a shell-shocked "That's really interesting" as they backed out of the house, he realized that the tables had turned. Now Josh thought Roo was the weirdo.

6

Roo holed up in the basement, glued to the computer screen. He had delved into the K9disc forum. The site was run by a guy named Ron Watson, a top competitor who had experienced success with several of his dogs. Many of the users posted information, stories, tips, and video of their performances, and Roo soaked up the information.

He learned that the sport was more involved than he'd originally thought. At the most basic level it was what was referred to as toss-and-catch. In these competitions there were markers set up at ten, twenty, thirty, forty, and fifty yards. The dog received one point if it caught the disc at ten yards, two points at twenty, up to five points for fifty. If the dog had all four feet off the ground at the time of the catch, the team received an extra half point. In each round, the idea was to score as many points as possible in sixty seconds. Sometimes these contests had sidelines, and if the dog landed outside those lines, the catch was no good. That variation of the toss-and-catch category was known as distance-and-accuracy.

Then there was freestyle. If canine disc were figure skating, toss-and-catch would be the equivalent of compulsory figures and free-style would be the long program. In it, competitors performed a choreographed routine set to music that included jumps, lifts, vaults, short catches, and long throws. The participants were judged not only on how well the dog caught the disc, but on the entire team's presentation, athleticism, speed, leaping ability, body control, varia-tion (of throws and catches), difficulty, and "wow factor." Contestants usually had ninety or a hundred and twenty seconds to complete their routine.

Josh was strictly a toss-and-catch guy. All the events he'd par-ticipated in had been toss-and-catch and he'd steered Roo and Ajax down the same path. Roo, though, was mesmerized by the videos he saw of freestyle events. He thought the routines were incredibly cool, and the performances of both the dogs and the handlers were killer. As the night slipped past he watched one video after another. He focused in particular on Watson, studying his moves and mem-orizing his advice.

Finally, Clara came down to say good night. "You have to watch some of these videos," Roo said, his voice filled with excitement. Clara stood behind him. As she watched the dogs on-screen charg-ing around the course, leaping into the air, catching the disc, then twisting and flipping around to land back on their feet, she could think of only one thing.

"Wow," she said. "Those dogs look a lot like Wallace when he plays with the spring pole."

———————

At first, Roo couldn't quite put his finger on it. It wasn't technique or ability so much. It was something else.

The disc spun and rolled across the ground and Wallace took off after it, snatched it, and zipped back to Roo. He dropped the disc from his mouth, and his eyes locked on to the one in Roo's hand. Finally, it struck Roo. Intensity. That was the difference. Ajax enjoyed playing catch, and he was good at it, but he could not match Wallace's intensity level. That shouldn't have been a surprise.

It was the morning after Roo's video session in the basement, and he and Wallace were out in the yard. After Clara's comment, Roo had lain in bed seemingly all night thinking about what he'd seen on the computer screen and what he knew about Wallace. It made perfect sense: the athleticism, the prey instinct, the toy love, the endless, endless drive. Wallace might make a great disc dog.

As soon as they hit the grass, Wallace had displayed a keen interest in the blue disc Roo held. He didn't need to be taught or shown anything. Roo simply rolled the disc and Wallace got down to business. Not only did he grab the disc and return it to Roo, he waited anxiously for the next roll, bounding around Roo and even feinting as if he was starting to run. If Roo hesitated too long, Wallace whined and then jumped up and tried to grab the disc out of Roo's hand. When Roo finally rolled it, Wallace charged across the yard, grass and mud flying in his wake.

Wallace was off to a great start, and Roo knew he should stop— in training, the general rule is to always leave the dog wanting more. If it's short and fun, the dog will continue to be excited about playing, but if the training sessions drag on, the dog will lose interest. Stopping was definitely the right thing to do.

But those videos were fresh in Roo's mind. He wondered if Wallace would jump for the disc. Roo held one out in front of him and without prompting Wallace flung himself into the air and grabbed hold. Roo repeated the drill a few times, and each time Wallace rose for the disc as if it were a box of treats.

In a lot of the routines the handlers had stuck a leg out and the dog jumped over the leg to get the disc. Or they positioned themselves so the dog had to run between their legs and then leap to reach the disc. Roo tried both tricks with Wallace. Boom, boom. Wallace nailed both without hesitation.

Then Roo remembered the weave drill he and Wallace did with the tug toy. He wondered if that would work with a disc. He began passing the disc back and forth between his legs, and Wallace jumped right in, carving out figure eights around and between Roo's legs.

Wallace's tongue flailed out the side of his mouth and he huffed and grunted and chased, little bits of grass flying up behind him as he dug at the turf. Finally, Roo broke the pattern; he stood up, and although he knew he wasn't really supposed to yet, he lofted the disc into the air a few feet in front of his body. It hung there for a second before Wallace launched himself off the ground and grabbed the disc. Any trick Roo could think of, Wallace simply did it.

Man and dog had been working at least twenty minutes, and Roo knew that was too long, but his body hummed with adrenaline. He went to the computer and typed out an e-mail to Josh. "I don't totally know what I'm doing, but I might have another disc dog on my hands." He reached to hit the send button but stopped and added one more sentence.

"I think Wallace might be awesome."

7

The first meeting of the Minnesota Disc Dog Club took place in April of 2005 at Quarry Hill Park in Rochester. The membership was "exclusive." It included Roo and Clara, Josh and Jen, and another Josh—Weigel—and his wife, Melissa. To avoid confusing the Joshes, Weigel became known as JW, which eventually evolved into J-Dubs.

As the Yoris pulled up, JW tossed discs to his dog, Sambuca, who ran on the field tracking and catching them. Roo left Wallace and Ajax in the car and went over to watch and chat. When JW and Sammy, as they called her, were done, Roo retrieved Wallace. Roo showed Wallace the discs, and the dog's eyes lit up. He was instantly excited.

Roo wasn't sure what to expect. After that first session Roo and Wallace had practiced in the yard every day. And, as far as Roo could tell, they were getting better. One day Josh had come by with his camera to take pictures of them in action. "Very cool," Josh had said in his concise manner, but Roo still wasn't sure if Josh had bought into the idea of freestyle competition.

Regardless of performance, Roo had to worry about how Wallace would deal with distractions, which at the park could very likely include the presence of other dogs. For the occasion he had gone to Home Depot and purchased a hundred feet of clothesline. He carried it with him now as he and Josh made their way down to a lower field, which was more isolated.

Roo secured the line to Wallace's collar and left the mass of it coiled up near his feet. He started throwing the disc, going slowly, with a few simple tricks and catches. Wallace, as always, joined in with great abandon, but his performance wasn't up to the level Roo had been seeing in the yard. Roo figured he needed to get warmed up a bit and get comfortable, both with the new surroundings and the new appendage, the rope.

As Wallace began to settle in and do better, something flashed in the corner of Roo's eye: Sambuca. Roo thought JW had put her away, but she remained out and was now sprinting across the upper field toward JW's car. Roo took in the moment. His eyes flashed back to Wallace. He hoped he could distract Wallace with a new toss or a treat before he saw the other dog, but he was too late.

Wallace's eyes fixed on Sammy. The sight of her sprinting away across the field set off his highly developed prey instinct. He shot off after her. Roo called his name several times, but Wallace paid no heed. Roo looked down. The coil unraveled at a frightening pace.

Roo grabbed the line. It zipped through his hand. He knew it would hurt like hell, and he could tell that Sammy would easily make it to the car before Wallace caught up to her, but he felt that he needed to prove that his system worked, that he could bring Wallace to the park without putting other dogs in jeopardy.

He squeezed. A fire flashed across his palm. He gritted his teeth and clamped down harder. The rope burned against his skin, but Wallace slowed and then stopped. He turned around and looked at Roo, then trotted back, his ears lowered and his tail down.

Roo shook off the pain and started throwing discs. After the incident Wallace seemed more focused. It was almost as if he knew he had messed up and now he was trying to make up for it. The rest of the afternoon went by without a hitch. When it was done the group stood around comparing notes and making small talk.

"So, what do you think about Wallace?" Roo said to Josh.

"Oh," Josh replied. "He's great. He's a great dog." He hesitated, recalling the scene of Wallace bolting across the field after Sammy. "You'll never be able to compete with him, but he's a great dog."

"Well, I guess it doesn't matter," Roo said, "since I'm not keeping him anyway."

———

As much as Wallace seemed to enjoy playing disc—and as much as Roo did, too—he believed the dog's true potential lay in weight pulling. It was a sport for which he was built and for which he had already shown a capacity. Flying disc was for small, fast herding dogs, not large muscular dogs with heads like cinder blocks.

Weight pulls also offered other benefits: They didn't require Roo to turn Wallace loose on a field surrounded by other dogs, and they were a hotbed of potential adopters. So in the middle of May, Wallace competed in his second weight pull. After the last competition Roo had changed his training routine and worked on getting Wallace to understand what he needed to do when faced with a load that he couldn't immediately move.

The event took place in the parking lot in front of a large pet store near Rochester, so it presented a new set of challenges. There were more dogs and people around, cars going by, a lot of smells wafting in the air, but at least it wasn't as loud as the indoor competition had been. Before the competition Roo sat with Wallace, patting him on the flanks and talking softly. As Roo spoke Wallace jabbed affectionately with his snout and gave him big licks on the face.

When the competition started, Wallace looked tiny hooked up to the wagon, which seemed to be the size of a small car. On its own it weighed 325 pounds and Wallace pulled it easily. After each round, they added another 75-pound bucket. As the bed of the wagon filled up, the vehicle looked even more imposing, but as long as Roo had a squeaky toy, Wallace had all the focus he needed. He moved easily through the early rounds and kept on going.

The weight kept piling up and Wallace kept grinding down the platform with the cart in tow. After each successful pull Roo and Clara were there with hugs and kisses and praise. And of course the squeaky toy, which Wallace tore into with particular fury after having worked so hard to acquire it.

Finally, the weight approached nine hundred pounds, the amount Wallace had maxed out at in his first competition. Roo worked hard to get him pumped up and then broke out a brand-new squeaky toy. Wallace stepped into the pull. He strained against the harness and the cart rocked but did not start to roll. Roo got down on all fours, squeaking the ball as hard as he could and holding it in front of Wallace while urging him forward. Wallace bore down, squatting a little. His body canted forward and his legs spread a little wider, pulling at the ground. The cart jumped and Wallace exploded forward; having broken the inertia, he churned down the run one step behind a retreating Roo.

When Wallace crossed the line, Roo was pumped and so was Wallace. He wagged his tail and jumped up on Roo and chewed the squeaky toy apart. He was far from done, though. He kept going until he reached a final 1,375 pounds. When all was said and done, Wallace had pulled more weight than any other dog in his weight class. In his second try Wallace was a weight-pull winner. Roo and Clara shared a high five and a hug but they were cool about the win—in truth they had expected Wallace to pull even more than he had.

Still, it was a high, and even when the rush began to wear off on the car ride home, the good feeling underneath it didn't. Roo and Clara sat in silence, each marveling independently at where the road had led and what still lay ahead. As the trees sped by, Roo spoke: "Not bad for a dog nobody wanted."

Clara laughed and looked at Wallace, sitting in the back gnawing on a chew toy, the fourth one he'd gone through that day. "Not bad at all," she said.

At the end of the month, Clara and Roo leashed up Angus and

Wallace and went to the Paws & Claws Pet Walk, an annual fund-raising event. Since they'd taken in Wallace, a few more dogs had come in with behavior problems, and the shelter had put them down. Once again, Roo and Clara had disagreed with the board's position.

The situation had turned contentious, and Roo had grown frustrated and disenchanted. He'd begun to speak out and was soon banned from the volunteer message board. Shortly thereafter, he'd stopped volunteering. Clara had seen enough of the drama and politics, too, and in early May, she left her job at the shelter to start a dog-walking and -sitting business. The transition had created a bit of a financial squeeze for the couple. Clara hadn't been making a lot of money at the shelter, but it was steady. Her business would take time to grow, and until it did her income had dropped off almost completely.

Still, the Yoris counted themselves as supporters of the shelter, and they remained friends with many who worked and volunteered there. Plus, the walk was always a fun event.

This one was particularly delicious. Throughout the day, people would ask about Wallace's progress. Roo and Clara were careful not to gloat, but they didn't hesitate to tell all about his weight-pulling accomplishments and his burgeoning disc-catching career. In fact, they had recently entered him in his first canine disc competition.

They thought he'd behave well enough at it to prove even more of his doubters wrong.

8

Clara had a method for packing the back of their SUV; she liked everything to be just so. She and Roo were a lot alike in that way. She folded the second row of seats down, so she had one large expanse to deal with. Wallace's crate went all the way in the back, facing backward. He still couldn't be trusted with a doggie bed—he liked to shred them—so she lined the bottom of the crate with fleece blankets. Next to Wallace's crate she put a few folded-up spare crates. Then the stack of discs, a treat pouch, and a bag of treats went next to the crates. The discs also served as drinking bowls, so a big bottle of water went behind the treats.

In front of Wallace's crate Clara stacked a few folding chairs, a cooler, and a fold-out, freestanding canopy they used to create a little shade. A stash of plastic bags went into the door pocket, and in the open space behind the front seats she spread out a blanket, where Ajax took up residence.

On the morning of June 25, the car was packed and ready to go; she and Roo climbed in and started out for La Crosse, Wisconsin. Whatever else was going on in their lives—Clara's mom's illness, job transitions, the end of their relationship with Paws & Claws—they still had a shared love of dogs and an enthusiasm to do things together.

They had never been to the site of today's competition, but they had heard a lot about it. The Family Dog Center is a paradise for dogs—or at least for people holding dog-related events. The twenty-thousand-foot main building is air-conditioned and heated and has food services for both humans and canines, sound and video equipment, and extensive staging facilities. Clara and Roo thought the place was incredibly cool, which certified in their minds what they had already known on some level: They were dog geeks.

For Roo, the most appealing aspect of the place was the fenced-in field. It was the reason he had targeted this particular competition for Wallace's debut. He still didn't know how Wallace would react during a flying-disc event. Would he focus only on the disc or would he be distracted by the other dogs and people around the field? The incident with Sambuca weighed on Roo's mind. Clara could sense it.

"What's bothering you?" she asked.

"Just nervous."

"You guys will do great."

"It's not that. I think he can win. I just hope they don't let the other competitors inside the fence, you know. If they keep everyone outside, it'll be perfect. . . ."

"He's gonna be awesome, and everyone will see that they were wrong and we were right," Clara said. Roo nodded. That motivation still drove them, yet underneath the talk of redemption and vindication, there was a sense that they needed to prove it to themselves. They believed, but they wanted to be sure.

———

Roo took Wallace from the crate and gave him a few firm pats on the side. "Let's go, boy," he said. As they headed for the field Clara patted Wallace a few times too and wished them luck. She and Roo looked at each other and shrugged, fingers crossed. They had no idea what to expect.

Despite their instinct to encourage him, Wallace needed little psyching up. As soon as he saw the disc in Roo's hand he wanted to get at it, and Roo had to fend him off as they waited to enter the field. The competition was very casual, with a small group of competitors and plenty of camaraderie, so that helped calm Roo.

And the field had been set up just the way Roo hoped it would be. Everyone sat outside the fence except the pair throwing and catching. Many of the other spectators and dogs lined the fence; some of the dogs were in crates but others stood on a leash. They barked and circled and the smell of them wafted across the field, which meant there would still be plenty to test Wallace's concentration.

The challenge was a real one. A few other dogs had made their debuts already, and things didn't always go well. Several of the newbies had been confused and thrown off by the presence of the other dogs and people. A few had simply stood there watching the disc fly without any reaction. Roo had hopes of competing in a bigger regional competition a month later—one without a fence around the field—so he hoped Wallace could ignore the mayhem and focus on the disc.

As the first round progressed, the pair before them finished and an official called out: "Now competing, Roo Yori and Wallace." Roo walked out to the throwing line, Wallace jumping up on him and trying to grab the disc the entire way. Roo looked out; a white line painted on the ground connected the dots between two small orange cones at ten-yard intervals out to fifty yards.

Roo removed Wallace's leash and signaled that he was ready. The announcer said, "Go!" Roo drew back and flicked the disc down the field. He didn't throw it as far as he could because he wanted to make it easy, to let Wallace get into a little of a flow before upping the ante.

The disc sailed off and Wallace bolted after it. He raced down the field and snagged it out of the air. He brought it back and Roo gave it another toss, this one a bit farther. Again Wallace zipped down and caught the disc. Back he came. Roo let it rip again and

Wallace caught the disc, but when he turned to come back something went awry.

Wallace stopped, turned his head, and began sniffing the air. He dropped the disc and put his nose to the ground, following a scent that drew him off toward the fence. Roo called him, softly at first and then with a louder, more insistent voice. Wallace was unmoved. Roo whistled and clapped. Wallace hardly flinched, as time ticked off the clock. Roo tried everything he could think of, but Wallace would not come. Finally Roo took off. He sprinted down the field, scooped up the disc, and grabbed Wallace by the collar.

The forceful tug and the sight of Roo with the disc snapped Wallace out of whatever enchantment had befallen him, and he loped back up the field behind Roo. As soon as they made it across the line Roo flung the disc and Wallace retrieved it. The buzzer sounded. Roo walked off, winded from his unexpected workout.

Clara met them at the gate. "What happened?"

"Not sure. He smelled something down the far end," Roo said, panting and looking back over his shoulder at the field. "There aren't even any dogs down there. I don't know what it was."

Clara gave Wallace a few pats and told him, "Good boy," then took the leash as they began walking back to their seats. "You think he can do it?" she said.

"I don't know," Roo said. "We'll see." He looked at Wallace and looked back at the field, where the next dog was running after a disc.

"He looked great out there," Clara said. "You guys both did."

She took Wallace for a walk and gave him some water, while Roo assessed the situation. The lapse had definitely hurt them, but they'd still posted a first-round score of eight points, which put them in the top half of the field. Roo had watched almost all the other dogs perform, and he hadn't been impressed by any except two—a particularly agile German shepherd and an Australian shepherd mix named Ashley. Roo knew Ashley's handler, Sherrone, who ran the only disc-dog event in the state of Minnesota, the toss-and-catch contest that Josh and Wazee had won. Roo figured he and Wallace would need a nearly perfect second round to beat those two, but no one else in the field of about fifteen scared him.

He sat back in his chair to await his chance. Clara had returned with Wallace, and Roo leashed him up. He wanted to win, but he also wanted to assess Wallace, so he sat and watched how Wallace reacted to the passing traffic. To Roo's pleasure, Wallace ignored many of the dogs that walked by. Some of them, though, aroused his interest, and Roo had to manage those interactions carefully.

Clara broke the reactions down into different categories. Sometimes, she observed, Wallace simply wanted to play or interact with another dog, but he was such a social moron that he didn't know how to do it. He'd get right in the other dog's face and nudge and nip, which would almost always lead to the other dog's losing interest.

In other situations, a passing dog would do something Wallace took as a challenge. When another dog stared him down, Wallace didn't take it lightly. The big German shepherd, the one that Roo considered a potential winner, had given Wallace the stare, and Wallace had barked and postured toward the dog.

Roo had prevented any sort of incident, but he knew he would have to keep an eye on Wallace around that dog for the rest of the day. In the meantime he hoped to focus some of that energy on the disc as he and Wallace set out for their second-round performance. As with the first attempt, Roo took his place in the throwing area and when given the signal, he let loose.

When Roo and Wallace went out for the second round, Roo didn't know what specific score they needed to win, but he knew they needed a great round. He started with a medium-length throw to get Wallace going and it worked. Wallace caught the disc and rushed back. Each time Roo let the disc fly a little farther and Wallace was locked in, making catches and flying back up the field, no signs of being waylaid by whatever random scent had distracted him the first time out.

Roo zipped a rising throw down the field, and Wallace darted after it, his chest heaving and his tongue flying out of his mouth. When the disc reached the apex of its flight, Wallace leapt to catch it, but the disc, caught by the wind, wobbled ever so slightly and Wallace missed. Wallace snatched the disc up from the grass and ran back. Roo slipped in one more shortish throw and that was it. Time up.

Roo knew the drop—coupled with the brain freeze in the first round—killed any shot they had at winning, but he felt good. In the moment, out on the field, something happened. It was a feeling, a sense that he and Wallace were communicating, connecting. He'd felt it in little bits before, but something about the competition had brought it to a new level, and Roo bathed in its afterglow.

Back at their little encampment Clara petted Wallace and held his face, putting her nose right up to his. "That's a good boy," she cooed. "That's my good pittie bull." The rest of the dogs finished up and the announcer began to read off the winners. Ashley won. The big German shepherd took second. And in third, Wallace. On the podium Roo had to keep Wallace away from the shepherd, but when the contest official handed him his ribbon, he said, "If not for the distraction in the first round, you guys probably would have won."

The ride zipped by as Roo and Clara almost floated back to Rochester. The dog that nobody wanted had just finished third in his first flying-disc competition. They couldn't wait to tell the world.

Chapter 4

Justification

———●———

We're playing with the big boys now, aren't we?

Roo Yori

1

Wallace climbed out of the car and sniffed. The smell of lady's slippers and day lilies rushed up on the hot July air. He didn't immediately move to explore the park, and as Roo watched his dog he couldn't blame the pooch for hesitating. This was the fifth park they had come to in five days.

In the aftermath of their experience in La Crosse, Roo felt that he had to make sure Wallace would not be distracted again during a routine, especially by another dog. For the first week after that initial competition Roo and Wallace not only practiced their freestyle routine, but they did it in a different place every day. Roo wanted Wallace to be consistently confronted with new surroundings while they played, and each place had its own unique set of smells and distractions—joggers, walkers, food carts, kids' parks, dogs, cats, and squirrels.

As they played Roo worked on the tricks, but even more so he focused on training Wallace to stay with him. He didn't need to help keep Wallace focused on the disc when they were alone—that was never a problem—but he wanted to make sure nothing else would pull him away from the task when there were outside distractions. After a week touring the parks of Rochester, Wallace appeared to be locked in.

The following week, Roo upped the ante. He had Josh and Wazee come to the park with them, and they stood off to the side while Roo and Wallace worked. This replicated the sensation of other competitors and spectators standing alongside the field and provided not simply a generalized distraction but a specific one close by. Wallace handled the new situation without a problem.

A few days later Roo made things even more difficult. He recruited a few other volunteers—Josh W. and Sammy and some other friends with dogs—to stand on either side of the play area. Wallace paid them no attention. Roo asked his friends to move around beside the field. Still, no problem.

Finally, in the third week of practice, Josh and Wazee walked through the field as Roo and Wallace played. They cut across Roo's throws, and they walked up and down the field as the disc whizzed past them. Roo had not been expecting it, and the change surprised him, but Wallace never hesitated. He went after the disc every time as if it were the only thing that kept him alive. By the time the third week ended, Roo felt much better about taking Wallace back into competition.

He needed to. The Skyhoundz North Central Regional would take place the following weekend in Indianapolis. The top four performers would automatically qualify for the Skyhoundz World Finals in Atlanta. Roo planned to be there. And he wanted to win.

———

Roo had been working on a freestyle routine from the first day he and Wallace had ventured into the yard and started playing disc. From the beginning he imitated the tricks he saw in videos online. Pretty quickly Roo realized that Wallace could do almost anything asked of him. The weak link on the team was Roo.

He could do the basic Frisbee toss, the backhand, and he could even do the sidearm—in which the thrower puts his thumb on top of the disc and his index and forefinger underneath against the front rim and flings it the way someone would when skipping a stone. But that was it. The people in the videos he watched threw a disc many different ways. Roo needed to learn how to do that.

One day Clara was on her way to the library. "Hey," Roo said, "see if they have any books on tossing a disc." To his surprise Clara returned with something called *Frisbee by the Masters.* Roo flipped through it. The book had been put out in the 1970s, so the pages were filled with photos of guys in knee socks, short shorts, striped shirts, and floppy hairdos, but the information seemed solid. The dudes looked goofy, but they were executing the kinds of throws Roo saw in the videos he watched.

Roo went to the basement and tore through the book. The next day he went out to the yard to practice, and within a few days of that he could pull off the thumber (thumb underneath the front rim, fingers on top, similar motion to the sidearm), the overhand wrist flip (a combination of the thumber grip and a sort of discus throw), the behind-the-back release, the under-the-leg release, and the butterfly toss (end over end). And the ultimate move—one that he personally loved but had never before been able to replicate—the skip toss, in which the disc hits the ground and skips back up into the air.

As for Wallace, the dog never stumbled. He soaked up anything Roo showed him. As long as a sequence ended with Wallace getting the disc, he was on board. One day the pair was practicing in the yard. Roo had fenced off a small area where he was trying to grow grass with plastic mesh fencing. He threw a disc that floated down inside the fence. Wallace charged up to it and stopped. He circled once, looking for an opening, but there was none. He looked back at Roo, who started over to help out. Wallace couldn't wait. He had to get the disc. He lowered his head and crashed through the fence, grabbed the disc, and dashed back out. Roo was laughing when Wallace brought the disc to him. "Good boy," Roo said, patting Wallace. "Good boy," he said, looking over at the mangled fence, "I guess."

The moves were pretty basic, but it was about more than just the moves. For each trick Wallace had to learn and remember both visual and verbal cues. The approach was more difficult than simply having the dog memorize certain sequences or the entire routine, but Roo felt it would give them more flexibility. Either way, Roo knew in order to succeed they'd have to put their own spin on things.

Skyhoundz used what it called the PAWS scoring system, which stood for Presentation, Athleticism, Wow factor, and Success ratio (of catches). In order to score well in all those categories, Roo and Wallace would have to do more than basic tricks. They needed to innovate. Roo had worked out a few minor variations on some old favorites—an under-the-leg sidearm throw that he hadn't seen anywhere else—but his big creation was something he called the Power Spin.

To execute it, Wallace would grab one end of a disc and Roo the other. Roo would spin until Wallace actually lifted off the ground, his body levitating outward like one of the elephants on the Dumbo ride at Disney. Roo would then lift and rotate his arms over his head while Wallace held on. Wallace spun around Roo in the air for one complete revolution, then came in for a four-point landing.

It wasn't the greatest trick in the history of canine disc, but it showed off the pair's unique abilities: Not many other people would be strong enough to swing a fifty-pound dog around their head, and not many disc dogs would be strong enough to hold on.

Roo thought it could become their signature move and set it up as the final maneuver of their routine. It was unconventional, but he thought it would provide an eye-catching pop to their Athleticism and Wow scores.

Unless it got them laughed off the field.

2

They were up by six A.M. on Friday, July 29. By seven they were packed and on the road, a caravan of two cars. Clara had to work, so Josh's brother-in-law, Ed, rode with Roo. Josh and Jen followed. They had a solid ten hours of driving ahead, although they knew that breaks for both people and dogs would extend that time.

No one cared. As far as they knew, Skyhoundz regionals in New Castle, Indiana, near Indianapolis, was the closest event that had a freestyle competition. Through a combination of taunting, urging, and leading by example, Roo had sold Josh on the glories of freestyle, and in preparation for the trip, Josh and Wazee had worked out their own freestyle routine, so they too would be showing off their moves. The motivation for both men was a trip to the world championships in Atlanta, where Josh and Jen had had such a good time the year before. In addition to the freestyle there would also be a toss-and-catch (or distance-and-accuracy, as Skyhoundz called it) segment, so Roo figured he had two shots to qualify.

They checked into the hotel around six P.M. and after walking all the dogs and setting them up in crates, they went to check out the site of the competition in the fading light. Roo already had an idea of what to expect, because he'd been in touch with the organizers.

Although the Yoris had officially adopted Mindy Lou and were now up to four dogs, Roo had begun to look for another. He loved playing disc with Wallace and thought the dog had real skill, but when he watched the videos online he saw speed and jumping ability he didn't think Wallace could match. Most of the top dogs were border collies and Australian shepherds. No one had ever competed successfully with a pit bull, an athletic dog no doubt, but one thick with muscles and a sturdy skeletal structure.

Plus, Wallace was a foster dog, up for adoption. Roo planned to compete with Wallace for as long as he could, but he didn't know how long that would be. The thought of keeping Wallace had certainly crossed his mind. But deep down he worried that theirs wasn't the right home for Wallace. They felt guilty that they had to rotate the dogs in and out of their crates in shifts because Wallace and Ajax in particular didn't get along. He still hoped Wallace could find a home where he would be *the* dog, with the freedom to roam the house all day long.

Online, Roo had read about a dog up for adoption named Pogo, a year-old mixed breed thought to have great potential. Roo reached out to the woman offering the dog, Christina Curtis. She competed regularly in flying disc and was a member of the Indy Dog and Disc Club, which ran the event near Indianapolis. She and Roo had e-mailed back and forth, and Roo planned to check out Pogo while in town. But a few days before Roo arrived, another disc-dog enthusiast came to see Pogo and adopted him on the spot.

Still, Roo had not wasted the opportunity to gather more information about the event. In his e-mails, he'd peppered Curtis with questions about the location and setup as well as the way the competition would be run. Why did he want to know so much? she asked. He explained about Wallace—that he was basically a good dog but one that sometimes took exception to other dogs and often behaved poorly around them, provoking them without even meaning to. Curtis was accepting, but she forwarded the note to some others in the group, and long before Wallace ever set paw in Indy, word spread that an "aggressive pit bull" would be participating in the event.

Roo didn't love the idea that they'd arrive in town with a reputation, but he figured better safe than sorry. Despite his work with Wallace, Roo still worried about distractions. He was happy, though, when they arrived at the venue: a high school football field, with a fence around the perimeter, a track outside the fence, and bleachers beyond the track. If the event was set up so that only the competitors were inside the fence and any spectators sat in the bleachers, it would be a great comfort. Roo figured fellow competitors could control themselves and their dogs, but spectators were a wild card.

He even liked the field itself. Plush grass covered the ground and a nice pitch gave it a sort of crowned effect. Roo found it pleasing to look at. He needed to find reassurance anywhere he could. The competition would be split into two divisions: novice and expert. Although he and Wallace had been playing disc for only three months, Roo knew Wallace had talent and he wanted to test himself and his dog, so he had signed up for the expert division. Now he wondered if that was a mistake. He also didn't feel as if he knew his own routine as well as he should.

Back at the hotel, he, Ed, Josh, and Jen were sharing a room, so the cramped space held four adults and five dogs in crates. Getting to the bathroom from the far side required an act that was part gymnastics and part contortion, but eventually everyone got ready and settled in for the night. Of the nine creatures in the room, Roo was the last to fall asleep.

As he lay in bed he continued going over the routine in his head. From his soccer days he was a big proponent of visualization, of knowing what he needed to do and how he was going to do it so well that he could play it like a movie in his head. When he had reached that point, he figured, he no longer had to think about what he was doing. He simply did it, and when he performed without thinking, it always went better.

The hours ticked by. Roo watched the movie.

3

The Rochester crew were among the first to arrive, and they quickly set about assembling the canopy and folding chairs; setting out the coolers and crates; piling up the disc bags, food, and treats; and outfitting each crate with a small battery-operated fan that would help cool the dogs in the heat of the afternoon.

As others began to arrive, Roo could tell that the setup would work exactly the way he hoped—all the competitors would set up along one side of the field opposite the bleachers and spectators would sit in the bleachers behind the fence. As more and more teams arrived the field took on a completely different look. With the collection of tents, canopies, coolers, loungers, doggie baths, crates, grills, and sundry other outdoor gear it looked as if a tribe of Bedouins had knocked over a Walmart and set up shop. The morning filled with the near-constant sound of barking.

At one point, a fellow competitor pulled up in his minivan with the aim of setting up a few spots down from Roo and company. He opened the door to his van and let his dog, a big black Lab, run from the car without a care in the world. The dog headed right toward Roo, who held Wallace on a leash. Roo didn't want to see what would happen when the dog arrived, so he heaved Wallace up onto his shoulders. To Roo's relief, the guy in the van noticed and called his dog back.

Roo wondered if the guy had heard about the "aggressive pit bull," seen Roo's reaction, and put two and two together. There was no way to know, but for Roo it reinforced the point that he had to be extra careful, because no one else would. If that dog had come over and started trouble everyone would have blamed Wallace, even though he wasn't the dog running around off leash.

———————

The event would start with a distance-and-accuracy competition, but Skyhoundz had a slightly different approach to these types of events. The field was shaped something like a diamond: ten yards wide at the start line, stretched to its widest point at twenty-five yards, and narrowing again to ten yards wide at the end line, fifty yards away. The diamond was divided into five zones, each ten yards long, and points were awarded based on where the dog caught the disc. A catch past ten yards earned one point; twenty yards, two points; thirty yards, three points, but a throw-and-catch of more than forty yards garnered five points, so there was a bonus for completing a long throw to the narrowest part of the field. There was a half-point bonus if the dog had all four feet off the ground when it made the catch, but the dog needed to land with all four feet in bounds in order for any catch to count.

Before the first round started the human competitors were allowed to warm up on the field. As Roo stretched on the sidelines he watched a few of the others throw. Time after time, their effortless flings landed in the bonus area. He leaned over to Josh. "We're playing with the big boys now, aren't we?" he said.

Pressure to make great throws compounded his anxiety about potential distractions for Wallace. The fear of Wallace running off the field continued to eat at him enough that when their turn came, Roo had Josh, Jen, and Ed spread out along the line of tents where the other competitors sat. If Wallace went off the reservation, a friendly face would be there to intercept him.

As the pair stepped up to the starting line for the toss-and-catch, the announcer called out their names and mentioned, as Roo had requested, that Wallace remained available to any would-be adopters. They stood at the line awaiting the signal. Roo nodded at the line judge. She looked at Wallace and said, "Is he going to be all right?" Roo looked at Wallace and realized what had driven the question—the "aggressive pit bull" warning.

"He's going to be fine," Roo said.

The announcer yelled, "Go," and they were off. Roo threw the disc and Wallace tore off after it, as always, and made the catch. Wallace hustled back and Roo tossed the disc again. Wallace snagged it. Two for two. Roo felt a surge of adrenaline. Wallace seemed to be feeling it, too. He appeared to dig a little harder as he ran back. They were in rhythm now, connecting again like they had in La Crosse. Roo threw. Catch. Another throw. Another catch. Four for four with three aerial catches put them at 13.5 points. Roo rushed to get off one last throw. He considered something short, to play it safe and pad the point total, but he and Wallace had the vibe, they had the momentum. Roo launched the disc for the bonus zone, a knockout punch. Wallace chugged across the field, tail back, eyes fixed on the disc. He chased it down and caught it! But it had sailed wide, out of bounds.

When the final results were tallied Roo and Wallace's 13.5 points left them half a point below the top qualifiers. They missed the worlds by less than a point. Roo pressed his palm to his forehead. He couldn't believe it, but he looked for the positives. Wallace never so much as glanced away from the field and the discs. He seemed rock solid. That was a relief. Most important, he and Wallace still had the freestyle routine to look forward to.

Instead of two rounds for all the competitors, the freestyle started with an initial round. The top six performers would go on to a separate distance-and-accuracy round followed by a final freestyle round.

To prepare for their next appearance Roo took Wallace onto the practice field behind the bleachers. They executed a few throws to get loose but not too many, because the day had grown sultry, and Roo didn't want Wallace to overheat. Instead, Roo rehearsed alone, practicing in his head and miming the motions, trying to fix the routine in his head and hone his performance. Then he stood along the fence and watched the other competitors, observing what they did and how they did it in an attempt to pick up a few tricks. Some of the dogs were awesome—intimidating even—but for the most part Roo felt he and Wallace could hold their own.

One pair in particular that he took notice of was a guy named Danny and his border collie, Guinan. They weren't the best team he saw that day, but something about them stood out. They seemed to project some sort of canine disc ideal. Danny threw the disc with an ease and efficiency that belied how difficult some of his moves were, and Guinan represented the classic disc-chasing breed, fast, agile, and alert, with perky ears and an eager prance. They were all the things that Roo and Wallace could never be, and they brimmed with a potential that Roo took note of.

As Roo's own turn approached, Josh and the others again took positions along the edges of the playing field in case Wallace should go astray. Roo unclipped Wallace's leash but held on to his collar as he walked onto the field. In Roo's other hand he held the five discs he would use during the performance. He looked around for a moment and waited. Roo could feel everyone's eyes on them and knew they were all wondering if this pit bull could do as well in freestyle.

He heard the familiar screech of guitars and relaxed. He'd searched long and hard for the right piece of music to accompany their routine. He wanted something upbeat and exciting, but he'd learned that a really fast song can make a dog look slow, and he already worried that Wallace appeared too lumbering. He'd tried a lot of different options before finally settling on something called "Rawkfist," a heavy chord thumper that had a driving beat. As the first notes sounded over the speaker system his body relaxed and his instincts took over.

He tossed the first disc and Wallace caught it. The rest simply fell into place. Wallace went through his legs and caught the disc, jumped over his leg and caught the disc, spun in the air and caught the disc. Roo threw behind his back, under his leg, and over his head. Everything disappeared. The other competitors, the spectators, the other dogs, the concern about Wallace getting distracted melted away. It was simply Wallace and Roo, as if they were in the backyard, and Roo felt that connection, that whole body-and-mind engagement not only with what he was doing, but with Wallace as well.

Roo walked off feeling fantastic. They hadn't been perfect, but they'd been very good, and Roo found the experience invigorating. "Good boy, good boy," he told Wallace, patting him on the sides when they made it back to their encampment. Josh gave him a quick high five and then took Wazee and ran out for his own round. Roo went over to watch, gathering congratulations as he went. He continued to pulse with the remnants of adrenaline that had taken over his body during the routine. He had high hopes coming in, but now he felt that sixth place and a spot in the second round were within reach.

Even after Josh returned, Roo continued to run through his performance in his head again and again. Finally, he realized he'd made a terrible mistake: He'd forgotten the Power Spin, the big closing move that was supposed to be the cherry on top of their routine. He couldn't believe it. "Oh crap!" he said out loud. Josh looked over at him. "I forgot the Power Spin," he said, disbelief in his voice.

Josh looked away and stared out at the field for a moment. "That sucks," he said at last.

Roo wished he could shrug it off so easily. The mistake ate at him as he waited for the scores to post.

Finally the announcement rang over the loudspeakers. The standings had been calculated and posted at the scorers' table. Josh and Roo made their way over and shuffled to the head of the crowd so they could read the type. Roo's eyes scanned down the list from first to sixth. He and Wallace were not there. He kept reading. Seventh, Josh and Wazee; they'd missed the second round by one spot. Then came eighth—Roo saw his own name. Out by two spots.

Roo knew his failure to include the final move had hurt them. A few more points in the Presentation and Wow categories might have put them over the top, but he also knew that after only three months of work they had done about as well as they could have.

And there was a benefit to being eliminated. With the pressure off, Roo could relax and socialize. He chatted with the people camped next to them, a couple from Kansas City who had driven up with their dog, Leaping Lunatic or Luna. The woman told Roo that she'd had her doubts about Wallace; he didn't seem like disc-dog material. But once she saw them perform, she threw all her preconceived notions out the window.

Likewise, the judge who had been positioned on the starting line—and unnerved Roo by asking the question "Is he going to be all right?"—swung by. As soon as Roo had thrown the disc and she saw Wallace go after it as if nothing else in the world mattered, she knew he would be better than okay. He would be great.

That wasn't all. Roo wandered off among the encampments, seeking out people he knew from the K9disc forum, so he could put faces with screen names. Everyone he tracked down greeted him warmly, offering him food and beverages and a place to sit and talk dogs. Afterward, all the competitors hung around for a cookout. It was another chance to mingle.

Wallace had made quite an impression; everyone had something to say about him. At the end of the festivities Roo and Wallace were given a special award called Keepin' It Fun, meant for the team that best exhibits the ethos of the sport. People couldn't believe that Wallace had been playing disc for only three months. Despite all the praise, no one wanted to adopt him. Almost every person there had more than one dog at home, and the thought of introducing a new dog—a pit bull—that didn't always play nice proved too much to overcome.

Roo had set out to prove that Wallace was worthy. That he and Clara had been right to save him and that Wallace could not only survive but thrive in the real world. And he felt like they were proving their critics wrong. On two or three occasions at the event, people admitted that seeing Wallace out there playing disc had opened their minds to pit bulls in a way that they hadn't been before. A few even pulled Roo aside and said, "I think what you're doing is great."

And while Roo was enjoying the positive feedback, this comment struck him as a little odd. It was the kind of thing you would say to someone who was running a soup kitchen or dressing up as Santa Claus at a family shelter. Was that the equivalent of competing in canine disc with a pit bull? Were the odds against them so outrageous? Were they a charity case, out there for the sole purpose of sending a message?

Even Roo assumed that Wallace would never reach the highest levels of the sport—he had come to look at Pogo, after all—but he also felt as if he and Wallace had already proved they could hold their own as serious competitors, and they were only getting started. When he returned to the hotel that night he called Clara. Between the competition and the camaraderie he'd had a great day. He told her that they had not made it to the second round but that the afternoon had still been a great success. He told her about the award and the dogs he'd seen and all the conversations he'd had. He was more impressed than ever with Wallace but had come to embrace a new reality.

"Maybe there's no one out there who's willing to take him," he said.

"Maybe not," Clara responded. She could hear the underlying happiness in his voice and knew where he was heading.

Wallace's original name, Ranger, was given to him by a child in the neighborhood.

From the start, Wallace loved to chase and play.

Clara's passion and willingness to fight helped keep Wallace alive when he was in the shelter.

When they got married in 2005, Clara and Roo already had two dogs and they were working with Wallace.

Even the chill of a Minnesota winter can't keep Wallace down. He launches himself off Roo to grab a disc.

Whenever there's a disc around, Wallace keeps his eye on the prize.

Wallace mastered the art of vaulting (launching himself off his handler), but Roo refrained from using the move often to reduce the wear and tear on his dog.

Wallace and Roo put in some practice time at their favorite disc-playing spot, Soldiers Field in Rochester.

Roo launches into one of his signature moves, the up-and-over roll, while Wallace charges underneath.

Whenever Wallace finishes off a move, his ears perk up as he listens for the next command.

A big part of Roo and Wallace's success came from Roo's athleticism, which included a series of jumping, under-the-leg throws.

Wallace may not have the speed and agility of other dogs, but he makes up for it with intensity.

Roo holds Wallace up to the crowd after their FDDO Freestyle round at the 2006 Cynosport World Games in Scottsdale, Arizona.

Wallace runs underneath Roo to nab a disc at Pork in the Park 2006, a festival in Jordan, Minnesota. Wallace took second in Distance/Accuracy (Ajax won) and first in Freestyle.

After running under Roo for a disc, Wallace turns around to soar over Roo's legs for another.

Wallace and Roo accept the first place prize at their first UFO Major Competition in Naperville, Illinois, on Labor Day weekend 2006. The medal stand is from the original World Championships and "signed" by Ashley Whippet. Jason Holland finished second with Dash while Matt Diano and Maggie took third.

Clara, who is certified in canine massage, helped keep Wallace stretched and warm during competitions.

JOSHUA GRENELL

COURTESY OF ROO AND CLARA YORI

Roo and Clara relax with (clockwise from bottom left) Scooby; Angus; Hector, a former Michael Vick dog; and Mindy Lou, the boss.

Josh and Roo have a seat on the back of the "Dogulance" while Hector and Wallace say hello.

Wallace became a well-known figure in the canine-disc world, and there was no way not to recognize him when he wore his custom collar.

The disc is your friend; after you're done ripping it out of the air it helps you cool off.

Wallace and Roo returned to the 2009 AWI World Championships in Naperville to make one last run at the Lander Cup.

Happiness is a day of disc, and Wallace is all smiles after a session in the park.

Roo went on. "Maybe it doesn't matter. Maybe we should just keep playing disc because he loves it so much."

"He's been with us for six months already," Clara said. "I feel like he fits into our home."

"Maybe this is where he's supposed to be."

"Let's keep him," Clara said.

"Yep," Roo said. "Yep."

———

On Sunday morning the group found themselves back at the high school field setting up the canopy and the crates again. The atmosphere was noticeably more relaxed: The day was all about fun. There were extreme distance toss-and-catch competitions, time trials, and freestyle exhibitions. Roo and Wallace participated in all of them and had a great time.

At the end of the day, Josh, Jen, and Ed piled into one car and set out for Rochester. Roo took Wallace and turned toward his parents' place in northern Illinois. He arrived a few hours later, feeling good about everything, especially the decision about Wallace. He brought the dogs inside. It was the first time Roo's parents would meet Wallace. As Roo's dad petted him, Wallace leaned against the man's legs. Roo seized the moment. He told his dad that he and Clara had decided to keep Wallace.

"Ahhhhhhhhh." His dad let out a long sigh. "If you're going to have another dog, shouldn't it at least be one that if something goes wrong you're not going to get sued for everything you're worth?"

4

Roo launched a disc into the sky and Wallace bolted after it. Two weeks after the trip to Indianapolis, the pair had fallen back into their old routine: daily workouts in the yard and weekly trips to the park. Today was a park day and they gathered there with the other members of the Minnesota Disc Dog Club—both of them. Wallace finished up his workout and Roo put him back in the car. J-Dubs took off but Josh G. stuck around, and he and Roo stood in the parking lot talking.

Roo had come home from his first foray into freestyle full of ideas and confidence. He knew he and Wallace could compete, and he now had a better idea of what they needed to work on. For starters, they simply had to get better, smoother, more efficient, with better transitions and fewer drops, but they also needed to improve their wow factor.

Josh agreed with all of that, but he had another idea, too. While in Indy they had watched some of the pairs' freestyle competition, in which two people and one dog performed. It was a brand-new event, and no one they'd seen was very good. The teams had forgotten their moves, they'd gone onto the field with their routines written on pieces of paper, they'd generally stunk. Roo and Josh had actually laughed watching some of it. "If we had practiced at all we would have finished top two in the category and made it to worlds," Josh said.

"Yep," Roo said. "Probably."

"So let's do it," Josh said. "They have an open qualifier in Atlanta. You go down a day early and compete. The top two finishers get into the world finals."

"Which dog?" Roo asked.

"Both. Wazee and Wallace. One of them has to make it."

Roo looked in the car. Wallace jumped from the front seat to the rear and paced back and forth across it. "All right," Roo said. "Let's do it."

————

When Roo arrived home, Clara was lying on the couch. Lights off, air conditioner running. This didn't surprise him. More and more these days he would come home to find her like that. Her business continued to struggle. She had a few dog-walking clients and an occasional day-care assignment, but otherwise things were slow. Clara and Roo knew it would take a while to build up a clientele, but they'd agreed that this was okay. Being her own boss would allow Clara to earn income and tend to the household stuff while Roo held down the full-time job. Roo had always looked at their marriage as a partnership in which they each carried equal weight. That weight was not measured in dollars earned but in shared responsibility, and this arrangement, as they had imagined it, seemed equitable.

But Clara spent most of the day rattling around the house, caring for the dogs and not much else. The place was never a wreck but not really tidy either. Roo didn't expect to walk in and find her cooking, hair coiffed and clothes perfect, but often there wasn't even a plan for dinner or food in the house.

Roo said nothing. Clara said nothing. They weren't confrontational types. Time slipped by. An unspoken tension developed between them. They drifted—Roo into Wallace, Clara into her thoughts. She'd put on more weight. Roo didn't understand what was happening or why. He felt let down, like Clara wasn't holding up her end of the partnership, but he tried to be patient and under-standing. Sally Setzer's last round of chemo had ended but the spec-ter of future relapses lingered. Roo had never had a parent suffer through anything like that; all four of his grandparents were still alive and well. He figured Sally's struggle had to play a role in Clara's.

In part, he'd agreed to drive to Atlanta and attempt to qualify for the world finals because he thought it would be good for them. It would get Clara out and give the two of them something to do together—a weekend away doing dog stuff. The dogs, it sometimes seemed to Roo, and their address were almost all they still had in common.

Clara barely moved when Roo came in. He told her about the plan. Clara raised up on an elbow and listened with interest. She seemed genuinely excited about the possibilities and even began talking about what they would need to bring and who could watch the other dogs for them while they were away. She worried a bit about Josh's wife, Jen. They'd only met a few times, but on those occasions Jen had been extraordinarily quiet. Clara wondered what they would talk about for an entire weekend, including an eighteen-hour car ride each way. Roo saw a flash of the old Clara, and he felt good about the plan. He hoped it would spark something that would get her going again and diminish the chasm that was grow-ing between them.

He got up from the living room and went into the kitchen. A stack of dishes—Clara's lunch—sat in the sink. Roo loaded the items in the dishwasher and started the machine, shaking his head as he went downstairs. He turned on his computer and when You-Tube appeared on the screen he searched "canine disc pairs free-style." As the dishwasher rumbled he sat watching one video after another. When he looked up it was dark.

Upstairs he rummaged in the fridge until he found some left-overs he could snack on. It was nine P.M. Clara had gone up to bed and Roo went back downstairs to watch more videos. At midnight he turned off the computer, put away the dishes, and went upstairs. He slid under the covers without waking Clara and drifted off to sleep.

5

The Chevy Suburban felt like it ate the road, taking up at least a lane and a half and stretching out behind them like a school bus. It belonged to Josh's father, and big and clunky though it was, it served a purpose—it could transport four adults, three dogs, and all their stuff during a ride that would last the better part of a day. Roo had felt like he was playing a game of Tetris while packing the car, and he needed every bit of his meticulous nature to make all the stuff fit. And although all seven creatures shared the space, they quickly divided into pockets.

The dogs—Wallace, Wazee, and Zipper the mini-dachshund— lounged in crates in the back. The women sat in the backseat, separated by piles of luggage, gear, and an uneasy silence, broken only by little snippets of forced conversation as they attempted to get to know each other. For entertainment they had Roo and Josh, who sat up front and talked nonstop. Despite the oddness of their first meeting the two men had become fast friends. During all the time at the park playing disc together, they realized they liked the same music, had a similar sense of humor, and were both fitness freaks.

From the forums and the videos they knew the names of the dogs and people they'd be competing against, and they tossed them back and forth, assessing the strengths of each. Only ten days earlier they'd gathered for their first pairs practice. They had to see if pursuing pairs was even possible. Sometimes a dog will only bring the disc back to the person who trained him.

Sure enough, both Wallace and Wazee tended to focus on their usual playing partner. If Josh threw a disc, Wallace would go after it, but he would return it to Roo. And if they tried to do a trick in which Wallace had to run past Roo to Josh, Wallace wouldn't do it. He'd get to Roo and stop. Pretty quickly Roo and Josh realized the task would require some ingenuity. They had to choreograph around the built-in obstacle. If they needed Wallace to bring the disc to Josh, Roo would have to position himself behind Josh.

The entire thing became a project of trial and error. They would simply try stuff—attempt some trick or another and see if they could make it work. Once they had something, they'd practice it until they had it down. After they'd gone through a training run with each dog they'd have a brainstorming session, during which they dreamed up new things to try, debated potential improvements, and choreographed transitions between tricks. After repeating the procedure every day for ten days, they had a bunch of tricks and the outline of a routine for each dog, but they were far from polished.

As the miles wore on, they continued to iron out the details. One of the first things they did was name all the tricks. Up until that point they'd discussed them by describing them, as in "Next we'll do that one where you throw it over my head and Wallace will run between my legs to catch it."

Having names would allow them to call out the tricks as they progressed through the routine, making sure each knew what was happening and that they could transition smoothly from one element to the next. That could only help, because with such little practice time under their belts, something was bound to go wrong.

Plus, designing and naming the new tricks turned out to be half the fun. Some were obvious, like the Short-Long, in which Josh and Roo stood next to each other while one made a long throw and the other made a short throw. Wallace would catch the first one, drop it, and continue on to the second one. Then there was the Double Throw, in which Josh threw two discs at once, and Roo caught one while Wallace caught the other. After that it got more interesting. They did another trick in which Josh ran in a ten-yard-diameter circle, firing discs at the center, where Roo stood holding Wallace in his arms and spinning around so Wallace could catch the discs. This was called the Turret. In their big finishing move, Roo and Josh linked arms and then each grasped the same disc with his free hand. Wallace then latched on to the disc and the two men would spin until Wallace lifted off the ground and sailed around them. The name? Circle of Trust.

As they rattled off the names and descriptions, their momentum built. And they began trying ever more bizarre inventions. "Oh," Roo said, "how about this: I start out in a headstand with a bunch of discs in my hands. You come over and grab my ankles and start spinning me around, and I'll throw discs to Wallace?" He laughed as he finished and mimicked the act of tossing discs out in a large circle.

"Right," Josh said. "You know what we call that?" He paused. "The Sprinkler."

6

It was a long walk from the parking area to the field, so the two couples began hauling all their stuff across the grass. On their second or third trip Roo and Clara carried a load of crates and bags. The morning was hot and Wallace, who had accompanied them back and forth on each trip, had begun to get flush and pink, as he often did when he got warm.

As they passed another guy, who was making his own trips back and forth, the man stopped to say hello to Wallace. "Hey, Pinky," he said, noticing Wallace's color. "How's it going, Pinky?" Clara and Roo said Hi and the three of them chatted for a few minutes. The guy's name was Danny Venegas, and Roo was happy that the first person they ran into had a positive reaction to Wallace, although something about his giving Wallace the nickname of Pinky stuck with Clara.

Only the top four finishers in distance and accuracy and freestyle, and the two finishers in pairs freestyle, would move on to compete in the finals. It was possible neither Wallace nor Wazee would qualify. Josh would get sixty seconds, and Roo would spend two minutes on his freestyle routine, plus another minute and a half each in pairs. If neither made it to the finals in any event, it would mean that the crew from Rochester blew a four-day weekend and thirty-six hours in the car for six minutes of competition.

Those numbers added a bit of tension to the proceedings on Friday morning as the Suburban rolled onto a field adjacent to a small cluster of houses. The development was a fly-in community, and the houses lined a central airstrip. A large hangar sat at one end. The field stretched across a plateau above the neighborhood. One of the prominent members of the community was Jeff Perry, a pioneering disc dogger and a cofounder of Hyperflite, a brand of disc popular within the sport and the sponsor of the Skyhoundz circuit.

Despite the heat a relaxed atmosphere prevailed. Jeff hurried around warning everyone to use bug spray to fend off the native chiggers. Others began producing beer from their coolers and kicking up their feet. Clara sat back to watch; it was her first time at a freestyle competition, and she was curious to see the other teams perform. She thought Wallace and Roo were pretty good, and as a pairs team Wallace, Roo, and Josh seemed solid as well. But she didn't really have anything to judge them against.

As she watched the individual freestyle teams compete, she was impressed by some of the stuff she'd never seen before. Tricks like foot stalls, in which the dog balances atop the handler and then jumps off, surprised and delighted her. And although Roo and Wallace couldn't do everything some of the others could, she felt that overall their stuff compared well. Watching the others also provided a welcome diversion from what was happening around her.

Roo and Josh were dealing with their nerves. The two of them paced around under the canopy, muttering to themselves and pantomiming moves. Every now and then one of them would suddenly fire a question into the air. "Under-Over and then Over-Under?"

"No," the other would say, "with Wallace it's Over-Under, Double Throw. With Wazee it's Over-Under, Under-Over," making an abbreviated replica of the throw or catch that went with each trick. At the same time the other guy would make the corresponding move, while nodding his head and saying, "Right, right."

Given the newness of pairs freestyle and the teams competing in it, the playing field was relatively level. That should have made them more confident, but somehow it increased the pressure because it meant that if they didn't screw up, they had a real chance.

It didn't help that the individual qualifying rounds seemed to drag on forever. Roo and Wallace gave the category a shot, and they did okay, but their performances weren't their best, and they finished in the middle of the pack. By the time the pairs competition started, the light had already begun to fade. Wazee went first.

Josh and Roo took the field, and their music came on. The song Josh had chosen was something called a Crazy Frog remix. It started out with what was supposed to be a cartoon frog imitating the sound of a motorcycle starting but resulted in a high-pitched nattering that could have easily been mistaken for Alvin from the

Chipmunks doing some sort of Mel Torme–like scat. The intro led into a dance tune done in the same voice. It was fun and upbeat but definitely different sounding. As Roo waited for the music to start, he saw people packing up their stuff. It was late, the signature event was over, and the pairs were still enough of an unknown that folks had little or no expectations. Then the first notes crashed against the quiet Georgia dusk. Around the field people stopped what they were doing and looked up.

Josh launched the first disc and Wazee reacted. The three of them settled into their routine as if they were back in the park. Wazee was in a zone, moving fast and catching nearly everything. When at last he snared the final disc, and the music came to a stop, Roo looked around. The people who had been packing up stood watching. The song had grabbed their attention, and the trio from Minnesota had held on to it. Roo and Josh jogged off the field laughing and high-fiving.

A few other dogs went before Wallace's turn came up. As a precaution, Clara and Jen positioned themselves along the side of the field, and as Clara waited her anticipation grew. She wondered if Wallace would do well, if there would be any sort of problems, what others would think of him. As always with Wallace she felt as though they had something to prove. The music started and the threesome went into their routine. Clara thought they looked good.

When they all returned to their camp, they agreed that Wazee had been better. They felt good about Wazee's chances, but Wallace was a question mark. Could they take the two top spots? The day neared sundown by the time all the dogs had finished. The competitors huddled around the scoring tent as the judges tallied. Finally, one of them took the microphone and began to announce the scores, starting from the lowest. As the names went by neither Wallace nor Wazee was called. Roo and Clara locked eyes. Clara grabbed Roo's hand. Finally, the judge said, "In second place, qualifying for the finals, Josh Grenell, Roo Yori, and Wallace." The foursome let out a little cheer and shared a round of high fives. "And our top qualifier," the announcer said, "is the team of Josh Grenell, Roo Yori, and Wazee."

Roo and Josh began accepting congratulations from the others around them. "Where did you guys come from?" they were asked again and again. They were almost completely unknown on the national scene and yet here they were grabbing the top two qualifying spots. Even one of the judges stopped by their canopy and complimented them on their performance.

The Rochester foursome shared a sense of happiness as well as relief. The long trip down was officially worth it. Now, if they could grab a little finals hardware it would be a complete victory.

7

Piedmont Park is 189 acres of trees and fields and ponds dotted by athletic courts and walking trails that sits about a mile north of downtown Atlanta. From almost anywhere on the grounds the city skyline provides an eye-catching backdrop. When Roo, Clara, Josh, and Jen arrived on Saturday morning for day two of the competition, one of the more expansive fields was decked out for the event. Banners and flags hung everywhere. There was a judging tent with event logos on it, a merchandise tent, and an on-deck tent. The field was marked with small flags that also bore the name of the event, and the grass was thick and soft.

The sounds of unpacking and setting up—the shouting and grunting and clanking of poles—was drowned out only by incessant barking. A tangle of quick-fold canopies and portable crates spread across one end of the field. The park was one of the things Josh had loved about his first experience in Atlanta. It was simply a great place to hold the competition.

The field sat next to a large dog park, so there were a lot of dogs and dog lovers already assembled, and on a late-summer weekend a fresh crowd of passersby were constantly stopping to watch the action, mixing in with a crowd of spectators to create a competitive atmosphere that topped any other event Josh had been to. It felt like a world championship.

The pairs finals wouldn't take place until Sunday, so they settled in to relax and watch the day's events. Except Roo. He was still searching for a disc dog and had made arrangements to meet up with Dolly, another pup he'd learned about online. He also made small talk with other competitors and introduced himself to people he'd met on the forums. And while the day off helped them all relax, it also built anticipation for the next day. Especially that night, when they attended the Banquet of Champions.

A large tent had been put up back at the field where qualifying had been. White linen tablecloths covered the tables. A buffet dinner stretched across one end. Everyone received a plaque for making it to worlds and the individual winners from the day's action accepted congratulations.

The Rochester quartet found themselves at a table with a few other newcomers and they all talked about what they had seen and heard so far. As they ate, a man named Zak George, a seasoned competitor who would end up with a show on Animal Planet, stopped by the table. "Are you the guy with the pit bull?" he asked Roo, who nodded, unsure what to expect. "There's nothing like it out there. Very unique. You're doing a great thing."

The program moved on. A man named Chuck Middleton was presented with a lifetime achievement award. Middleton had been one of the pioneers of the sport, winning many titles with his dog, Donnie, and helping found the first disc dog club, in Dallas.

Middleton spoke about the good ol' days and about the advances in performance, and finally spoke about Donnie, who had since passed on. In the end, he said, he'd trade it all, all the trophies and travel and championships, for one more day in the park with his dog, one more afternoon in the sun throwing the disc to Donnie. The moment stood out for Roo.

They were staying with Jen's aunt and uncle, and later that night as Roo lay in bed the notion came back to him. He knew what Middleton was talking about, that feeling of freedom and connection that came from engaging with your dog. He thought about it for a long time before he fell asleep.

———

When the music came up Roo and Josh stepped onto the field. The afternoon had been another long one of waiting, the tension building. Roo's eyes were wide for most of the day, and Josh had never been jumpier. Now, finally, they were ready to go.

Wallace's turn came up first, and it started smoothly enough. But midway through Roo ran over to Josh and yelled, "Short-Long," the name of the next trick in the routine, in which they stood side by side with Josh making a short throw and Roo a long one before Wallace sped off to catch both. But Josh confused the trick with another one that required them to stand about twenty-five yards apart. So when Roo yelled, "Short-Long," Josh promptly turned and ran.

Roo wasn't sure what to do, but he knew he couldn't do the trick he was supposed to. He took off after Josh. When he finally caught him, he looked Josh in the eye. "*No*, Short-Long!" he said. Josh nodded, turned, and ran again. Roo shook his head and looked at the sky. He sprinted after Josh, Wallace following, eyes fixed on the discs, waiting for someone, anyone, to throw one of them. When Roo caught up to Josh this time, he said, "Stay here. You throw short and I throw long!"

"Oh," Josh said, realizing his mistake. "Shit." On the sidelines Clara watched in disbelief. They were visibly confused. But at last they got back in sync and moved on. The rest of the routine went well, but what would the Keystone Kops impression do to their chances?

When Wazee's turn came Roo and Josh were a little shaken but they started slowly and built up momentum. Their confidence returned and the round went smoothly. Not quite as well as his qualifying round, but pretty close.

The judges agreed. At the end of the first round Wazee was in first place. Wallace, even with the miscue, clung to third. A dog named Shiloh, a cattle dog mix, held second. Roo had never heard of Shiloh and her handlers. They lived in a different region and didn't participate in the forums. Roo had watched them play, and they were good, but he thought they could be beaten.

A one-two finish would exceed any expectations they had arrived with, but it suddenly seemed possible, although pulling it off would take a good round for Wazee and a great one for Wallace. At the same time, Roo knew another miscue with Wallace could easily knock them off the podium. Between pacing and muttering, Roo and Josh worked to make sure they had all the moves down. The cramming only ratcheted up the pressure and by the time they took the field for Wallace's second round they were each a jangly ball of nerves.

Then Wallace happened. Stepping onto the field something seemed different. As always, he had an energetic quality to him, jumping for the discs and shaking with anticipation, but Roo could sense something else in his bearing, see it in the way he carried himself. His tail was stiff except for the tip, which flicked steadily. His ears were perked, his eyes wide. The music kicked on, the discs began to fly, and Wallace did the rest.

He ran a little faster, jumped a little higher. He appeared, if it was possible, to move with a little more grace. He caught nearly everything. As the routine progressed, Roo felt that sensation, that connection and singularity of purpose that had struck him during earlier competitions. He could sense that Josh felt it too, and the three of them worked in perfect synchronicity, sharing an instant, almost nonverbal communication.

When the round ended the men floated off the field on a sort of blissed-out high. Back at the tent, the pair traded high fives and enthused with Jen and Clara about how great the performance had come off—from both on the field and off it. Other competitors offered congratulations, and more than one said that despite the first-round problems, Wallace had sealed the win with that performance. Roo hoped it was true, although he knew that Wazee had a big lead heading into his final round.

If Roo and Josh could repeat their first-round showing with Wazee, he would almost certainly win. But as the round unfolded, Roo found himself out of position at one point, making a mess of the trick they were performing. His misstep wasn't as bad as the Wallace debacle, but it certainly hurt. "I'm so sorry," Roo said coming off the field, but Josh waved him off. They convinced themselves that it wasn't a big deal, certainly not as big a blunder as they'd endured during Wallace's first round. Still, the mood in the tent had shifted. Whereas an hour earlier they'd felt good about a one-two finish, now they wondered if either dog would claim one of the top spots.

Roo tried to temper his anxiety later when everyone gathered around the scorers' tent to hear the results. Since the field was larger, only the top three places would be announced. Roo stood with Clara, holding Wallace on a leash. Josh, Jen, and Wazee were next to them. The announcer stood on a small stand above the crowd and beside him was an Olympics-like medal stand, with three distinct levels. "In the pairs expert division, third place goes to Josh Grenell, Roo Yori, and Wazee." The crowd applauded, and Josh let out a little whoop as the four of them traded hugs.

Roo wondered if he should go up to accept the trophy with Josh and Wazee. Was it possible that Wallace finished ahead of Wazee? The second round was incredible, but the first was almost equally bad. In the eyes of the judges, Roo figured, Wazee had probably been better overall. He left Wallace with Clara and stepped onto the stand with Josh.

After they had accepted their trophies the announcer went on. "In second place, with the highest single-round score of any team, a second-round total of forty-one point five points out of fifty, we have Josh Grenell, Roo Yori, and Wallace." Roo's fist shot into the air. He hopped off the podium and hopped over to Clara, who gave him a long hug, then bent over and grabbed Wallace's face, cooing at him. Roo scooped Wallace up and they took their place on the stand and accepted the second-place trophy. Josh and Wazee moved over to join them, and the pair high-fived. All the pressure had receded now. Roo had wanted to win, but he was thrilled with second. And third. They were going home with two trophies, but he felt as though he'd gained more than that.

As they were packing up, Roo saw Chuck Middleton, the man who only the night before had accepted the lifetime achievement award, walking toward them. Middleton introduced himself. He'd been one of the judges of the pairs competition, and he wanted to meet Wallace. As he petted the dog, he said, "He's a great dog, and it's great to see him out here. Just watching him, you can see how much he loves to play."

"Yep," Roo said. "He's the highest-drive dog I've ever seen."

Middleton went on. "Don't let anyone ever talk you out of competing with him. He's a winner. He would've won today if you guys didn't spend twenty seconds of the first round yelling at each other."

That night, after a celebratory dinner at Aunt Carol and Uncle Frank's, Middleton's words came back to Roo. He thought not only about Middleton's post-awards visit but also about his speech the night before—*he would trade it all for one more day in the park with his dog.* Roo loved playing disc with Wallace. He loved how much Wallace loved it, and he loved how it showed that Wallace had been worthy of their effort to save him.

He also loved those times when they were out there alone, and everything else dropped away. Nothing existed but the two of them and a few plastic circles. In a deeper way, on a level he maybe only half recognized himself, he'd come to identify with Wallace. As a soccer player he'd been discounted and overlooked, too. He was the type of player, his college coach would say, who did the little things necessary to win but that only someone with a trained eye would notice. He made all the other players better.

Still, most coaches looked at him and saw only a kid who was a step slow and about three sizes too small and wrote him off. The only team that had given him a chance was rewarded with a four-year starter who became good enough to at least consider making a run at the pros, even if it hadn't worked out. Roo knew about being prejudged based on appearances and assumptions and left for dead. He'd saved Wallace from that fate once and didn't want to make the mistake of giving up now.

As they lay in bed that night, he and Clara talked in whispers so as not to wake anyone. She had been instrumental in saving Wallace, and her connection to the dog was as strong as his. She had played a key role throughout the weekend, too, taking care of Wallace between rounds, making sure he was fed and walked and watered, keeping him stretched and warmed up, so that Roo could focus on his job. Being together, engaged in a common purpose, had brought them closer again, and even spending time with another couple, doing couply things, made them feel more like a couple again.

"Not bad for a pit bull nobody wanted," Clara said, repeating the line that had become their standard acknowledgment of Wallace's achievements.

"Yep," Roo said. "He's earning it."

"Watching him, he's just . . ." Clara searched for the words. "He's so determined. He sees that thing he wants, and he's not going to let anything stop him from getting it. And once he has it he's not letting go. I love that about him." She looked at Roo, and he slid his hand across the covers until it found hers.

"He never gives me less than a hundred percent," Roo said. "No matter how bad I throw it, he never quits. He never gives up." Roo sounded like he was going to say more, but he stopped and the room went quiet. They lay there like that for a while—silent, lost in their own thoughts, but connected—until they drifted off to sleep.

The next day Roo called Dolly's handlers and told them no thanks. Maybe Wallace would never win first place, but Roo would take his chances with the dog that nobody wanted. He'd seen enough already to think that maybe they could shock the disc-dog world. And either way, he was smart enough to recognize something special when he had it.

On the long drive home, the group stopped off at an Italian restaurant in Janesville, Wisconsin. As they ate, the conversation ebbed and flowed. One lull in the chatter stretched until, out of nowhere, Josh spoke. "That last round with Wallace," he said. "That was one of the greatest experiences of my life."

8

Roo stepped in from outside. November in Minnesota had brought the kind of cold that made their trip to Atlanta feel like a distant memory. The temperature inside didn't do much to rekindle that weekend either. Clara lay on the couch, lights off, TV on.

In the months since Wallace's showing at worlds they'd returned to their old patterns.

There were a few blips of connectivity. In October Wallace and Angus competed in another weight pull, and Wallace won for most weight pulled as a percentage of body weight. Shortly afterward, Roo, Josh, Wallace, and Wazee appeared in the Rochester *Post-Bulletin*. They were exciting moments, but the connection they fostered between Roo and Clara didn't outlast the following week.

Clara seemed to have slipped into full-on depression. She had little energy or enthusiasm for anything. Every minor difficulty brought her down, and she cared about almost nothing. She still gave all she had to the dogs—they wanted for nothing and suffered no neglect. But her temper flared like it never had before. If she were trying to walk through the house and the dogs were in her way she might yell at them, which seemed strange even to her.

Roo, she never yelled at. Neither of them was inclined to fight, and they once again retreated to their neutral corners. In his heart, Roo knew this wasn't the real Clara. She wasn't the type to lie around and watch TV all day or lose her cool. He hoped that with time and patience she would be able to shake off whatever was dragging her down. He forged on. At night and on the weekends he worked with Wallace, both with the discs and on the spring pole. While Wallace dangled and pranced around the garage, Roo read about dogs and more specifically about pit bulls. He had begun to feel more strongly than ever that the breed had gotten a bad rap.

"Hi," he said to Clara as he shook off the cold and took off his coat.

"Hey." Clara's voice came from the darkness.

"How ya doin'?" he asked.

"Okay."

"I'm starving," he said. "We got a dinner plan?"

"No."

"Well, we got anything in the house?"

"Not sure," she said. "Take a look."

Roo rummaged in the kitchen, but there was nothing. He decided to make a run to the store to pick up some stuff. When he was done shopping he made his way to the register and slid his debit card through the machine. It was rejected. Roo tried again. He and Clara had always been careful to manage the money in their account so it wouldn't be overdrawn, but even if it was, it carried an additional $3,000 line of credit that should have covered any overdraft. The machine processed for a moment, and the notice came up again, "Insufficient funds."

Shocked and embarrassed, Roo quickly produced a credit card and zipped it through the machine. His mind raced. What could have happened? Was there an error at the bank or had they fallen that far into the hole? He knew that since Clara had left Paws & Claws their income had gone down, but not by much. Not enough to cause this, he thought.

The credit card processed: rejected. What? Roo couldn't believe it. He swiped the card one more time. He didn't even want to think about what this might mean. The limit on the card was $10,000. Again, the card was rejected. Roo apologized. "Something must be wrong at the bank," he told the girl at the register. "I'll have to get it checked out and come back tomorrow." He looked at the packed bags on the counter. "You want me to put that stuff back?" he asked.

She looked too, and then flipped a hand at the bags. "Nah," she said, "we'll take care of it. Happens all the time."

Roo flew home. He was angry and humiliated and scared. He blamed himself for not knowing what was going on. He had always taken care of the banking, but when Clara left Paws & Claws it was one of the things they'd agreed that she would handle. She seemed to have it under control, so he had let it go. Now he had no idea where things stood. He charged through the door.

"Clara," he called, but there was no answer. He looked around.

She was out walking a few of the dogs. He went to the computer and pulled up their account information. "What the hell?" he said. It was no mistake. They were broke. He walked away from the computer in a kind of shock and slumped down onto the living room couch.

When Clara returned he was calm. "Where did all our money go?" he said. "Why are our credit cards maxed out?"

Her face dropped. "I'm so sorry," she said, putting her hands over her eyes.

"What happened?" Roo said with a trace of insistence in his voice.

"We started falling behind. . . ."

"When?"

"Months ago, beginning of summer. I just wasn't making enough, but I kept thinking my business would get better. That I'd get more clients and we'd be able to catch up."

"But you haven't done anything to get new clients. You just sit around all day."

"I know," she said, starting to cry.

"Why didn't you tell me?" Roo asked.

Her voice got small. "I didn't want to disappoint you," she said. Roo shook his head and let out a long exhale, then got up, walked across the room, and went upstairs.

He sat on the bed, arms crossed, stewing. Trying to work through his anger. Trying to figure out how to get them out of debt. The house they'd bought was at the high end of the range of mortgages for which they'd been preapproved. The payments were a burden. They had just adopted another dog, a rat terrier named Scooby Snack, with whom Clara had started to play disc. Five dogs, all of which needed food and shots and trips to the vet. The excursions to Indianapolis and Atlanta had cost money, too. He felt overwhelmed.

Finally, the door creaked open. Clara came in slowly and sat on the edge of the bed, her face in profile. She folded her hands in her lap and looked down at them. Neither of them said anything, and a pained silence filled the room. Finally Clara spoke. "Are you going to divorce me?"

Chapter 5

World Beater

What are you feeding that dog?

Chuck Middleton

1

It started simply enough, with a kid and his dog. In this case, a nineteen-year-old kid from Ohio named Alex Stein. As a student at Ohio State, Stein received the dog as a gift, a male whippet that he named Ashley, or more formally Ashley Whippet. He took Ashley everywhere, and they did everything together. It was the early seventies and the Frisbee craze was taking off around the country, especially on college campuses, and Alex discovered that Ashley could catch discs like no other dog around. Alex and Ashley weren't the first man and dog to play catch with a disc, but they started playing regularly and before long they became the most famous disc team ever.

Ashley was so good, in fact, that Alex decided they could make it in showbiz. So one summer he and Ashley made their way out to L.A. He tried approaching talent agents and even Wham-O (maker of the Frisbee), but no one was interested in Alex and Ashley. Alex took matters into his own hands.

On August 5, 1974, Alex smuggled Ashley into Dodger Stadium. Between the seventh and eighth innings of a nationally televised Monday-night baseball game between the Dodgers and the Cincinnati Reds, Alex launched Ashley over the fence and onto the field, jumping the rail right behind him. He hit the ground and pulled out a few discs. He began throwing them and Ashley began catching them. The crowd was instantly enthralled. Most people had never seen anything like what was happening on the field, and they cheered every catch.

Ashley was a sight to see. Whippets, thin and fast, are not typically great disc dogs, but Ashley was rocket quick and a great leaper and he catapulted himself into the air, twisting and arching to snag discs, to the delight of the people in the stands. When security appeared to stop the intrusion, the crowd booed so forcefully that they stepped back and let Alex and Ashley go at it.

They were still going when the broadcast returned from commercial and analyst Joe Garagiola began doing commentary as the cameras captured what was happening on the field. Finally, after eight minutes, security took Alex away. He was arrested, but in a remarkable stroke of luck, a man named Irv Lander, who worked in promotions for Wham-O, had been at the game. He bailed out Alex, but he didn't solve Alex's biggest problem: Ashley was missing. Alex spent three days in a near panic until finally he received a call from a family who had been at the game and found Ashley roaming the stadium parking lot.

Man and dog were reunited and with Lander's help, and a sponsorship from Alpo, they founded a world championship for canine disc in 1975. The first year saw only a handful of entrants but the sport grew quickly. Ashley won the first three world championships, and a few years later the event evolved into a circuit with the championship named after him: the Ashley Whippet Invitational, or AWI. Alex and Ashley went on to perform at numerous events, including the Super Bowl, and on *The Tonight Show* and *Merv Griffin*.

Nothing has been as simple since. For a variety of reasons, the world of competitive disc dog has continued to splinter and re-form itself since the early eighties. Besides the AWI, there are at least five major circuits, including Skyhoundz, the Flying Disc Dog Open (FDDO), the United Frisbee-Dog Organization (UFO), the U.S. Disc Dog Nationals (USDDN), and the Purina Incredible Dog Challenge (IDC).

Each offers its own world or national championship. For years many players considered AWI the top prize, but that perception has faded somewhat and the question of which title is most prestigious depends on whom you ask and when you ask them. Roo didn't have much preference. He'd compete in any of them. He made most of his decisions about where to compete based on the travel requirements.

Still, he had some goals. The AWI had the Lander Cup, and each year the winner's name was added to it. Roo thought it would be cool to have *Wallace* etched on the sport's oldest prize. And he was drawn to the Purina Incredible Dog Challenge. He liked that it was mostly an invitational, which meant you had to be considered a top performer to even make it there, but even more so he liked that the finals appeared on national television. As he became more aware of the politics surrounding pit bulls and Wallace's ability to help change attitudes, the idea of appearing in front of a national audience with his dog, showing the breed in a positive light for a change, had great appeal to him.

At the start of 2006, something else caught his attention: the Cynosport World Games. For whatever reason, AWI, UFO, and FDDO all decided to hold their championships over one weekend in September in Arizona. Each would crown its own independent champion, but at the end of the weekend the dog with the best composite finish among the three events would be given a separate overall award and named the Cynosport World Champion. It was the closest thing the sport had to a unified title, and Roo wanted to win it.

The first year on the circuit had been about proving Wallace had been worth saving, but this year would be about proving that a pit bull could be one of the best disc dogs in the country. Roo had an idea about how to accomplish these goals, but a few obstacles stood in his way. Namely, his free time, his dog, and his personal life.

2

Roo had no idea when he and Wallace would find the time to make themselves into a world-class disc team.

The immediate solution to the Yoris' financial distress was not divorce. Instead, Clara took a job at a local coffee shop, Dunn Bros., which would bring in some extra income and allow her to continue her dog walking and sitting. She had also embarked on a canine massage class, hoping the added service would help her business. And Roo would begin taking real estate classes, which they would pay for, in part, with the money Clara earned. If all went well, he'd have his license by spring and would start earning extra money selling houses nights and weekends.

The real estate classes took place on the weekends. All day, eight A.M. to five P.M. up in Minneapolis, an hour and a half away. Besides the classroom time there was homework, too. And the classes advanced in sections, which meant there were exams along the way that required serious cramming. And of course there remained Roo's nine-to-five job at Mayo, the dog walking, the spring pole sessions, and the fractured marriage. Things hadn't changed much between Roo and Clara, but they were at least making progress in putting their life back together.

Other than the time crunch, Roo sort of liked the plan. Before he got the job at Mayo he'd come close to getting into real estate. He'd always been intrigued by the prospect. He liked exploring houses, assessing the market, and working with people. He looked forward to doing the job, but he had to get through the classes first.

He also had to figure out what was wrong with his dog. In early December, Roo had gone downstairs to get Wallace out of his crate. As he put on Wallace's leash he'd noticed a spot on the dog's side. The fur had thinned and the skin beneath it appeared pink and raw. Roo thought maybe he'd been rubbing up against the bars of the crate. "Clara," he called. "What's going on with Wallace?"

She came down to take a look but could make no more sense of the spot than Roo. They scheduled an appointment with the vet, who determined Wallace was having an allergic reaction. The prime suspect: Wallace's food. Clara and Roo changed brands. The new stuff hurt their finances but they charged ahead and hoped for the best.

For a while it seemed to work, but then Wallace's allergies flared again—even worse. As the calendar turned, his reaction spread. He developed sores on his head and he itched all over. He scratched tirelessly until his sides were nearly bald. Clara gave him oatmeal baths in an attempt to relieve the discomfort, but the effect was temporary. Eventually he wore bloody patches into his skin and staph infections broke out.

The trips to the vet—and the bills—piled up. The experts treated the sores and the infections with antibiotics and put Wallace on antihistamines to ward off the allergic reactions. Finally, in February they made an appointment with a dermatologist. He ran a panel that would test Wallace's reaction to almost fifty different substances. The doctor explained that each potential allergen would register on a scale of one to four, with four indicating the highest level of sensitivity.

Clara and Roo waited for the results, doing everything they could to make Wallace comfortable. Roo had planned to work with Wallace throughout the winter, but that was proving difficult. His condition and the cold, dry air did not mix well. One snowy night Roo received a call from Josh: They were having a snow jam. All the members of the fledgling Minnesota Disc Dog Club gathered at the park. They positioned their cars so the headlights illuminated the field and charged out into the still-falling snow. Discs soared and dogs romped. Music blared from someone's car.

Roo was having a blast at the park, and so was Wallace. But after a handful of tosses, Roo saw dark spots on the snow as Wallace ran back with the disc. After Wallace returned the disc and danced around him waiting for the next throw, Roo looked closer. The dark spots were actually red spots. Wallace was bleeding. The dry air had caused his skin to harden and crack. Wallace didn't seem the least bit bothered and wanted only to chase the disc, but Roo wouldn't have it. That was the end of the snow jam for them.

Roo wondered if Wallace would be able to keep on playing disc. He certainly still had the same energy and drive—he continued to be a terror on the spring pole—but would the drugs and the distraction of the itching affect his ability to perform or concentrate? It felt like one of those head-shaking ironies. Roo had finally given up the pursuit of a "classic" disc dog and had committed to accomplishing the impossible with Wallace, and before they even got started Wallace's competitive days might be done.

Finally, the results came in. Wallace tested positive for allergies to eleven of the substances. On four of them his sensitivity measured at four, including dust, ragweed, wool, and cotton mites. Roo and Clara couldn't believe it. The special bedding they'd given Wallace to make him more comfortable had exacerbated the problem. They immediately switched to fleece blankets and changed his food again.

They waited.

3

On his trips to Indianapolis and Atlanta Roo noticed that the rage in canine disc seemed to be vaults—tricks in which the dog uses the human as a platform to launch itself high into the air on the way to catching the disc. Roo and Wallace didn't have any vaults in their routine; Roo knew that to compete for the top prize they'd have to add a few.

Roo suspected that vaults would never be their strong suit. He had begun a weight-loss program for Wallace, hoping to take him from fifty-eight pounds down to somewhere around fifty, but even if Wallace could lose the weight and master vaults, Roo wondered how good a fifty-pound pit bull would look soaring through the air and landing.

By late February Roo had received his real estate license and lined up a job with a local broker that would start in March. Free of classes and studying, he took advantage of some unseasonably warm weather to play disc with Wallace. With the treatments and environmental changes they'd made around the house Wallace looked liked his old self, and Roo was eager to see if he still had the desire and ability to catch the disc. It didn't take long to find out.

As soon as Roo picked up the discs, Wallace's body wiggled and his tail went stiff. He leapt up on Roo, trying to get at them. Roo pushed him away and let one fly. Wallace jetted after it with an intensity that was impressive even by his usually high standards.

Roo made another throw and despite how fast Wallace ran, the disc sailed far ahead of him. But Wallace never gave up. He lowered his head and kept charging. As his face, the disc, and the ground converged, Roo could see Wallace wouldn't make it, but Wallace wasn't constrained by things like the surface of the earth. The ground was still soft after the thaw, and at the last second Wallace plowed his face into the dirt, burrowing underground to grab the disc just as it landed. He trotted back to Roo, dropped the disc, and coughed up a big chunk of sod. He looked up with a muddy grin that Roo could only interpret as, "How's that?"

Roo figured his dog was ready.

Roo had already taken to the Internet, watching videos and querying on forums, to learn how to execute vaults. He and Wallace had started to work on them toward the end of 2005, so they had something of a head start. After Wallace ran through his stable of old tricks, Roo began to work on the vaults. He turned over a large plastic bin and then held a disc on the other side. "Take," he said, giving Wallace the cue that he should grab the disc and hoping Wallace would jump on the bin, then leap to get the disc.

Wallace, being Wallace, plowed right through the bin and grabbed the disc. Roo reset the bin and tried again. Same thing. After a few more failed attempts, Roo held the bin in place with his foot, and instead of running through it Wallace began to jump over it. That was progress. After each try Roo attempted to correct Wallace and he would tap on the bin to indicate he wanted Wallace to jump on top of it.

Finally, Roo held the disc up so high that Wallace couldn't get it. Roo tapped on the bin. Wallace jumped on the bin, then launched himself into the air and grabbed the disc. "Good boy," Roo said, and let Wallace chew on the disc, since getting the toy was the reward he coveted most. A few more repetitions and they were off and running. Within days all Roo had to do was tap on the bin and Wallace would jump up on it. Then Roo could tap on his thigh or his back and Wallace would use one of them as his launching pad.

It wasn't always easy or pretty. There were some successes; there were some wipeouts. Roo took those as confirmation of his initial thought. The team could work in one or two vaults just to show they could do them, but for the most part they'd have to come up with something else—a different style for a different type of dog. Exactly what that would be, Roo didn't yet know, but he liked the idea of innovating.

As they played he took particular delight in watching Wallace. It wasn't simply that the dog excelled at catching discs; it was that he loved it. The thrill of the chase made him so happy. Wallace continued to compete in weight pulls—he'd become quite good—but he never derived the joy from it that playing disc seemed to bring him. That enthusiasm led to the next breakthrough.

Typically, after Wallace caught a disc he would run back toward Roo at breakneck speed. One time, as Wallace charged toward him, Roo thought, *If I jumped in the air, I bet he would keep going right under me.* So Roo jumped, and Wallace went under. Roo threw another disc, and as Wallace charged back Roo leapt up and did a sort of scissor kick. Wallace buzzed underneath him.

Roo had another idea. He threw a disc. Wallace caught it and charged back, and as the dog approached Roo jumped, but not straight up. He sort of dove up and forward, as if he were launching himself off a diving board. Wallace raced under him and Roo canted toward the earth headfirst. At the last instant he tucked his head, rolled directly into a somersault, and popped up onto his feet. This, he thought, could be it. This could be their signature twist. It felt right.

He and Wallace continued to work on all their new tricks—the vaults, the new throws, the jumps and dives—for the next week or two. Then Roo hooked up with Josh to get a second opinion. He ran through all the vaults and the other small improvisational changes he'd made. Josh nodded his approval. "Pretty sweeeet," he droned. Finally, Roo tossed the disc and when Wallace returned he did the dive and roll, popped up on his feet, and did another toss that Wallace ran and caught.

He looked over at Josh. His buddy stood silent for a moment. Then he burst out laughing. "What the hell was that?" he said at last.

"That's our new move," said Roo.

"Well," Josh said, "it's either awesome or ridiculous." It was certainly new. No one had ever done anything like it as far as either of them knew. Roo ran through a few variations on the trick. The more Josh saw, the less outrageous it seemed. As they talked about it, they realized Roo's jumping and rolling could create the perfect mix. Wallace would bring the drive, power, and disc-catching prowess, while Roo could accent their athleticism and wow factor. It was a different approach, but the judges didn't grade only the dogs; they assessed the whole team.

As March began, Roo felt great about their competitive odds. His dog's health had stabilized. He had a new twist for his routine and two months to hone it before the competitive season started. On top of all that, he had sent a tape of himself and Wallace to *The Late Show with David Letterman* and the duo had been invited to appear on a "Stupid Pet Tricks" segment in May.

One night he sat in the basement watching videos, hunting for ideas and inspiration. Wallace sat next to him and dug his nose into Roo's thigh, seeking attention. Roo reached down and began petting Wallace. As his hand passed over Wallace's front right shoulder he felt something, a slight indentation. Roo looked closer, moved Wallace into a different position, and rechecked. He was right. There was an indent, not much larger than a quarter, but unmistakable. Maybe it was supposed to be there. Maybe it was always there and he'd simply never noticed before. He checked the other side, felt the other shoulder up and down, side to side. No indent. There was nothing on the other side. Roo felt his heart sink.

"Clara," he yelled. "What's up with Wallace?"

4

The University of Minnesota College of Veterinary Medicine started in 1916 as part of the School of Agriculture and became a freestanding entity in 1947. The school employs more than two hundred staffers and sixty vets. Roo and Clara arrived with Wallace on a sunny day in mid-March. The day after Roo had discovered Wallace's odd problem they'd taken him to a local vet, but that doctor had been short on answers. So they'd made an appointment at U of M.

After an examination, the vets determined that Wallace had infraspinatus muscle contracture. The condition typically arises from overuse, especially in relatively inactive dogs that suddenly do a lot of running. It occurs when one of the muscles in the shoulder— the infraspinatus—which flexes as the dog pulls its leg back toward its body, gets stretched or torn, causing inflammation. It's not painful, but as it heals scar tissue forms, and since the scar tissue is less flexible than the muscle it can cause the muscle to permanently contract. It usually causes a noticeable limp or odd gait. It can be fixed by surgically severing the tendon that attaches the muscle to the bone, relieving the tension. Other muscles take over for the infraspinatus, so the dog can walk and run normally again with little impact. Unless the dog is a world-class competitor.

In Wallace's case, no one quite knew what the prognosis would be. "To be honest," one doctor told Roo and Clara, "I can't believe he's walking as well as he is." But since Wallace wasn't limping, the vets didn't think he was a candidate for surgery. They also didn't think he should play disc anymore. Those words hit Roo like bad sushi. His stomach flipped. His body went stiff. For the second time in a few months he faced the possible end of Wallace's competitive life.

Roo and Clara began the long drive home in silence, each of them wondering what the news meant. And then the questions began. If the vets were right about Wallace's condition, why wasn't he limping? Just a few days earlier Roo had been playing disc with him, watching him run at top speed and even successfully complete vaults, and there had been no signs of trouble. Wallace moved naturally and did nothing to indicate he was in pain. And what had caused the condition? Was it all Wallace's activity, the running and jumping of playing disc, the spring pole, the weight pulling? No one could say. Was it the vaults? Maybe he simply weighed too much to endure the landings after launching his body that high in the air.

Clara and Roo struggled with what to do. The U of M vets thought surgery was not appropriate, but should they do it anyway? Wallace didn't seem bothered and they didn't even know if the diagnosis was correct. Should they let him compete or shut him down? Should they attempt physical therapy, special exercises, medication?

They took Wallace to a neurologist who worked with animals. He thought that some sort of trauma had killed the nerve attached to the muscle and that had caused the muscle to atrophy. Beyond that he couldn't answer the how or why or what-it-meant questions either, but he suggested physical therapy might help stimulate the nerve and bring the muscle back.

Together with the woman who had been Clara's canine massage instructor, they designed a program of exercises meant to target the fine-motor movements of the muscle. The tasks included walking sideways, pivoting around on the front legs while his back legs stayed put, stepping one leg at a time over low obstacles, sidestepping over crushed soda cans. They hoped the combination would bring the muscle back.

Roo had stopped playing disc with Wallace the minute he discovered the indentation. Now he drilled Wallace for fifteen or twenty minutes a day on the therapy exercises. He hoped they would work. He didn't want to think about the consequences if they didn't. To keep himself busy, to steer his mind away from those bad thoughts and feel like he was still making progress on his goals for the year, he started practicing disc alone.

Every day after he worked with Wallace on the therapy exercises, Roo would go into the yard with a handful of discs and practice throwing for twenty or thirty minutes. Wallace would see Roo heading out with the discs and bark in indignation that he was not being invited along.

Roo worked on distance, on accuracy, on technique. He also studied the subtleties of disc handling on the videos he watched. To the casual viewer, the handler simply threw the disc, but to competitors and judges there was more to the action. Did the player flip the disc, roll it off his knuckles, spin it off his teeth? Roo worked on spinning the disc on his fingertips or his elbow or his knee, then batting the edge of it so it shot off as if it had been thrown. He did flips and rolls. He added flair. He created an obstacle course in his yard that required him to throw under, over, or around things to hit his target.

He also worked to master the air bounce, a type of throw in which the disc angles downward as if it were going to burrow into the ground but then, as if by magic, changes trajectory and rises into the air. Roo again took to the Web and had soon mastered the toss. Then he perfected a version he'd seen elsewhere in which he took a running start that led to a sidearm throw, which made him look something like a pitcher in a game of cricket.

Roo had already begun to forge a more athletic throwing style. He regularly did jumps and spins leading into his throws. He lifted high into the air, kicked one leg up, and threw the disc under his thigh. He threw behind his back. His pedigree as a college athlete showed.

The experience of connecting with his dog made playing disc fun, but the competitive spirit brought him back to his soccer-playing days. He enjoyed that. Even more, though, playing disc became a refuge for him, a way to make his troubles fade away. He had poured himself into the sport, and he wasn't ready to give it up—even if Wallace couldn't be with him.

Clara had begun to play disc with Scooby and Roo occasionally joined in or helped out, but not that often. Clara, after all, had been an athlete too, and she had her own competitive drive. In February, Clara's mother had gone for a second cancer surgery, at Mayo. Roo and Clara had been regular visitors while Sally was at the facility, and she now came back regularly for follow-up treatments and exams. Whenever she did, Clara would meet her for lunch. Sally seemed very strong and remained all business when discussing her health, so Clara felt insulated from it. But Roo knew it weighed on her, and he figured Sally's health had a lot to do with his wife's funk. Still, Clara was her mother's daughter. She gave Roo scientific updates but steered clear of feelings. At one point, Sally's treatments were making her hand hurt. She came to visit and Angus scratched her hand, which was excruciating for Sally. "I felt so terrible," Clara told Roo later. "It was awful that it hurt her so much and awful that it happened here."

That was the closest Clara came to letting her feelings out, and Roo figured that if playing disc with Scooby could help her get through, he didn't want to mess with it. He hoped, too, that it would jump-start Clara in other ways and that playing together, taking both dogs to events, would bring them closer again.

That was if Wallace could still compete. A month passed. Six weeks. Two months. Roo and Wallace continued to do the therapy exercises every day, but they weren't working. The muscle wasn't coming back. Both the first competition of the season and the *Letterman* appearance approached. Clara and Roo needed to make a decision.

They watched Wallace closely. He didn't seem to be in pain, and the condition didn't appear to limit his mobility. It certainly didn't limit his desire to run and chase and play. Even if the therapy hadn't alleviated the condition, it had at least strengthened the adjacent muscles, preparing them to better pick up the slack for the missing flexor. In reality, no one knew exactly what the problem was or what had caused it, and no one knew how competing would affect Wallace.

Roo and Clara agonized as the days went by, but they kept coming back to one thing: Wallace loved playing disc. Even more than that, he needed it. The sport gave him the mission and focus he so desperately had to have. Without it, he'd likely revert back to his Paws & Claws days. He'd come so far since then; Roo and Clara felt as though they couldn't stop now.

They would try to be smart about the strains and keep an eye on Wallace, but they would go for it. Clara became a fanatic about stretching and warming up Wallace. The first event of the year, the local Skyhoundz distance-and-accuracy event in La Crosse, Wisconsin—the event at which Wallace had made his debut the previous June—took place two days later. It was the middle of May and Wallace and Roo hadn't played disc in two months. Clara packed the car and the three of them headed to La Crosse with very low expectations.

5

The takeoff was rough, but it was the landing that rattled him—the stuff in between didn't help either. By the time Roo caught up to Wallace in the airport baggage area it was late, and Roo could immediately tell that the dog was stressed. The three-hour flight from Rochester to New York City for the *Letterman* taping had been Wallace's first, and Roo could see that it hadn't gone well. Maybe Roo should have seen trouble ahead when he had to lie about Wallace's breed just to get him on the plane: The airline had an embargo on pit bulls. As quickly as he could, Roo got Wallace to the hotel, and they both crashed.

When they had a room to themselves, Roo would let Wallace sleep on the bed, although there were two things he had to watch out for. Sometimes Wallace would have an allergic reaction to the type of detergent used on the covers. And every time Wallace would try to sleep right on top of Roo. If Roo moved, Wallace would move right along with him. Tonight, though, Wallace crashed hard and stayed in one place.

The next day Wallace seemed better, if still a bit uncertain. Their hotel sat only a few blocks from Central Park, so Roo hoped a leisurely walk and a little disc would settle Wallace down before they arrived at the *Late Show*. The previous week Wallace had been great: After five and a half months with almost no practice, he had won the La Crosse event handily. His first victory. The infraspinatus had not gone away, but it didn't seem to affect Wallace. He ran fine. He jumped and landed without any apparent pain. Roo tried to be cautious, making sure the dog was warmed up and stretched before every session, but he didn't see any reason to stop. He even competed in another weight pull, hauling a personal-best 1,725 pounds, which put him second overall and earned him a certificate for pulling more than thirty times his body weight (33.8).

Roo considered the La Crosse win step one on the march to the Cynosport World Games, but beyond that he tried not to read too much into it. Now that he had been to regional and national competitions he saw the local events for what they were—a lot of good people and good dogs who were still figuring out the sport. As Roo and Josh found out when they'd started the Minnesota Disc Dog Club, disc-dog fever hadn't yet hit the Upper Midwest. Therefore many of the competitors weren't that seasoned.

The spring had been a huge time of growth for the club, as Roo and Josh had worked hard to build membership. Every time they played disc in the park people would stop to talk, and they would go into full recruitment mode. They also held a competition during Rochesterfest, an annual outdoor festival, that drew a large crowd and received coverage in the newspaper. Roo had even pulled his car over once or twice when he saw people throwing discs to their dogs and told them about the club.

Now their group outings consisted of about twelve people and their dogs playing together. The club had started its own forum to talk canine disc, and over the coming months it would become the most visited canine-disc forum on the Web. They had even founded their own local Skyhoundz event.

So Wallace's win was nice, but Roo had bigger plans, the most immediate of which involved getting a few compliments out of David Letterman. When Roo and Wallace arrived at the side door of the Ed Sullivan Theater, they certainly made an impression. The security guard was so petrified of Wallace that he didn't even check Roo's ID. He simply opened the door and got out of the way, actually stepping into a separate room to get clear of Wallace. Roo found it funny and even made a mental note: If you're in New York and want to get into *Letterman,* just show up with a pit bull.

During rehearsal all the animals performed with a Letterman stand-in. The stand-in was terrified of Wallace, too. Roo and Wallace were there, mainly, to catch a few discs and do the Power Spin, but for whatever reason, whenever they tried the trick Wallace let go of the disc. The dog wanted to do it. He was eager and as soon as he slid off, he'd come right around in front of Roo, ready to try again, but he simply couldn't hang on. *So much for the locking-jaw myth,* thought Roo. Still, at one point he needed to run back to the greenroom to get a toy, and no one would even hold Wallace's leash. Finally, Biff Henderson, the deadpan stage manager, stepped forward. "Don't worry, Wallace, I got ya," he said.

When rehearsal ended, Roo knew they wouldn't be on the show, since they hadn't managed to complete the trick, although in the end the show was running long so none of the "Stupid Pet Tricks" made the cut. By the time the show aired Wallace was fast asleep. Upon returning to the hotel, the dog had curled up and passed out. That was four P.M. He didn't flinch until four A.M. Only then did Roo realize how freaked out his dog had been. Wallace never went twelve hours without stirring.

Still, the trip had not been a waste. For Roo it was both an indicator of how far he and Wallace could go together and also a reminder that no matter what else happened, he needed to put his dog first.

6

Taking second place at the 2005 Skyhoundz World Championships had been great, but Roo considered pairs a back door into the top ranks. The category was so new that not many people had competed, and those who did weren't terribly well practiced. It would take a few years for people to figure out what worked in pairs and become smooth at performing it. For all those reasons, Roo really wanted to excel in singles against established teams with classic disc-dog breeds and a track record of success.

Given all the time they'd lost, he and Wallace turned up the intensity of their workouts. Every day they polished their old tricks and added new ones. All Roo's solo practice started to pay off. His longer, more accurate throws would help them in toss-and-catch competitions, while his more varied and athletic trick throws added something to their freestyle efforts. Wallace was down to fifty-two pounds, and he looked sleeker and faster.

The La Crosse win had built Roo's confidence and confirmed that they were on the right path, but they were still learning and practicing on the fly. Roo signed up for a full slate of local events leading up to the Skyhoundz regionals, set for the end of July near Indianapolis, but he didn't care about winning them. They were trial performances, places to test new stuff in a competitive atmosphere.

On June 18 they took third in freestyle at an event in Rochester. Six days later, they won the freestyle category and placed second in distance and accuracy in Jordan, Minnesota. Roo and Wallace were

beginning to make a name for themselves and more and more people stopped by for a chat at events. Roo, never one to shy away from
a conversation, traded tips and ideas and encouraged the hesitant to
join the sport. But many came by simply to get a look at Wallace.
Veteran disc doggers had never seen a pit bull play before, and they
were impressed. Newbies were surprised to see the breed out there
at all.

During Wallace's downtime, Roo read up on pit bulls. He joined
several forums, asked a lot of questions, and read a few books. He'd
set out to understand Wallace better but quickly became aware of
the full scope of the situation. The incident with the airline had
tweaked him, as had his failed attempts to buy homeowner's insurance after adopting Wallace.

He learned how only a hundred years ago, in the early 1900s, the
breed had been a well-regarded, all-purpose family dog known for
its solid temperament and particular affinity for children. In England they were known as nanny dogs. Buster Brown's dog Tige was
a pit bull, as was Petey of the Little Rascals, chosen specifically to
work with the child cast. But now the dogs were considered inher-
ently vicious and shunned.

Roo and Wallace were living proof that it didn't need to be that
way. Thousands of pit bulls lived long lives without ever causing a
problem, and Roo continued to show that even a pit bull with a
behavioral problem—in Wallace's case a questionable ability to get
along with other dogs—could be managed so that it could live
peacefully in a house with other dogs, go out in public, and even
compete. It took effort, though. Sometimes responsible ownership
was more than simply going to a few obedience classes and fencing
in the yard. It meant a commitment for the life of the dog to do
everything necessary to ensure that nothing went wrong.

7

Roo and Clara did not like what they saw. The field had bare spots. Rocks poked out of the ground and litter dotted the landscape. They briefly considered not competing but felt that they had to support the event. Plus, everyone else seemed unbothered, so why should they complain?

They had come to a new event, another local Skyhoundz tournament. This one took place in Highland Park, but it wasn't run by the Minnesota Disc Dog Club. Roo had decided to compete because he thought they needed a final tune-up before regionals the following weekend. The competition was distance-and-accuracy only, but there would be a freestyle demonstration, and Roo wanted to lock in his singles performance. He and Josh needed to iron out a still-evolving pairs routine. Just the night before, as he was lying in bed, Roo had envisioned what he thought would be the ultimate pairs stunt.

In it, two people stood side by side. One got down on hands and knees while the other bent at the waist, so they formed a mini staircase. The dog would run up, jump on the first person's back, hop onto the second person, and then launch himself into the air and catch the disc flipped by the person standing. Roo told Josh about it, and they immediately named the move: Stairway to Heaven. Unfortunately, Roo and Wallace weren't doing vaults anymore and Josh had decided not to do them with Wazee either, so they couldn't actually try it. They agreed to keep the idea between themselves, though, because who knew what would happen down the road.

On the field, Wallace's freestyle performance went okay but not great. The distance-and-accuracy performance went much better. As Roo improved as a thrower, he had come to understand how much of a team effort these competitions were. The throws needed to be accurate, but they also needed to fly a precise distance. A forty-five- or fifty-yard throw-and-catch would net the same number of points, but the longer the throw, the longer it took the dog to return with the disc. And the farther the dog ran, the more tired it got, slowing it down.

When a team was working well, the throws would come down just beyond the scoring line, maxing out points and minimizing wasted time and effort. Roo needed to be particularly sharp because Wallace often ran slower than most other competitors. Still, when that disc was in the air, he pinned his ears back and hauled. Once he secured the disc, he made up time by hustling back. He may not have matched every border collie out there in speed, but he could outwork them.

And he did. Wallace took home another win. But there was a problem.

Shortly after Wallace's round, Clara went over to his crate to give him some water. "Roo," she said. "Wallace is bleeding!"

"Oh, no," Roo said, jogging over. "Did he get his tongue? Sometimes he bites it when he's running." He held Wallace's face and they looked in his mouth but his tongue appeared fine. Roo took him by the collar and led him out. Wallace limped. The blood came from his front right paw. When they cleaned it away, they saw that a small chunk was missing from one of his paw pads. Roo was pissed. "I knew we shouldn't have run him on this field."

"Maybe it'll heal," Clara said.

"Six days 'til we leave for Indy," Roo said, pacing around the tent. "Six days."

"When we get home I'll clean it out and soak it," Clara said. "It'll be okay."

"Man," Roo said, looking out at the field, where other dogs ran.

For the next week he woke up every morning and checked Wallace's paw. The wound seemed to improve a little every day, but it was sore and Wallace stayed off it as much as possible. Roo didn't even try to practice. Instead, Clara soaked the paw and hoped for the best. "It'll be okay," she said day after day, but she didn't know if it was true.

———

The following Friday morning Clara packed the car for the long drive to Indianapolis. In went Ajax. In went Scooby. And in went Wallace. He hadn't run or practiced all week, but in the last twenty-four hours the wound seemed to have closed up and he walked without a limp. Clara and Roo had no idea if Wallace would be able to participate, but they were going with the other dogs so they figured they might as well take Wallace along and see what happened.

Last year's trip to Indy had been their first taste of big-time competition, and they had arrived as clueless dreamers. This year would be different. They knew where they were going and what they were doing. In 2005 Roo thought they had a chance; now he *knew* they did.

As they mingled among the competitors, they quickly picked up on a change in the atmosphere. After Wallace's second-place finish at worlds and his strong showing in all those local events, he arrived as a clear front-runner. Other competitors within the region knew who he was, and they were out to beat him.

Roo bumped into Danny Eggleston, whom he had first watched perform with his dog, Guinan, last year in this very event. The pair had impressed him as the perfect disc-dog team, steady thrower and classic breed. Since then Roo had come to know Danny as one of the most competitive people out there. "We've been practicing," Danny said.

"Practicing?" Roo said.

"Yeah," Danny said. "Guinan, Christina, and I are entered in pairs. We wanna win worlds." Christina, Danny's longtime disc-playing partner, had been the club member whom Roo had pestered a year earlier for information about regionals, which led to a certain fear of the "aggressive pit bull."

"Ah," Roo said. "Wallace hurt his foot, so I'm not even sure he'll be able to play." Roo shrugged and walked away. This was going to be fun. He could see that the pairs category had become more competitive. There were perhaps twice as many teams and, Roo imagined, this time around they'd actually had time to develop and hone their routines. He hoped Wallace would hold up.

In truth, though, he was more focused on singles. He wanted to win and to qualify for worlds. First, he had to figure out if he had a dog to compete with. Shortly before the contest started he took Wallace off to a side field. As soon as Wallace saw the discs in Roo's hand he began to jump and grab at them. After a week off he was raring to go. Roo tossed a disc and Wallace chased it down. He tossed a few more. He checked Wallace's paw. It seemed to be okay. He continued with the warm-up, and Clara came over to help Wallace stretch until it was almost their turn.

As they waited in the on-deck area, Wallace literally shook with anticipation. As always, his ears stood up, his tail flicked in a blur. He let out a little whine. Finally, they hit the field. Roo turned him loose, waited for the music to come on, and launched into the routine. Wallace's paw didn't seem to bother him at all, but it soon became clear that something wasn't right.

Roo had feared that Wallace would be rusty, but he was the one struggling. Some of his long throws were too low, so that Wallace had no chance to catch up to them before they hit the ground. When he threw a series of short quick tosses, some were too close to each other and others too far apart, making it impossible for Wallace, who did his best.

Roo came off the field shaking his head. After all the doubt, all the worry about Wallace's health, all the practice, he'd choked. They needed to finish in the top six to advance to the next round and have a chance at earning a trip back to Atlanta, but he doubted they'd make the cut. As he waited for the rest of the field to finish, he shifted his focus to pairs.

He and Josh hadn't worked on their routine much in the previous month and not at all while Wallace nursed his injured foot. They huddled now and ran through the moves again, one by one, making sure they had the sequences down and all the names straight—they especially focused on the names.

Finally, the scores came in. Roo pressed forward among the crowd next to the scorers' table. There at the top of the list were Danny Eggleston and Guinan. Roo scanned down. He saw his name and zoomed in. It was there, but it wasn't on the sixth line; it was on the seventh. He had just missed again.

Roo slumped back to the tent. He knew he could still go to the last-chance qualifier on the Friday before worlds and attempt to earn a spot, so he tried to look on the bright side. At least Wallace and his injured paw wouldn't have to compete in a second round of singles. Danny and Guinan were a growing concern, though. They'd clearly gotten better over the last year, and Roo wondered what their pairs routine looked like.

It didn't take long to find out. Danny and Christina took the field a few spots before Roo and Josh, who stood to watch. Danny hadn't been kidding. They had been practicing, and they moved well. There wasn't much in their routine that was new or different, but what they did was clean and polished. Roo nodded in approval. Then, toward the end of the routine, Danny and Christina lined up side by side. She dropped to her hands and knees, and he crouched next to her. Guinan vaulted off their backs and shot into the air, grabbing a disc. Roo and Josh stared at each other, eyes wide open.

They'd just done the Stairway to Heaven! "They stole our move," Roo said.

"Unbelievable," Josh said.

"You didn't say anything, did ya?" Roo asked.

"No, did you?"

Roo groaned. "Guess it wasn't so unique after all."

Now Roo and Josh would have to nail their routine to win. After he'd done so poorly during singles, Roo was anything but confident. They trudged onto the field, but once the music started Roo pumped his fist in the air a few times. The crowd cheered and Roo threw the first disc. Wallace was off. By the third trick they were in a zone, feeling again like they had in Atlanta the year before. They were connected and everything flowed.

Roo wished he knew how to make that feeling happen or understood why sometimes everything came together and other times they were more ragged. He knew it wasn't Wallace. The dog was the same no matter what, whether they were in the yard, at the park, or on lined fields surrounded by people. It had to be him, something he was or was not doing that made the difference, but he didn't know what.

Roo and Josh came off the field exhilarated. They didn't know if they'd win, but they sure as hell put themselves in the running. When the judges announced the scores, all of the Rochester crew ran over to check. Every team scored in the twenty-to-thirty-point range except for two. Danny, Christina, and Guinan had earned a score of 31.5; Josh, Roo, and Wallace had 32.0. They had won by half a point.

They raised their arms and let out a short whoop. He and Josh high-fived and other competitors started offering them so many congratulations and handshakes and pats on the back that Roo felt like a football player who had scored a touchdown in the Super Bowl and was being mobbed by his teammates. As always, he tried to stay cool on the outside but inside he was pumping with joy and satisfaction. Danny and Christina were nearby, and Roo and Josh went over to shake. "All right," Danny said. "I guess we'll see you in Atlanta."

Roo laughed. "Yep," he said, "you will."

8

Roo and Clara's relationship had become something of a roller coaster. Events and outings seemed to buoy them. When they went to competitions or club meetings, they would work together and the old feelings would resurface. And Clara's job at Dunn Bros. helped too, getting her out and making her feel like she was contributing. But she was still never quite the old Clara, and there were periods where she seemed to sink back down and wallow on the couch. Roo's reactions fluctuated, too. Mostly he was filled with sympathy and patience, but at times he felt as though he were shouldering an unfair share of the burden and wondered if he needed to push her. What was the right balance?

He sat next to Clara on the couch. Between his job at Mayo, his efforts to sell houses, and the task of competing in and getting ready for national competitions with Wallace, Roo had reached a breaking point. To make it worse, the real estate job had started slow. He was putting in a lot of effort without much to show for it yet.

"Clara," he said, "I need help."

"With what?" she answered, not looking away from the TV.

"Is there any way you can get a job that pays more? I'm struggling."

Clara turned to him and he could see the hurt in her eyes. "I don't know what else I could do." She had a degree in studio art and little other experience. A few "creepy" interactions had turned her off of working as a massage therapist.

"Could you get more dog-walking clients?"

"I've tried. It's not easy. It's not like people need that much help around here. I'm sorry," she said. "I'm trying."

In the days after Clara sank lower than she had in a long time, and Roo could see that she was doing everything she could, but she simply didn't have the background or the wherewithal to do more right now. He felt bad about having pressed her, which made it even more difficult to talk about their relationship.

Roo practiced hard with Wallace. After the pairs win at regionals, he knew they had great potential, but they had yet to prove it in singles. He wanted to make sure they were ready for their next chance—the AWI Classic in Naperville, Illinois, about forty-five minutes from where Roo grew up. This would be their first non-Skyhoundz event, which meant a new crowd and a new format and wider competition. The Skyhoundz events were great, but because they were grouped by area, teams ended up in a sort of round robin, often facing off again and again.

Roo wanted to see how he and Wallace stacked up against the wider world of disc doggers, and he also wanted to get back a little of his anonymity. He and Wallace had become well-known within their Skyhoundz region; they couldn't sneak up on the competition anymore.

That became clearer every day. In the preceding months Roo and Wallace had appeared in two different dog magazines, as well as the local newspaper. As August moved along they popped up in an Italian magazine and on a local NBC-affiliate show. Clara's mom had come to see Wallace perform in Rochester and become an instant supporter. A library director, Sally sought out any published material about Wallace, printed it out, and saved it. Sally hardly wanted to talk to Clara about her own health, but she always asked after Wallace's.

"How's your mom?" Roo asked one day when Clara came in from lunch with her mother.

"She's good. She's making a scrapbook about Wallace," Clara said.

"Really?"

"Yeah, she can't get enough of him. She thinks it's an incredible story."

Roo shrugged and nodded. He had Wallace out of the crate and as Roo crouched down Wallace came over to him. Wallace sniffed at Roo's hands, then started nudging and biting at Roo playfully. Clara watched them.

"He really is different," she said.

"Yep," Roo said, looking up at her.

"I used to think of him as simply our dog, but he's not. He's special."

"He's got something inside him, like no other dog I've ever seen," Roo said. "People see that, they get that when they watch him. He's not just good for a pit bull; he's *good*." As he had when he was a puppy, posing in that garage among his siblings with his odd demeanor and partially blue eye, Wallace stood out.

At the end of August, Roo entered another local event, in St. Charles, as a tune-up for the AWI Classic. He and Wallace won the freestyle division. They headed for Naperville on the upswing.

———

The field sat on a plateau in a city park; a creek with a jogging path cut past the far end. Bleachers lined one side, while on the other, open side, contestants were setting up camp. Clara had to stay home to deal with a few dog-walking clients, so Roo, Josh, and Jen hauled down without her. The five-hour ride felt like a trip around the corner by this time. They spent Friday night with Roo's parents but woke up super early on Saturday to get a good spot next to the field.

As they started to unpack their stuff and carry it across to the far side of the field, Roo decided to put Wallace to work. He filled a plastic travel crate with gear, then grabbed the weight-pull harness out of the truck. He strapped the harness on Wallace and clipped it to the crate. As Roo walked across the field Wallace went with him, dragging the crate behind him.

The parking lot began to fill with license plates from as far away as Florida, Texas, and Colorado. Many people were shocked to see a pit bull at all, but to see one pulling its own stuff across the field came off as bizarre. A few people steered clear but many chuckled and came for a closer look. "Isn't that something?" the line usually went. "He's a good helper."

"Yep," Roo would say, "he does it all." It would take a moment to sink in.

"You mean he plays disc, too?"

"Yep."

"That's so cute."

Roo found the reaction condescending, but he had to admit he would probably feel the same in their situation. No one expects a pit bull to play disc, never mind compete at a top-level event. Certainly, the two people among the onlookers who Roo cared about most had low expectations. Roo's parents, Ron and Lynda, didn't arrive with him at first light, but they came later in the day to watch Roo and Wallace. "You think they'll be okay?" Ron asked Josh.

"If they're on," Josh said, "they can win."

"Really?" Ron responded.

Having his parents in the crowd caused Roo no anxiety, but something else did. A top-four finish would qualify them for the Cynosport Games. Roo still had his eye on that championship as a crowning achievement. But before he could hope to win it, he had to get in it.

The AWI Classic had a slightly different format than Skyhoundz. During the freestyle round players could use up to seven discs, compared to the five Skyhoundz allowed. And the toss-and-catch portion had slightly different rules. There was no out-of-bounds (Roo liked that); lines marked fifteen meters, twenty-five meters, and thirty-five meters. A catch beyond fifteen earned one point; twenty-five earned two points; thirty-five earned three. Beyond the thirty-five-yard line sat the outline of a semicircle with a five-yard radius. Any catch in the semicircle brought a one-point bonus.

Roo had plenty of time to see exactly how it all worked. His turn didn't come up until somewhere in the middle of the pack of about fifty competitors. He preferred that spot. He felt the judges were reluctant to reward high marks to the early competitors, because they needed to leave room for others to come along and do better, and by the end they had lost their perspective on what had already been done.

The only other thing that could hurt them was the wind. Certain throws, like the air bounces, needed to be made into the wind, and Roo had carefully constructed their routine so that those throws all went in the same direction. The trick then was to understand where the wind was coming from and to start out facing in the proper direction.

Otherwise, he tried to enjoy the day. The event drew the biggest crowds he'd ever seen at a disc-dog competition. It coincided with the city of Naperville's annual fall festival, so people were out and regularly came by to watch. When he took Wallace for a stretch and a warm-up, the dog seemed eager but unusually calm. His body was taut and primed, the tip of his tail swished, but he wasn't jumping up like a puppy chasing a butterfly.

When they took to the field, the wind was light and shifty. A few people moved their dogs away from the edge of the field, and one family with children pulled the kids off to the side. Roo blocked everything out, made his best guess on the wind direction, and let fly. The throws were on target and Wallace responded well, catching almost everything and moving with speed and fluidity. The crowd began to cheer and Roo fed off it. Most of the people there hadn't seen them perform, so Roo's jumping, twisting, and diving was as new to them as seeing a pit bull on the field.

Roo didn't know exactly why but the entire routine seemed to run more smoothly than usual. Perhaps it was the two extra discs. They allowed him to round out the transitions and keep up the pace. For someone who had grown accustomed to performing with only five, the upgrade was a true bonus.

When Roo came back to the canopy, he was pumped. His parents were still clapping. Josh and Jen were excited, and his mom gave him a big hug. His dad squatted down to pet Wallace. After a minute he looked up at Roo and said, "He's awesome." A few competitors swung by to meet Wallace. He didn't seem like a cute sideshow attraction anymore. "You guys are making this hard for the rest of us," one guy said to Roo. Another said, "Other people have tried to do that sort of athletic presentation before; it's not new. But you're the first one to make it work."

Everywhere he went people were buzzing about "that pit bull" that had seemingly come out of nowhere. Roo knew the toss-and-catch round, which came next, would be key. At the moment, he and Wallace stood in fourth place, but any trouble in T & C could knock them right out of contention.

Since the toss-and-catch wasn't set to music the announcer provided running commentary during each performance. Wallace nailed the first catch beyond the thirty-five-yard line. The second throw hung up in the air a moment and Wallace launched after it, landing in the bonus zone. The third throw bent a little left and Wallace tracked it down, another thirty-five-yarder. "Everyone should realize," the announcer said, "Wallace is a banned breed in many parts of the country." The fourth throw zipped through the air. "But he's proof that there are no bad breeds, just bad dog owners." Wallace leapt to catch the disc, another bonus grab. As he ran back the announcer began the countdown. Ten seconds left, nine, eight—as long as Roo got the throw off before time ran out it would count—seven, six, five. Wallace hustled back to Roo, who quickly launched another throw. Four, three, two, one. Wallace snagged the last disc. Five thirty-five-yard catches and two bonus points, a total of seventeen points. "That's it. Show 'em how a pit bull really does it, Wallace," the announcer said as the dog trotted off the field.

Roo knew they had done well and moved into first. The next-best competitor had earned only thirteen points, and Roo held a six-point lead. A two-point win was considered a blowout, so Roo and Wallace's advantage loomed over the field. As Roo wandered around, he crossed paths with the same guy who'd earlier come to meet Wallace. "Not gonna give anyone a chance, are you?" he said. Roo smiled and shrugged.

The hardest part lay ahead. Roo knew that a simple solid performance in the final freestyle round would clinch the win, but that was easier said than done. Roo often improvised during a routine or from one round to the next. He didn't like to repeat himself, and sometimes in the flow of a routine he would feel some opportunity or see some possibility to do something different. Usually, he'd go for it, on the fly. When a trick worked—when he and Wallace were in sync and feeling connected—it could create magic and led to some of their best rounds. When it didn't work, it was ugly. Roo knew this was why his results were a roller coaster, why he could rack up wins and then follow with middle-of-the-pack performances. But it was hard to temper his creative and improvisational impulses.

Running onto the field for the final round, he kept repeating to himself, "Follow the routine. Follow the routine." The wind played nice, the crowd cheered, the discs flew, and the dog ran. Roo and Wallace weren't perfect, but they were good, and that was good enough. They won the event by a resounding six points.

For the awards ceremony the organizers brought out the original medal stand from the very first AWI tournament, which was decorated with Ashley Whippet's paw print. Roo took pictures of Wallace holding his paw up next to Ashley's signature. Roo also agreed to appear at the awards banquet that night. He'd planned to go to his parents' house, but as the winner he felt like he needed to make an appearance. Josh and Jen went with him.

At the event everyone wanted to know who they were and where they had come from. They had questions about Wallace and about some of Roo's tricks, too. He met a lot of people he'd talked with online or read about. Not all the talk was positive, though. One of the judges and a few competitors expressed fears about the Power Spin, Roo's closing move, worrying that it was potentially unsafe. If the dog let go or the disc ripped, it could lead to a serious injury. Roo explained that for Wallace, the move was safer than vaulting, but he understood that if others tried to copy him—people whose dogs weren't built like Wallace—things could end badly. No one condemned him, but they suggested he think about eliminating the trick.

Roo also met Tom Wehrli, whom everyone called "the Historian." Wehrli had brought the old medal stand to the competition that afternoon and had a museum of Ashley Whippet and canine disc memorabilia in his basement. Roo had learned earlier that evening that an almost mandatory part of a trip to Naperville included a visit to Tom's cellar. Although it was after hours, Wehrli agreed to let Roo and Josh come by after the affair and have a peek.

In Tom's basement they signed the guest book—a who's who of disc doggers—and stepped back in time. The place was covered with posters from Ashley's performances, pictures, commemorative discs from every year of the competition, an old vest Ashley used to wear when he performed, newspaper clippings, ticket stubs, and dozens of discs, including one that looked like a cow pie and something called the Buzzbee, which had a small compartment for holding illicit materials.

They flipped through the stuff while Tom told stories about the old days, including his dog Murray. When they had seen everything there was to see and stood on the doorstep saying good night, he offered them one final piece of advice. "Appreciate your dog while you got him," he said, and he closed the door.

9

Atlanta brought on a feeling of déjà vu. The same four people packed in a Suburban. The same long ride. The same destination. The same accommodations with Aunt Carol and Uncle Frank. This time, Scooby joined the list of competitors and therefore the list of travelers. Clara had competed with Scooby at regionals and qualified for the finals in the micro-dog category. Scooby didn't need to compete on Friday, but when they arrived at the field Clara and Roo each took him out for a performance to keep him sharp. Roo finished first and Clara second.

Then came Wallace. He'd already qualified in pairs, but Roo wanted a shot at the singles title. After the success in Naperville, Roo arrived feeling good about their chances. Their renown had begun to spread outside their region—not that they were household names; it was more like "that pit bull" and "that guy with the pit bull"—and their arrival on the field brought with it an air of expectation.

Roo had spent the three weeks since Naperville working hard to prepare for this singles qualifier. He didn't want to become complacent, and after his improvisational approach had backfired in the last round he wanted to lock in a routine. They started out fine, but one of his air-bounce throws didn't bounce. Then Wallace dropped another throw. Feeling like he had to make up ground, Roo went off the program. He added a few twists that he hoped would impress, but more mistakes followed. Coming off the field, he knew he'd blown it.

When the standings came out, Roo and Wallace were twenty-first of thirty-three competitors, not even good enough to get a shot in the second round. Roo couldn't believe it. After the win in Naperville he expected to qualify for the Skyhoundz worlds and even, honestly, expected to win. Now he was finished. His mood suffered. For the rest of the day and even back at the house that night, he was uncharacteristically quiet.

By the following day he'd regained his perspective. He still had pairs to look forward to, but that competition wouldn't take place until Sunday. What lay ahead was a day of socializing and watching other teams play. As Roo made the rounds he ran into Jeff Perry, the Hyperflite cofounder and unofficial host for the weekend. Earlier in the summer, maybe back in July, Jeff had asked permission for Hyperflite to use a few photos of Wallace. Roo had said yes without giving it much thought. He assumed the company wanted to use the photos on its website.

Besides being one of the major benefactors of the sport, Jeff was a Hall of Famer. As they chatted, Jeff asked Roo if he would be at the Banquet of Champions that evening. "Yep, yep," Roo said. "Wouldn't miss it."

"Make sure you don't," Jeff said. "There's going to be a big surprise." As he walked away, Roo tried to imagine what he could be talking about.

He also ran into Danny and Christina, the couple with whom he and Josh had dueled in Indy for the top spot in pairs. "We're gonna get you this time," Danny said.

Roo wasn't much of a trash talker, but he did his best. "I don't think so," he threw back with a chuckle.

Danny went on. "We got some new stuff, and we've been working on it."

"Same with us," Roo said.

The rest of the afternoon passed pleasantly as Roo continued to roam around, relaxed in the tent, and spent some time with Josh reviewing their routine.

At the Champions Banquet, Roo, no longer a newcomer, talked with everyone and watched the awards ceremony. Danny and Guinan had won the singles title, and Roo felt a pang of something, not jealousy but missed opportunity, as he watched Danny give his acceptance speech. He became so engrossed that he forgot about his encounter with Jeff earlier in the day. So when the ceremony came to an end and the emcee announced a special presentation, Roo wondered what it could be. On the main stage stood a large object draped with a sheet.

Jeff came up to the podium and started talking about one of Hyperflite's lines, the Jawz disc, which was a little heavier and more durable. It was the type of disc Roo used. For years the disc had been sold in a package that had a picture of a disc-dog regular on it, a boxer named Gretchen. "Well," Jeff announced, "for the newest version of Jawz we've come up with new packaging." He held up a disc attached to cardboard packaging, which featured a picture of Wallace running across the field, Jawz disc in his mouth.

Then he pulled the sheet off the hidden object. There stood a point-of-purchase display, a rack on which Jawz discs would hang in the store, and that too featured a picture of Wallace. In the shot Wallace jumped toward the camera, and the display had been designed so that it looked like Wallace was jumping over the rack, with his head coming over the top and a paw on either side.

The crowd let out a loud cheer and everyone turned to look at Roo, Clara, Josh, and Jen. Roo kept his eyes on the display. When he gave Jeff the okay to use the photos he hadn't realized it would be for brand packaging, but he didn't mind because playing disc was never about money. Plus, the finished result was so cool. He couldn't believe it. They had officially arrived.

Afterward, he wondered briefly if he should be concerned about the message. Was using a pit bull to sell extra-durable discs reinforcing the sorts of stereotypes he sought to overcome? But his goal was not to hide the true attributes of a pit bull—the dogs tend to be strong and athletic and energetic—it was to make them acceptable as they were. To show people that despite what they had heard and what the dogs could be manipulated to do, the breed was capable of greater things.

Later that night, back at Aunt Carol and Uncle Frank's house, Roo went downstairs with one of the new discs and showed it to Wallace. He gave the dog a scratch and a solid pat on the side. "Way to go, buddy," he said. "Way to go."

———

Roo and Josh had some significant changes planned for the pairs event. None of the new tricks they had added were visually stunning and the routine wasn't markedly more difficult than the previous one, but in the new arrangement everything flowed better, ran smoother, came off cleaner. Within the context of the new routine some of the same old tricks looked better and cooler. Wallace appeared more athletic, and Roo and Josh looked less spastic. They hoped that would be enough to put them over the top at the pairs event.

Of the three favorite teams, defending champs Frank Buckland, Shannon Bilheimer, and Shiloh were up first. Roo and Josh looked on as the threesome tore up the field. When the scores came up, they had earned four 9.0s and one 8.5 for a total of 44.5. A great round.

The tension grew, but Roo and Josh tried to stay loose. Finally, they were up. Wallace was flying and they executed a round that felt at least as good as what Shiloh and company had done. They came off the field pumped up, and when their scores were posted the men had been proved right: Although there was greater variation in the numbers—from a low of 8.0 to two 9.5s—the total came out the same, 44.5.

Finally, Danny, Christina, and Guinan had their turn. They looked great, and as their act wound down, Roo thought they very well could jump into first. They set up for their closing move, the Stairway to Heaven they'd rolled out in Indy, and Roo knew if they hit it right they were golden. But as Guinan approached he appeared to slip on the field and slid into Christina. They covered it up well, but they wound up a half point behind, with a score of 44.0.

Heading into the second round the scoring couldn't get any tighter: Two of the top three teams were tied, the other a half point behind. Roo and Josh felt their competitive drive kick into high gear. They wanted it.

As they wandered between rounds they ran into Danny and Christina. Roo prepared himself for a little more trash talking, but looking at them, he could see something wasn't right. "We're out," Danny said. "On the slip, Guinan hurt himself. He can't go out again."

"Oh, wow," Roo said. "Is he okay?"

"He's all right long-term, but he can't run right now, never mind jump."

"Sorry," Roo said.

"Well, now we're rooting for you guys. You have to win. We can't let Shiloh do it again."

"We're gonna give it a shot," Roo said.

Having one of their main competitors drop out could have relaxed Team Wallace, but it had the opposite effect. "This is our chance," Roo and Josh kept telling each other through gritted teeth. "Right now, this is it. This is when we do it." A year earlier they had paced around the same tent, in the same spot, trying to ward off fear and nerves; now they did it to get pumped up. On the field,

Shiloh's team turned in another stellar performance and the atmosphere in the tent grew more tense.

Roo and Josh bounced around. They thrust their fists downward next to their sides, as if they were cowboys jamming guns back into holsters, and the tension played on their faces. When they finally jogged out, it was as if they were marching into battle. And it showed.

Technically, the round went fine. Roo and Josh made the throws and Wallace made the catches, but they were so charged up that their movements came off as stiff and mechanical. The flow that had marked their first performance, that they'd worked so hard to make a part of their routine, disappeared. There was no energy or joy in the performance.

They knew it, too. The whole thing felt wrong. They knew they had blown their shot at the title and had broken the cardinal rule of disc: Have fun with your dog. Back at their tent, Roo looked at Clara and Jen and said, "If you ever see us get that serious again, slap us in the face." The title had been theirs for the taking, and Roo couldn't shake one question: Would they ever win? But he tried not to dwell on it, because taking it too seriously had caused the problem to start with. He forced himself to smile and look forward to the next event.

When the final results were posted they had once again scored a 44.5. Frank, Shannon, and Shiloh came in at 46.0. For the second year in a row Shiloh took first and Wallace second.

10

Among the many things the win in Naperville had accomplished for Roo and Wallace—it spread their names across a wider sector of the disc-dog world, building their confidence and earning them a trip to Arizona for the Cynosport Games—it also sucked in Ron and Lynda Yori.

Roo's parents had become huge Wallace fans, and Ron had begun to read up on the sport, diving into the forums and websites. They had taken great pride in Wallace's win at Naperville, but even more so they had been enchanted by the sportsmanship—the true camaraderie among the participants and the way they all cheered for one another. Roo knew that spirit didn't always prevail, but he didn't want to burst their illusions.

That proved a smart move, because when Roo mentioned that he might not haul out to Scottsdale for the Cynosport Games because he could not afford the trip, his parents wouldn't hear of it. They offered to drive and pick up meals and hotels along the way. Roo couldn't refuse.

And so he found himself rolling along an endless succession of highways as the sun passed overhead and his parents chatted and napped. Clara had to stay home to work and care for the other dogs, so Roo felt a little like he was reliving his childhood. His mom pointed out the scenery and his dad asked questions about the disc dogs and handlers he'd read about online. They motored along

Route 66 and even stopped at the Route 66 Museum. For the better part of three days the Yoris' maroon Chevy Tahoe made its way across almost two thousand miles of road while Wallace, to Roo's relief, chilled out in the back. Roo enjoyed the time but felt a little uneasy because it had become clear that his parents now expected Wallace to win every time out.

Finally, late in the afternoon of Thursday, November 2, they checked into a small dog-friendly hotel in Scottsdale, where Josh waited for them. He'd flown in a few hours earlier to provide support and film the event. The city was filling up fast: The Cynosport Games were a sort of Olympics of dog events, featuring not only the disc competitions but also championships in dock diving, fly-ball (a relay race), course-a-lure (an obstacle course), and agility. Overall more than a thousand dogs from eleven countries and almost every state would compete. For the disc-dog competition alone there were nearly eighty dogs from five countries, including the European champ from Germany and an entire contingent from Japan.

As soon as everyone was settled, Roo wanted to go check out the venue, a place called WestWorld, the massive three-hundred-and-fifty-acre equestrian center outside of town, with stables, multiple open-air arenas, offices, and a parking area that included room for a hundred RVs. Roo and the others made their way out to the polo field, a nineteen-acre plot that had been divvied up into sections for the Cynosport Games. As they looked they saw a maze of obstacles, walls, hoops, tunnels, and a giant pool. The disc events were set up at the far end, split into four separate fields lined with banners. At the center, grandstands and tents surrounded another field, where the finals of each event would take place (except for dock diving, since the pool couldn't be moved). With any luck, Roo thought as he looked out across the vast expanse, he and Wallace would be performing in front of those grandstands on Sunday.

———

On Saturday morning Roo sat atop a giant berm that circled one end of the polo grounds. As was their custom, they'd arrived early, before seven o'clock, to secure a good spot for their tent and a parking spot right behind it. Roo figured the heat would require him to take Wallace in for a cooldown or two in the air-conditioning.

From up here, maybe thirty feet above the playing surface, he could see the entire field, divided up into sections like a farm in the Irish countryside, the people and dogs scurrying about and the workers, silent from this distance, putting final touches on the equipment. Behind the entire expanse rose a ring of brown mountains, jagged and huge against the blue backdrop of the sky. Roo had always loved those sorts of outdoor scenes, the rugged landscapes of old Westerns, and he soaked up this one.

It was, it seemed, the first time he'd been alone in four days. Later that morning his uncle Robert, his mom's brother, was scheduled to fly in, too. The support buoyed him, but at the same time it took him out of his normal routines and somehow made him feel more isolated. He thought of Clara.

They were still in debt, although their financial troubles had at least stabilized. He'd sold only two houses during 2006, just enough to cover his expenses, but he felt he was set up to make a profit the following year. She was doing well at Dunn Bros. and she had finally started to accumulate more dog-walking and dog-sitting clients.

Not having her there made him miss her in a way he didn't when they were at home living their nearly separate lives. From the start she'd played an important role in their success by handling Wallace during events, and playing disc remained one of the few places he could still find the old Clara. That made her absence more notable. They really were better as a team.

Roo also worked through everything that had happened the day before, during the Friday qualifier. Though Wallace had already earned a spot in the finals, Roo had entered the qualifier, to get the dog a little exercise after the long car ride and to work through their routine one last time. Good thing he did. Instead of lines painted on the ground, a ring of banners outlined the field. They were about three feet tall and attached to a framework of metal poles so they hung like a curtain in front of a stage.

The effect was visually appealing, but the presence of the banners meant that an errant throw did not simply result in a catch outside the lines, it created an unsightly crash into a wall of fabric. To make it worse, the field was a little smaller than those he usually played on, and he found on several occasions that either he or Wallace came too close to the edge for his comfort. He'd have to make a few adjustments.

The night had ended with a cookout for all the competitors. Teams regularly showed up in custom T-shirts. One guy from Texas with a few cattle dogs wore gear touting the Texas Heelers. Another team Roo saw was the Disc Connected Canines. Roo had started using discs with Wallace's image printed on them, and for the trip to Arizona he'd made up a bunch of shirts emblazoned with the words *Pit Crew*. He was glad to have them, because as that party began to break up, the Japanese contingent produced a supply of shirts and discs and hats and began offering trades.

Pretty soon an all-out swap meet erupted. Roo didn't have many extra shirts, but he scrounged up what he could and a few of the customized Wallace discs, and got in on the action. The session went on so long that the final trades were made by flashlight.

The following day Roo rose early, and he tapped into the stillness and peace of the morning as he sat on the hillside and thought back on all of it. Sometimes he could be uneasy before a competition, but not today. That calm would serve him well, because the day promised chaos. The joint AWI-UFO championship included three rounds of freestyle and a toss-and-catch round, while the

FDDO competition featured four individual events: freestyle, pyramid distance, obstacle course, and speed disc. During Saturday's action alone, Roo and Wallace would have to crank through one round of AWI-UFO freestyle, the toss-and-catch session, the obstacle course, the pyramid, and the FDDO freestyle. More than fifty other teams would be doing the same over three fields.

Roo and Wallace started with the first of the AWI-UFO freestyle performances. Roo hoped his adjustments to account for the smaller playing area would work. As they hit the field, Roo focused on the moves and Wallace flew. Roo had to hustle a little more to get into the right spots, but that actually accentuated the athleticism that had become his hallmark.

Roo and Wallace scored 36.7 points, which put them in third place, one point behind the leaders, Junichi Hara and Fine, and half a point behind Yoshihiro Ishida and Rusty, both of Japan. Roo felt they were in perfect position to make a run at the top spot, since the next leg of the competition was the toss-and-catch, which they had dominated in Naperville.

Waiting for their turn, Wallace was his usual self—anxious, pesky, hyper. Roo tried to keep Wallace calm. He knew they probably wouldn't be able to replicate the seventeen-point round they had in Naperville—really, a dream round—but they wouldn't have to. Ideally, they could make up some ground on the leaders, but as long as they did well enough to stay close he'd be happy.

During warm-ups Roo had tried to get a bead on the wind. It was light but shifting and hard to predict. As soon as he thought he knew what it was doing, it changed. As they stood in the on-deck circle, Roo attempted to get an update, but the sight of the discs in Roo's hand made Wallace nuts. He whined and barked and jumped, trying to grab the discs.

Before Roo could get the dog settled, the judge motioned for them to take the field. Roo noticed a group of Japanese players standing alongside watching. Clearly, they were surprised to see

Wallace. "Pit bull," Roo heard them saying to one another in accented English.

Roo threw the disc and it spun off down the field, but about halfway to its target it began to sink. Because Wallace was such an ardent chewer, Roo used heavier, more durable discs. They lasted longer, but they fell from the sky a little faster than others. Before Wallace was even halfway down the field, the disc hit the ground. Wallace picked it up and charged back. Roo heard a burst of chatter from the Japanese. Most dogs trotted back after retrieving the disc. Wallace ran just as hard on the way back as on the way out.

Roo snapped his attention back, cursing himself. He needed to focus. He took the disc from Wallace and let it rip again. It soared off but very quickly settled into the same trajectory. Roo shook his head. Then, as Wallace rushed back, Roo felt it. The wind was behind him. A downwind throw always fell quickly, as the wind tended to push it down, especially with heavier discs.

He usually had time for only five throws during a toss-and-catch, and he had now wasted two of them because he'd allowed himself to be distracted, first by Wallace and then by the onlookers. He bore down and made the third throw on a higher trajectory. Wallace raced down the field and snagged it, a three-pointer, with a half-point bonus. Roo threw again. Another three-pointer. Finally, as time ran down, Wallace leapt into the air and grabbed the disc—three more points. A total of 9.5 points.

Roo slumped back to the tent. He could only watch as others took the field. The next team jumped from way back into first with a round of 19.5. Ishida held on to second with a round of sixteen. Two others posted big scores. By the time the toss-and-catch ended, Roo and Wallace had fallen to fifth place, almost seven points behind the leader.

Roo knew he had no shot at the AWI title, but he didn't have much time to sulk. The FDDO title remained up for grabs, as did the overall Cynosport Games combined title. He needed to make up as much ground as he could in the remaining two AWI-UFO freestyle events and go for broke in the FDDO events, which would be starting in a few minutes with the obstacle course.

All the FDDO events were new to Roo, but he felt best about the obstacle course. In it, dog and handler stood on one side of an obstacle—a tunnel, a round set of posts, a hoop, a bar—with a five-yard-by-five-yard square painted on the ground on the other side of the obstacle. The handler had to throw the disc over, under, around, or through the obstruction as described by the rules so that it flew into the square, where the dog had to catch it. Roo had re-created some of the apparatus in his yard, or at least he'd tried. He'd never seen an actual FDDO competition, so he built the stuff based on descriptions he found online. How close it came to the real thing, he still didn't know.

In the end, Roo's backyard course proved similar enough that they did well, scoring twelve points out of a possible fifteen, which left them tied for eighth. They went back to the tent to rest up for the distance pyramid.

"Nice job, man," Josh said. He'd spent most of the day glued to his chair or attached to his camera. Roo appreciated having him there in case he needed to work out any technical problems, but for the most part Josh seemed determined to stay out of the way. The same held true for Roo's parents. He could see that they were full of questions, but they had learned enough about him over the years to realize this was not the time to ask.

The distance pyramid presented another new challenge, but it involved skills they already had. The event took place on a large triangle painted on the ground. The base of the triangle stretched thirty yards and it came to a point sixty yards away. Every ten yards a line cut across the triangle, dividing it into six zones. As the triangle grew narrower the odds of staying in bounds on a catch got longer, but the farther the catch the more points awarded. But there was a trick. Each team had three discs, but only the last throw counted. So if a dog caught the disc in the fourth zone on the first try but dropped the next two, his score would be zero. If he stopped after that first catch, his score would be four.

That's what Roo did. Wallace caught a four on the first try and Roo stopped there. It proved to be a wise choice. One team recorded a five, but no one scored higher and six teams pushed their luck and came up with zeroes, effectively taking themselves out of the competition. Roo and Wallace's four points moved them up in the standings so that they sat in fifth place in both competitions, the AWI-UFO and the FDDO.

Where that put them overall in the race for the Cynosport title was impossible to tell, but Roo noticed that few teams were doing well in both competitions. The AWI-UFO dogs tended to be pure freestylers that struggled in the FDDO games. Those that excelled in FDDO didn't seem to have the freestyle skills to impress the AWI-UFO judges. Roo's preparation was paying off, and he felt like they had a chance. He simply needed to stay confident and relaxed and throw the disc where Wallace could catch it.

That's what he told himself as he headed out to the FDDO freestyle round. This was the part of the event he felt most comfortable with, but he would be performing for a new set of judges using a slightly different standard. He had no idea how they would receive Wallace. He intended to put on a good show and hope for the best.

They hit the field and Wallace burst off with his usual energy and enthusiasm. Roo made good throws. And as good as they had been in the morning, they were better in the evening. Not great, in Roo's opinion, but very good.

Roo sat with Josh and waited for the scores. "Whaddya think?" he asked.

"Only saw three or four others that were even close to you guys," said Josh, without looking away from the camera. "Gotta be a decent score."

"Yep," said Roo. "Hope so."

"How's Wallace holding up?"

Roo laughed a little. "I'm sure he's tired, but he'd be back out there right now if he could." Roo couldn't say the same about himself. He'd been up since six A.M., and he was weary.

Josh peeled the camera from his face and looked at Roo. "He's an incredible dog." Roo nodded. Josh knew dogs, and Roo valued his opinion, so the compliment meant a lot. It made him think about Wallace, too. Where he had come from, what he had been through, and how much he had accomplished.

When the scores went up, Roo and Wallace had tallied eighteen points, the third best in the freestyle, and it jumped them to solo possession of third place in the FDDO competition. It would all come down to Sunday. The FDDO would be decided by the speed-disc round, an event with three distinct zones marked on the ground, one ten yards away, one twenty yards away, and one thirty yards away. The dog had to catch a disc in each zone and get back across the line as fast as possible. Roo had never worked on anything like it with Wallace. It was the event Roo feared most coming in.

He went back to the hotel and called Clara. They spoke for a while before Roo went to sleep. She posted the news on the forums, where many of Wallace's supporters were following along. Word began to spread. A pit bull had a shot at a canine disc world championship.

11

Only the top eight teams would compete in the final AWI-UFO freestyle round in front of the grandstands, packed with about a thousand people. A solid second-round score—36.7—earlier in the day had moved them up from fifth to fourth, but just barely.

Roo knew they needed another great round to hold on to their spot and maintain any chance at the overall Cynosport championship.

At the start of the round, the eight teams were announced one by one, and as their names were called they trotted onto the field waving to the crowd. They would perform in reverse order, from eighth place down to first, and as Roo awaited his spot in the rotation, he decided to approach the round as if they had nothing to lose. He was simply going to have fun, play to the crowd, and show everyone what he and Wallace could do. He even considered adding the Power Spin back to their routine, but one of the judges had been among those in Naperville who'd advised him against it, so he feared the move would do more harm than good.

He led Wallace out onto the field, and when the music started he pumped his fist in the air a few times. The crowd cheered. Roo began and Wallace weaved between his legs, chasing discs. Roo flipped a short throw to the side, and Wallace leapt, spun in the air, and snagged it. Roo did it again and again, and Wallace continued to rise up after the red discs like a kid on a pogo stick, spinning and twisting with each jump.

Roo made a series of short flips and Wallace bounced into the air catching one after another. Roo made several long throws and Wallace tracked them down. As Wallace rushed back Roo went into a near split. Wallace jumped Roo's leg and as he charged by, Roo flipped a disc in the air that Wallace caught. As the dog came back Roo switched sides and did it again. The announcer chimed in after the tough catches: "It's good!"

Roo jumped and threw the disc between his legs—"It's good!" He threw it behind his head—"It's good!" He dove over Wallace and tossed a disc: "This dog is hot. Look at the head on those shoulders." Roo unleashed an air bounce, and it shot up into the sky. Roo could see that it got under the breeze just a little. The disc was carrying too far. It soared toward the banners that lined the field.

Wallace charged toward a banner at full speed as the disc started dropping.

Unlike the banners around the outer fields, these ones hung from the support system of the grandstands, so if Wallace crashed into the banner he wouldn't just hit a wall of fabric, he'd hit the heavy wooden beams and metal poles that held the stands up. Roo couldn't tell if there was enough room for Wallace to make the catch and stop. The disc angled toward the top edge of the banner.

"It's an air bounce," the announcer called. "It's up. . . ." As always Wallace looked at nothing but the disc. He sped across the field, ten yards from the stands. "It's up . . . ," the announcer repeated as he could clearly see that Wallace might run out of space. Five yards. The disc continued to drop. Three yards. Roo put his hands to his head. Wallace launched himself up, and Roo wondered if their weekend might be about to come to a horrible end. The announcer had gone quiet, but a low murmur spread through the crowd.

At the last second Wallace twisted his body in the air, reaching his head up to snag the disc and fall sideways into the banner, like an outfielder catching a fly ball against the home run wall. His shoulder and ribs crashed into the scaffolding, but he bounced off and landed on the ground. "It's good!" the announcer yelled. Wallace began charging back to Roo, who pumped his fist.

Roo made a behind-the-head throw. He bridged up on his hands and feet, and Wallace barreled underneath him. He spun the disc on his finger and then batted it off with the other hand. Wallace tracked it down. Roo loaded up one more throw, with two discs. They separated in the air, one going short and the other flying long. Wallace caught the first and let it go. He took off after the second one, which drifted far across the field. The distance seemed impossible, but Wallace lowered himself and charged. The disc turned and began to fall. Wallace jumped to snare it. "It's g—" the announcer began, but the disc bounced off Wallace's mouth and fell to the ground. Roo threw his head back in disbelief.

Wallace picked up the disc and ran back. Roo waved to the cheering crowd as they walked off. With a 37.8, their best score of the weekend and a tie for the best mark any dog had scored in any round in the competition, they took fourth place in the AWI-UFO. But Roo couldn't help but wonder what would have happened if Wallace had made that last catch.

————

Roo opened the cooler and looked inside—ham sandwich, Gatorade. That's what he needed. For the second day in a row he'd been up since six A.M. He was bone tired. On top of that he had not eaten all day. Some combination of nerves, adrenaline, anxiety, and anticipation had kept him from wanting or needing to consume anything, but those other fuels had now run out. As soon as the freestyle round ended, the hunger hit him. He began to feel light-headed.

Before he could unwrap the sandwich, though, his father rushed up. The speed-disc competition had been moved to the grandstand, and the time had been pushed up as well. Roo and Wallace needed to get over there. The FDDO championship and Cynosport title waited.

Roo put down the sandwich, took a granola bar, and ran. Once again, the top eight dogs performed in reverse order, so Roo watched the way the other competitors approached the three zones. Some went for the farthest zone first and worked their way back; others went closest to farthest. Because the event was timed, the trick seemed to be to keep the dog from coming back after each catch.

A few of the teams had already failed to complete all three catches. Roo decided he would start with the closest zone and work his way out, easiest to hardest. When Roo yelled *out*, Wallace knew he was supposed to drop the disc he had and get ready for a new throw, so Roo figured he'd complete the first, yell *out,* complete the second, then do it again.

Their turn finally came, and Roo gave a shrug. *Here goes nothing; here goes everything.* He threw the disc toward the first zone. Wallace caught it and turned to come back. "Out!" Roo yelled. Wallace dropped the disc and looked up. Roo threw again. Wallace turned and ran. There was nothing elegant about the dog's movements. This was where he was at a true disadvantage. Stopping, starting, turning. Those things were easy for small, quick dogs. They were tasks for Wallace, with his big head and bulky body.

Still, as always, Wallace had desire. He lumbered forward, accelerating. Roo could see that his throw would land in the zone, but he didn't know if Wallace would get there in time. Wallace charged. The disc descended. At the last second, Wallace lunged and grabbed the disc before it hit. To be sure, Roo looked over at the judge, who held a flag in one hand. If the flag went up, it meant no catch. If the flag was thrown on the ground, good catch. The flag dropped.

"Out!" Roo yelled. Wallace dropped the disc and stared back at Roo, who had already begun to launch the next disc. Wallace again came about and started after it. Once again, the throw was on target but there appeared no way Wallace would be fast enough to make the catch. Roo began to jog out on the field toward Wallace. It looked like an instant replay. Again Wallace lunged and snatched the disc. This time it was even closer to the ground, and Roo couldn't tell if the catch was clean or if the disc touched first. He looked to the judge, who stood motionless staring at the spot where Wallace had made the catch.

Wallace had turned and begun to head back toward Roo when, finally, the judge dropped the flag. Roo began to clap and call Wallace. The clock didn't stop until the disc crossed the start line and Roo knew Wallace would run faster if the dog were chasing him. As Wallace accelerated, Roo sprinted back toward the line. They crossed almost together and Roo looked up at the clock. Their time: 18.46 seconds. The best of anyone on the day and good for 9.5 points. They instantly shot into first place, but either of the two remaining competitors could pass them with a good performance.

Roo wanted to watch, but he had to eat. He ran back to the tent while Josh and his parents stayed to watch the action. The next team took the field. Roo tried to listen to the crowd and judge what was happening by the sound, but he couldn't tell. There were some cheers, some *aw*s, and a round of applause. Time ticked. Finally, Josh appeared, breathing heavy.

"They were a disaster," he said. "You've got second locked up." Roo pumped his fist, and Josh turned and ran back toward the grandstand. Roo couldn't believe it.

The last team remaining had started the round 1.75 points ahead in the FDDO competition, so they'd need at least eight points to hold on to the lead. They'd have to complete all three throws in no more than forty seconds to get that many. If they didn't, Wallace would win. Either way, Roo felt great about the Cynosport title. No one knew the grand totals for each team yet, but as far as he could tell no one else had done as well in the combined events as he and Wallace.

Roo heard the *wah wah* of the announcer's voice and the cheer of the crowd. He knew the final team had taken the field. He had finished eating now and sat back in his chair listening. He wished Clara was there. Not only to enjoy the moment but because these events drew them together, the way they used to be. Adopting Scooby had helped by getting her more involved in disc, but it hadn't solved their problems.

The news from Red Wing did not help. Clara's mom was not doing well. Her doctors had recommended another surgery, her third, but Sally had decided against it. She wasn't done fighting, but she was through with medical intervention. Clara feared what that meant.

The day's results could make a difference; a win would give them something to celebrate together. More goals to pursue together. Another year on the disc circuit, spending time together. He was hopeful.

Josh and Roo's parents appeared in the foreground, walking quickly. They rushed into the tent. The final team had finished. Their time: slightly more than forty seconds. For that they earned 6.5 points. It wasn't enough. Roo and Wallace had won. Wallace was an FDDO champion. Roo jumped up and high-fived Josh. He hugged his parents and let out a loud whoop. He went over to Wallace's crate and opened the door. "Hey," he said, "good job, buddy. You did it. You did it, Wallace!" He scratched the dog's head and patted him on the sides. It had all finally paid off. The chewed-up furniture, the constant havoc, the rotating crates, the trips to the vet. All the days dragging tires around, the nights tending the spring pole, the endless hours in the yard and at the park playing disc had led them here. Wallace had already justified his existence in Roo's eyes, and now he had proven that they truly belonged.

A few minutes later they gathered for the announcement of the Cynosport winner. As Roo expected, Wallace won that, too. At the award ceremony Roo stood with Wallace on his shoulders. Next to him stood Chuck Middleton, the Hall of Famer Roo had crossed paths with throughout the year. As the crowd cheered, Middleton looked over at Roo. "What are you feeding that dog?" he asked.

Roo laughed. Back at the hotel he called Clara. Their dog, the dog that no one wanted, the pit bull that a "no kill" shelter had wanted to kill, had outrun, out-jumped, out-hustled, and out-hearted all the herding dogs and retrievers and shepherds. In not just one event, but in a grueling series of games and contests that tested every aspect of a dog's abilities. Wallace was a world champion.

12

The ride home seemed to go much faster than the ride out. Roo's parents finally got to ask all those questions they had been holding in, and the three Yoris took turns reliving their favorite moments of the weekend.

The competitive season had come to an end, but Roo and Josh were just getting started. They decided to make a training video with Wallace. It was a tribute to another underdog story, Rocky. Roo dressed Wallace in a gray sweatshirt made for dogs so that it fit like a tracksuit. Then he outfitted himself in a gray sweatshirt and sweatpants, and the pair went out running. As the distinct trumpets of "Gonna Fly Now" came up, the pair ran through the park at daybreak. They moved on to the streets of downtown Rochester. Wallace did the canine equivalent of push-ups, pulled a tire up a hill, jumped up to grab a tire swing with his mouth and hung on. Finally, he and Roo mounted a long concrete staircase behind the Mayo Civic Center, and they danced at the top, Wallace up on his hind legs with his front legs raised in the air. It ran three minutes, and Roo and Josh thought it was hilarious. They posted it on YouTube on December 11, 2006, sent the link to a few friends, and moved on.

The disc-dog people found it first. They knew Wallace and Roo, and they loved the video. It circulated quickly. Along the way it came to the attention of the pit bull community, a collection of rescue groups, advocacy organizations, and fans of the breed. They had begun to hear stories of a pit bull doing good things in the disc world, and now here he was, showing up in their in-boxes, funny, athletic, positive. The video took off. By the end of the day it was the number one video in the Pets & Animals category. The stream of comments included many that thanked Roo for showing the breed could be something other than what the headlines portrayed.

Roo and Josh were floored: They never expected *that* sort of impact. They quickly decided to put together another video. This one was a highlight reel of Wallace, both playing disc and pulling weights. It began with driving guitar music and white text popping up on an orange background: "To all of those who would never give me a chance. . . . To all of those who talk badly about my breed. . . . To all of those who say I should be dead simply because of what I am even when you know nothing about me. . . . I cannot defend myself with words, but actions speak so much louder. . . ." What followed was four minutes of Wallace at his best, intercut with a list of his achievements. At the end, the music stopped, and the orange screen came up again: "All of this in under two years. Not bad for an unwanted pit bull." By the end of the day that video, too, had hit the top spot for most-watched in Pets & Animals.

Roo's old college buddy Beaker helped him build a website for Wallace, and the traffic spiked. Wallace had become a hero in the pit bull world. He was a regular topic of discussion on the four sizable pit bull–related forums that existed on the Web. In one of them, someone took a poll: If you could adopt any other pit bull, which would it be? Virtually every respondent listed Wallace among his top five picks.

Roo took Wallace's newfound status seriously, and he wanted to continue to spread the word. He contacted a local TV station, which agreed to come out and do a piece on Wallace. Roo and Wallace showed off all their best tricks and Roo talked about Wallace's past, the struggles he faced because he was a pit bull, how rare it was for a pit bull to succeed in canine disc, and the unfair perception of pit bulls in general. When the story aired the next night, full of positive images and local pride, the phrase "pit bull" never came up. Wallace's breed had been completely cut from the piece.

Two weeks later a local mailman was bitten by a pit bull. The story appeared everywhere in the local news, and the dog's breed was almost always the first thing mentioned. Roo suddenly realized the depth of the problem, the persistence of preconceived notions about pit bulls, and how far he still had to go. He wanted to win the AWI and get Wallace's name on the Lander Cup. He wanted to finally win that Skyhoundz pairs title. But more than anything he wanted to get into the Purina Incredible Dog Challenge and show off Wallace on national TV.

If people didn't want to see pit bulls for what they really were—simply dogs—he and Wallace would force them to look.

Chapter 6

Going Big

Talk less, do more.

Roo Yori

1

Roo rushed to complete the paperwork. He'd been helping Josh's father hunt for a new house, and one of their offers had been accepted. Great news, but bad news, too. Roo was scheduled to leave early the next morning on a ten-hour drive to Wichita, Kansas, for the regionals of the Incredible Dog Challenge. That meant all the forms and contracts for the real estate deal had to be filed before he left.

At ten P.M. he finally got everything filled out. He took the papers to Mr. Grenell's to be signed. Afterward, Roo looked the file over one more time, then dropped one copy off at his office and the second copy at the listing agent's office. By the time he got home it was almost midnight. He wouldn't be getting a lot of sleep tonight— again.

The new year had been prosperous, but it also set a new standard for busy—even for Roo. He'd found a sweet spot for his real estate business in the halls of the Mayo Clinic. The place swarmed with new hires—college grads, medical residents, and nurses—who took a job, rented for a few months, then decided they wanted to stay. Word had spread: If you want to buy a house, see Roo.

So Roo continued to work forty hours a week at Mayo, although he'd moved to the evening shift, which stretched from two P.M. to ten P.M. Before heading into the lab he'd hit the real estate office from eight A.M. to one thirty. On weekends and during his dinner break he'd look at and show houses. Often the dinner excursions ran long, so he'd have to work extra hours to make up the time, staying past ten several nights a week. He also continued to take Wallace and Angus to the occasional weight pull. In late April Wallace competed in his final pull and topped out at 1,735 pounds, an even thirty-four times his body weight, to win first place and earn enough points to merit a champion classification.

Roo's nonstop routine helped the Yoris' financial situation—they started to dig themselves out of the hole—but it didn't do much for his face time with Clara or his practice time with Wallace. Roo tried to compensate by becoming more efficient. Rather than practicing the old moves over and over, Roo would dream up new tricks on the drive to work and practice them intensely in the short time he and Wallace had. If a new move worked and Wallace got it in practice, that was it. Roo would assume it was battle-ready. If it didn't work, he'd dump it. The previous week he'd come up with a twist on a trick called the Japan Over. To execute the move a handler flashes a disc behind his back to get the dog to run behind him, and then he flips the disc in front of himself and the dog has to spin and jump back over the handler's outstretched leg to catch it. Roo took that sequence and added a jumping flip throw.

Roo didn't know how this new on-the-fly approach would hold up in competition, but he didn't have any other options. It had a chance because of Wallace. Once he got something down, he had it forever. It also reflected on Wallace and Roo's connection. Dogs are expert at reading body language and when they are really tuned into their companions they can tell everything from the person's mood to what is wanted of them. Wallace could read Roo from fifty yards away and often knew what Roo wanted him to do before Roo had even given the command.

Part of that traced back to the way Roo had trained him. Many disc players train their dog to memorize routines from start to finish. Roo never did that. Each individual trick had its own verbal cue and often a hand cue as well. Roo always had a plan going into a competition, but this approach allowed him to improvise as he went along (although that sometimes got him in trouble), and he often did. It also forced Wallace to pay attention and keep his focus on Roo throughout, which helped build and reinforce that unspoken connection.

Roo knew that their bond would be put to the test in Wichita. Roo planned to use the Japan Over in Wallace's routine at regionals. He hoped it would work.

———

The Incredible Dog Challenge (IDC) is an exclusive affair. Only four dogs are invited to each of the two regionals. On the Friday before the competition, those four get practice time on the game field. After they're done, a small number of walk-ons are allowed to try to qualify for the event. They're let in on a first-come, first-served basis, and if the line is too long not everyone who shows up will necessarily get a shot. Either way, only the top two qualifiers get into the regionals. And of the six dogs that participate in the regionals, only the top two make it to nationals, where they're joined by the top two dogs from the other region and the defending champion. Five dogs; that's it.

Roo didn't want to get that far ahead of himself. As always, he felt hopeful and felt that if they did their best they could compete with anyone, but he had no idea how they would perform. It was the second week of May and they had not competed yet this year. Would the rust show? Would the new move fall apart in live action?

Roo pushed the questions aside and focused on the goal: Place in the qualifier and get into the regionals. He wanted that at a minimum, because each of the regionals got its own show, televised on Animal Planet. The finals aired on ABC, ESPN2, and Animal Planet, so at the very least Roo wanted to get some TV exposure. It was part of his goal for the year.

His media experience with the local reporter who had covered up Wallace's breed at the end of 2006 had left a bad taste in his mouth. Roo wanted to use Wallace to get attention and spread a new message about pit bulls, and he wanted to do it in a different way. He'd spent so much time on pit bull forums, where breed defenders talked endlessly about the problems and injustices facing these dogs, that he could no longer listen.

He adopted two new mottos, which largely made the same point. The first: Don't talk, do. And the second: Let the dog's actions speak. Roo had found that he could give someone all the information in the world on pit bulls, and it might make no impact, but let the same person see Roo and Wallace play disc, and their outlook changed. The wall that supported the conventional wisdom started to crumble, and they were much more receptive to Roo's message.

Others were finding the same thing. Roo started to get requests for Wallace videos from pit bull owners around the country who were fighting breed bans. These people found that it was one thing to stand up at a council meeting and say, "My dog's a good dog." It was another to show a video of Wallace, working out, showing off his great training, and performing stunts that most people don't associate with pit bulls. It altered the conversation.

Roo was happy to help. The breed bans were a growing problem. A short time before the IDC regional, Wichita itself had considered one. The measure had failed, but had it not, Wallace would not have been allowed to enter the city, never mind compete.

In general, Roo believed in the stance promoted by the ASPCA and others: A general dangerous dog law was better and more effective than one that wrongly criminalized an entire breed. Problem dogs come in all shapes, sizes, colors, and genetic backgrounds. Authorities should have the right to act against any dangerous dog, not simply ones that look a certain way. As a popular phrase around the movement stated it: Punish the deed, not the breed.

As Roo and Wallace rolled into Kansas, Roo knew that one good round could spur the process of upending all the bad headlines and negative perceptions. The first step was both the simplest and most difficult: Waking the next morning at five A.M.; getting everyone dressed, showered, fed, and walked; and getting to the venue by six A.M. He had no idea how many walk-ons would be allowed to compete, so he wanted to make sure he was first in line.

2

Roo had spent most of the drive to Wichita on the phone while Josh stared out the window. Mr. Grenell's real estate deal had hit a few snags, and both sides were in full wheeler-dealer mode trying to salvage the bid. As the miles rolled by Roo acted as negotiator, counselor, financial adviser, construction inspector, and therapist. The talks extended into Friday, and as Roo stood waiting to take the field with Wallace he was glued to his cell phone.

They had been first in line among the walk-ons, which made both Roo and Josh feel better about getting up so early. Once inside, the field made Roo yearn even more to get a spot in the regional. The IDC people had set up large stands on two sides of the field. A long pool for the separate dock-diving competition stretched along the third side and a series of tents and booths rimmed the fourth side. A giant video screen rose above the tents. Together the elements of the setup made Roo feel as though he was competing inside an arena. The place was empty for the qualifier, but that didn't dampen the effect.

The competition itself had a unique set of rules. Each team had two minutes to perform a routine, but that was it. No second round.

However, at each end of the field sat a five-yard-by-five-yard square. After its round the team went to one of the squares. The handler would throw two discs, one at time, toward the other square. If the dog caught a disc while in the opposite square, the team got one bonus point per catch. Roo and Wallace had never specifically practiced this game, but Roo figured it was similar enough to the other distance-and-accuracy events that they'd be able to wing it.

Six or seven walk-ons would get a chance to fight for the two open spots, and Roo and Wallace were up first. Minutes before their turn, Roo told the lawyers and brokers on the other end of the phone that he had to step away for a few minutes, but he'd call back as soon as possible. He put down the phone, led Wallace onto the field, and stuck the routine. Nothing spectacular—he wanted to save something for Saturday—but very good.

He jogged back to the tent where Josh waited, put Wallace in his crate, and got back on the phone. He talked while the other teams competed but hung up again when the announcer began reading off the scores. One by one the names went by—fifth, fourth, then "in third place," the voice in the speakers stated, "Josh Grenell and Wazee." They'd missed qualifying by one spot. Second place went by, and then, finally, came Roo and Wallace, with the top score in the qualifier.

Roo hissed an excited "Yesssss." He high-fived Josh and gave Wallace hugs and pats and scratches behind the ears. They were in. They would definitely be on TV. Even if they lost, they would show the world what pit bulls were really all about. If they won again tomorrow, they'd reach even more people.

Roo and Wallace had to hang around to tape interviews for the TV show and introductions, which would be shown on the video board before their round the next day. Roo was on and off the phone through the night, including a joyous call to Clara, who immediately posted the news on the forums. By nightfall, the real estate deal had been settled and all the distractions slipped away.

Roo, exhausted, slipped off to sleep. Wallace curled up nearly on Roo's head and did the same.

———

Roo's first impression proved true. The IDC field looked like an arena when he saw it, and now it felt like one. It was Saturday afternoon and Roo peeked out from the competitors' tent. The stands were packed, holding a crowd of about two thousand people, certainly the biggest crowd Roo had ever performed in front of. And unlike a lot of other events, these people hadn't wandered over from a state fair or harvest festival or stopped by while strolling in the park. They came to watch the dogs perform, and they were into it. Their steady buzz added an electricity to the air.

And then there were the cameras. Everything that happened would be recorded for use in the show, and every performance appeared on the video screen as it was happening. Two cameramen patrolled the field, and a third camera swung back and forth above the action on a long jib. Their presence amped the atmosphere up another notch, and Roo struggled to hold back the adrenaline.

He and Wallace were up second, and as Roo prepared to head for the field Wallace stood up at the sight of him, especially since he was carrying discs. As always, Wallace's ears perked, his tail stiffened, his muscles twitched. When Roo opened the crate Wallace began lunging at the discs. The familiarity of it all enhanced the sense of nervous excitement that he'd been feeling all morning.

Walking out, he saw himself and Wallace appear on the video board. He heard the roar. The announcer rattled off a few facts about them. Roo took a deep breath. Wallace jumped up on him, trying to get the discs. As the music started, Roo tossed the first disc. The wind swirled and the disc wavered. Wallace jumped and snatched at the disc, but it hit the side of his mouth and fell to the ground. The crowd "awww"ed and Roo's heart dropped.

He tossed the next disc and Wallace caught it. The crowd

cheered. He threw another; another catch, another cheer. They hit another and one more. Their momentum built, and Roo started to feel it, but the next move up was the Japan Over variation, the new trick they'd only learned the week before and had practiced fewer than a dozen times. For a second Roo considered dropping it, but he decided to go for it. He motioned with the disc and Wallace shot behind him. He put his leg out and flipped the disc in front of his body. Wallace turned and sprinted after it, but he missed. Roo couldn't believe it. Another miss, he figured, would give them only the slimmest chance at second place.

As his mind raced, Roo noticed that a little gust of wind had held the disc in the air. Wallace still had the hyperfocused look on his face he had when going for a catch. Roo watched as Wallace hit the ground and spun quickly. He lunged forward and caught the disc before it hit the ground. The crowd exploded.

They were on a roll now. Roo moved into the weaves, where Wallace dodged in and around his legs, then shot a long toss across the field. As Wallace charged back Roo dove over him, landed and popped back up off the ground, and fired an over-the-shoulder air bounce. The throw soared across the space, and Wallace accelerated over the grass, eyes fixed on the disc. As it neared the edge of the playing surface, Wallace launched himself into the air and snagged it. Again, the crowd roared.

They finished the routine in style, completing the rest of their throws. Roo moved to the end line and tossed his bonus discs. Wallace caught one of them for an extra point, and they jogged off to cheers. The scores came up almost immediately. They had jumped into first place and Roo liked their score. Now two of the final four teams would have to outdo Wallace to knock them off the qualifying list.

Roo watched the rest of the routines intently. The next two teams were good, but neither beat them. They were still in first with two teams remaining. Next up was Ron Watson and his dog Leilani, who were one of the invited teams. Ron and Roo were buddies. Ron had founded the K9disc forum that Roo had used extensively when he was getting into the sport, and Roo had studied many of Ron's videos in the early days when he was figuring out how to play. On the other hand, Roo had shared some of his innovative moves with Ron.

As Roo watched, any feeling of security he had waned. Ron and Leilani were on fire. They had some cool tricks and they nailed every throw. Suddenly Roo wondered if he and Wallace had been good enough. The atmosphere and the energy of this event were a notch above anything else he'd been to and maybe the competition was, too. When Ron and Leilani's score flashed on the board it was official: They knocked Roo and Wallace into second place. If the final team also surpassed them, Roo and Wallace would be finished.

Roo squirmed as he watched the last team. They were good. Roo could tell it would be close. After they were done, he stared at the scoreboard. It seemed to take forever. Finally, the freestyle score came up; it was half a point higher than Roo and Wallace's. But the other team had missed both of its bonus throws. Roo and Wallace's bonus put them over the top. That was it. They got second. They were going to the finals of the Incredible Dog Challenge. They were going to be on TV, twice. They were going to make a difference.

3

When Roo walked in, Clara was cooking and the house smelled great. In the few days since he'd returned home from Wichita he'd been inundated with e-mails and postings of congratulations, but there wasn't much time to bask in the glory. On Thursday, three days after returning home from Wichita, Roo, Clara, Josh, and Jen were leaving for Colorado, where the Skyhoundz West Coast Open would take place. They usually competed in the Skyhoundz regional in Indianapolis and used that as a springboard to qualify for the finals in Atlanta, but Roo felt like switching things up. The event in Colorado was an open, which meant he could simply show up.

He had other reasons for heading west, too. The Open would take place right outside Denver, a city known for having stiff anti–pit bull legislation and particularly draconian enforcement of it. Roo thought it would be cool for Wallace to appear on Denver's doorstep and win—proving to the nonbelievers that not all pit bulls were evil monsters that immediately needed to be exiled or put down.

Roo sniffed around the kitchen and Clara laughed. Helped by Wallace and Scooby and a steady stream of disc events, the couple had fought their way through 2006 together. By the end of the year at least some of the tension between them had eased. When Clara's mom announced that she would not continue to seek treatment, everyone in the family knew what that meant. It was only a matter of how much time she had left. For Roo it no longer mattered if Clara was a little depressed or unmotivated or isolated. He only wanted to make sure she and Sally could make the most out of whatever limited time they had.

Clara fought her sadness and coped as best as she could, talking on the phone and making trips to see her mom. One weekend her sister came in from Chicago, and the two daughters took their mom to the Twin Cities for a few days. It was a good-bye tour but not a sad one. They simply wanted to spend some time enjoying one another's company.

Around the house Clara had stepped up. With Roo out so often she had become the main caregiver for all the dogs. She had emerged as a cooking fiend, although the recipient of her efforts was Wallace. His allergies continued to be a problem and food remained a key source. The initial food switch had helped, but over time Wallace began to build up antigens in response to the new substances and eventually had reactions to that food, too. Roo and Clara switched again, which helped until the pattern repeated itself. They were up to the third or fourth change now, and Wallace's latest diet included home-cooked specialties. His meals varied but included pounds of white fish, steak, pork chops, and venison. These entrees were often accompanied by potatoes and even vegetables. Cooking had become almost a full-time job for Clara, so it was little surprise that when this regimen had run its course she planned to move Wallace to a raw-food diet.

Roo recognized the outline of the woman he had married, the track and basketball star, the dance student, the passionate shelter worker who put in far more hours than she was paid for because she wanted to help. Maybe, he hoped, she was pulling out of her funk. Maybe the old Clara was coming back.

She would have been happy to cook for Roo, too, but he was never around for dinner these days. Until tonight. "I think there's an extra pork chop that Wallace isn't eating," Clara said.

"Oh, gee," said Roo, looking at Wallace's feast. "I get a whole pork chop."

Clara laughed. "Well, he has allergies. And he's a world champion."

"I'm a world champion, too," Roo said.

"Yeah," Clara responded, smiling, "but you have the easy part." She patted Wallace on the head, then picked up a plate of food that looked as though it had come from the kitchen of a five-star restaurant and placed it on the ground before him.

———

If Roo could have dreamed up a perfect day to play disc, this would be it. They were in the town of Thornton, just outside Denver. The Rockies, white-tipped and menacing, rose up around them, like the breed ban itself. The sun shone and a few puffy clouds floated along

on a breeze that was just strong enough to feel but not stout enough
to affect the flight of a disc.

They had made the thirteen-hour drive out in one day—two
cars, five dogs, and a pair of walkie-talkies on board. Roo had
triple-checked the legal jurisdictions before arriving, and sure
enough Thornton was a little oasis of pit bull safety. The town
brought out a few friendly faces as well. Roo had a cousin, Jennifer,
who lived nearby and she came out to watch. Likewise, Roo and
Wallace had a few fans from the forums who showed up to meet
them and see them in action.

They made new friends, too. One woman came by and introduced herself. She had a pit bull of her own, and inspired by Wallace, she hoped to get into the sport. Roo gave her a few tips and
recommended a few online outlets where she could learn more, then
directed her to the merchandise tent, where she could buy what she
would need to get started.

Roo didn't plan to disappoint any of Wallace's fans. He'd entered
Wallace in both the distance-and-accuracy competition and the
freestyle. Distance-and-accuracy came first and Roo and Wallace
were solid if not spectacular: They scored thirteen points to put them
in a tie for fourth in D & A, but it had no bearing on the freestyle
competition, which started next with its own round of D & A.

Roo and Wallace tapped into the momentum they had built
during their freestyle round and took it even further. They went five
for five, all three-pointers, and Wallace got four half-point bonuses
for making four catches with all his paws off the ground. They
racked up seventeen points and took a commanding lead.

The actual freestyle performances were up, and Roo once again
found himself toward the end of the rotation. As dogs ran and
jumped and discs sailed, Roo passed time. He had a lot to watch,
since Josh and Wazee were playing as well as Clara and Scooby and
even Jen and Nova, their second Australian cattle dog.

As Roo and Wallace's turn approached the sky changed. Ominous clouds began to pile up around the mountain peaks. It wasn't a matter of if the gathering storm would hit them but when. Roo began to grow anxious. The team two spots before them took the field and the weather remained steady. In the tent Roo paced. The clouds continued to roll in. The team before them took the field; the weather held. The other team came off the field, and the judges quickly calculated their score.

Roo and Wallace stepped onto the field, and as if someone had been waiting to turn on a fan, the wind popped. It grew so strong so fast that the judges halted the competition, hoping it would die down at least a little. Roo and Wallace waited for a few minutes, but the wind continued to howl. The judges waved them back to the sidelines. Other competitors had gathered, and everyone milled around trying to figure out what to do. The rain seemed to have missed them but the wind persisted. Some of the other players joked with Roo: "Hey, the wind is your friend."

Roo laughed, but the truth was he felt fine. The idea of playing in the wind didn't bother him. A wave of confidence swept over him, and he felt like no matter what, he and Wallace were going to be good. As the debate raged on Roo spoke up. "Let's just do it," he yelled through the wind. Everyone else went quiet and turned toward him. "Let's just play," he said.

"Are you sure?" one of the judges asked.

"Yep, yep," Roo said, and he led Wallace onto the field.

For Roo, the round that followed was one of the most satisfying the pair ever pulled off. They missed a few that the wind messed with, but they made a few spectacular grabs, too. They wound up with the best score of any team, including those who had gone in the perfect conditions. They won the freestyle easily, and Roo loved the performance because he knew that as they started, everyone watching expected them to fail. The situation served as a microcosm for Wallace's entire career, his entire life really. No one had ever expected much from Wallace, and that made his achievements that much sweeter. Roo enjoyed proving the doubters wrong.

In the final D & A round Roo played it safe and he and Wallace were able to move up a spot, into third. In pairs, Roo and Josh and Wallace made it look as though they had been practicing for weeks, although they'd hardly done so at all. They won that, too. Roo was equally excited that Josh and Wazee finished third in freestyle, meaning that for the first time they had qualified for the Skyhoundz finals in freestyle.

Not everything was perfect, though. The woman with the pit bull who'd stopped by earlier to learn how to get into disc came back. She told Roo that she had purchased some discs but in the process had a bothersome conversation with the guys in the tent. When she told them what type of dog she had, they told her not to expect much, pit bulls can't really play disc. "What about Wallace?" she had said.

"He's a fluke," they had told her.

Roo shook his head. Still, for tonight, nothing could sour his mood. The two couples went out to dinner to celebrate. Roo was giddy as he looked around. A mile in almost any direction and Wallace would have been impounded and put down simply because of what he was—a criminal by genetics. But in this little spot he was allowed to run free, and in doing so he won two firsts and a third against some of the best competition in the West. For Roo, there was no louder or more convincing way to say breed bans are ridiculous.

4

Both Roo and Josh had sworn off local competitions, until today. Their abstinence came about not because they didn't want to compete but because they were helping organize the contests. The Minnesota Disc Dog Club had grown to twenty-five or thirty members. And those members officially hosted five events throughout southern Minnesota, which the club organized into a series. There were enough members now that each event had enough participants to make it fun and competitive even if everyone didn't show up.

Besides founding the club, Josh now served as president and Roo was a member of the board. As such, they took a role in running each event, doing everything from setting up the field and bringing and hooking up the sound system and scoring computer to lining up judges and scorekeepers. They were too busy to compete with their own dogs. They were also afraid that if they did compete and win, others would complain that they were putting on the events simply so they could show off.

Their goal, in reality, was to spread the sport throughout the state and attract more participants. They had done incredibly well already, considering that only two years earlier there had been only one small toss-and-catch event in the entire state and no organized means to create or support new ones or bring together people who were interested in doing so.

Now they not only had the club and all its members, but also over the course of 2006 and 2007 Roo, Josh, and other members of the club had begun to give demonstrations and performances around the state. They appeared at the Twin Cities Pet Expo, Doggie Palooza, the Mall of America, and a few schools. Sometimes they got paid, and they used that money to support the club. They bought the sound system and the computer. They paid the expenses. When the demos ended, they encouraged people from the crowd to come down and get a few tips on how to play with their dogs. When they could, they talked about dogs in general and pit bulls in particular.

The club's competition during Rochesterfest, the city's weeklong outdoor celebration, had become the anchor of its schedule. In its first appearance, in 2006, the disc-dog event had drawn a surprisingly large crowd. The entire field had been lined with people, and it was two or three deep in some spots. Coming into the 2007 event, Roo and the club had received inquiries about whether or not Wallace would be competing. He was, after all, a world champion now, and the club had been using him to get attention and spread the word. Roo didn't want to disappoint.

Then it got personal. Roo's parents announced they would come up for the day and bring with them his grandparents, who were visiting from California. In addition, Clara's parents made the trip down from Red Wing.

Out on the field Roo and Wallace did their best to show their hometown what the rest of the country was seeing. It was a park they practiced in all the time. It felt good and comfortable to be out there with his friends and family watching. Wallace, eager to the point of being a pest as always, didn't disappoint. The pair won the event by ten points.

Afterward, Roo brought the dog over to meet his eightysomething-year-old grandfather. Wallace, distracted by all the people and smells around him, looked everywhere but at the man, who sat in a chair. "Hey, Wallace," he called as Wallace ignored him. "Hey, Wallace," he repeated. Suddenly, as if someone had turned off his iPod and restored his hearing, Wallace tuned into the call, turned toward the direction of the sound, and tried to climb into Grandpa's lap, almost knocking the chair over.

"Well," Roo said, "now you've had an official Wallace greeting."

––––––––––

Back at the house Clara's mom approached Roo. Sally continued to carry on as if she was in perfect health, and she was still working as the director of the Red Wing Public Library. She asked Roo for a favor: The library had a program for kids, and she wondered if he and Wallace and others from the club would come give a demonstration and talk. Roo said yes on the spot.

On the day of the event Sally met them at the library and oversaw everything. The building had a large open basement where the event would take place and she scurried about directing the setup. At times, though, Roo noticed, she grew tired and needed to sit.

When the doors opened more than two hundred kids piled in. Roo and the others grasped the opportunity to do something a little different. They talked about dog safety—how to approach a dog and what to do when one approaches. They worked reading into it by holding up cards with words on them—*sit, lie down, spin*—and when the kids read them off in unison, the dogs obeyed.

Then they threw the discs and the kids loved every second of it. Wallace came out last, the star, and put on a show worthy of a Skyhoundz final. He jumped and twisted and ran. He went under Roo and jumped over Roo. When they were done, he wiggled and jumped up to try to get the discs from Roo, and the kids roared. Roo never talked about pit bulls, but he didn't have to. To these kids Wallace was just a dog, and he differed from other dogs only in that he could do cool tricks.

Roo spent the rest of the summer spreading the message. He and Wallace appeared at a few schools, the Minnesota Vikings Fan Fest, a camp, and two minor-league baseball games. The shows gave Roo and Wallace a chance to stay in shape, but in truth the crowds simply liked to see long throws and catches. Roo tried to work in some new material here and there, but his opportunities were limited. He hoped all their past work would pay off, because the fall championship season had arrived and he and Wallace hadn't truly practiced all summer.

In early September Roo decided to sneak in one last practice before the slew of fall competitions started in earnest. It was late, almost nine forty P.M., and Roo knew the lights at the park went off at ten. He grabbed his stuff, leashed up Wallace, and jumped in the car. The day had been warm but the night was cool, even for Minnesota, and a fog had settled over the grass. As they walked onto the field, Roo realized it would be hard to see, even with the lights. Then, as he dropped the bag full of discs on the ground, the lights clicked off.

Roo and Wallace stood in almost complete darkness for a moment, before some light from the overheads in the parking lot filtered through the mist. It wasn't much to see by, but Roo figured it was worth a try. He took out a disc and gave it a short flip. Wallace shot after it, quickly disappearing into the fog. Roo could hear Wallace's footsteps thwapping on the soft ground, then complete silence as the dog lifted in the air, and the sharp click of enamel on plastic. *Thud*—Wallace landed, the footsteps returned, and moments later Wallace reappeared, disc in mouth.

Roo threw the disc again and the process repeated itself. The experience felt surreal, disc and dog disappearing, Roo standing alone, isolated, listening, and Wallace reappearing, almost materializing out of the wet clouds. Visual cues were impossible and Roo dropped most of the verbal ones, too. Still, they connected and fell into a rhythm. Over the next ten minutes Roo and Wallace played almost flawlessly. Roo couldn't see the catches or the dog or anything around them, but he heard it all. He felt it.

When it was over, he knew they were ready for what lay ahead.

5

B etween the two jobs, the five dogs, and the steady string of demos and performances, Roo didn't think he could be any busier, but September promised an even crazier schedule. The first week he and Wallace would defend their title at the AWI Classic in Naperville. The next weekend they would go to Kansas City for the Canine Legislative Conference, where Roo had been invited to speak about ambassador dogs and how they helped change perceptions. The third week of the month they would drive to Atlanta for the Skyhoundz World Championships. All of it would serve as a buildup to their ultimate test, the Incredible Dog Challenge at Purina Farms in Missouri, where the potential for a star turn on national TV and the most coveted prize in the sport awaited.

The return trip to Naperville felt odd. So much had changed since their last visit. A year earlier, Roo and Wallace were a team with a lot of local success still trying to prove they belonged on a national level. The win at Naperville had served as a springboard toward that goal, and they were returning as world champions.

Now the target had moved. This year they wanted to show that their success hadn't been a fluke, but even more so they were dedicated to changing perceptions about pit bulls. On a personal level, Roo also still longed to win the AWI championship and get Wallace's name on the Lander Cup. A top-fifteen in Naperville would get them an invite back to the finals in Arizona, and Roo hoped that would be easy to achieve.

In truth, he didn't know how many more chances they would get. Wallace was five years old, and he'd been training and competing hard for more than two years. His body was not made for this stop-and-start, repeated-takeoff-and-landing sport. He had begun to show signs of wear and tear. He took longer to warm up and seemed a touch slower. When they played for a long time or for several days in a row, Roo noticed that Wallace would start to limp to protect the leg with the atrophied muscle.

Wallace's desire never wavered though, and when they hit the field in Naperville he wiggled with excitement. For the first round, Roo broke out a new opening move. He and Wallace started at opposite ends of the field, then charged toward each other at full speed. At the last second, Roo dove into a forward roll and Wallace raced underneath him. It came off perfectly and to great dramatic effect, and the pair never looked back.

They earned the highest score of the first round and in the second Roo went into showman mode. Before heading out on the field Josh helped him gel his hair into a faux-hawk. "You need some privacy so Josh can do your hair?" Clara joked. At the beginning of the routine, right before he and Wallace charged at each other across the field, Roo paused for effect and primped his hair. He and Wallace cruised to the win.

And this time the victory came with more than a trophy; they won a plane ticket to Arizona for the finals. That made it different than the year before, too. Back then Roo desperately needed the ticket, since he didn't think he could afford to get to Scottsdale any other way. This year, though, he didn't really need the help. He was happy to have it, but for the year he'd already sold about half a dozen houses and he and Clara were almost completely out of the hole.

After two years of doubt and struggle, financial stability felt good. They were not in the clear yet, but as early as the summer they had started to feel a lot better about their situation. They had made modest donations to a lot of small, local groups—first prize at a lot of weight-pull events was dog food, which Wallace couldn't eat, so the Yoris gave it to a nearby husky rescue—but maybe, they thought, it was time to do something bigger.

Hero Disc, the company that made the discs Wallace now used, offered an interesting program. Anyone could have a set of fifty custom collector's discs made at a steep discount. Once those fifty were delivered, the company would retire the artwork so the discs could never be produced again. Roo and Clara decided to make a Wallace collector disc and donate any profits from its sale to pit bull causes. It fit in with Roo's "don't talk, do" philosophy.

The discs came in, and the Yoris began to sell them through Wallace's website and at events. Demand wasn't a problem, as the discs quickly sold out, but Roo and Clara realized they had to decide something: Who should get the money?

———

The second Canine Legislation Conference brought together lawyers, law enforcement personnel, investigators, individuals, and organizations dedicated to improving current animal legislation and promoting new, better laws. Its particular focus was breed-specific legislation—the breed bans against pit bulls that were sweeping the country.

The first conference had taken place in Chicago the year before, but a group called Kansas City Dog Advocates had agreed to host the second edition after a controversial case in their city. In that instance a dog, Nikko, had been confiscated simply because it looked like a pit bull, despite the owner's documents showing that it was not. The legal fight over Nikko's breed lingered, even after a DNA test that the KC Dog Advocates helped arrange showed that it was not a pit bull. Finally, after eight months, Nikko was finally released.

The case pointed out the foolishness of everything about breed bans. It's often impossible to tell if a dog is a pit bull simply by looking at it, especially in the case of mixed breeds, which are numerous since purebred pit bulls are not that common. And if the dog is part pit bull, what percentage qualifies as meeting the definition of the breed? Half? Twenty-five percent? And where does the burden of proof lie, with the agency confiscating someone's family pet or with the owner?

The whole situation defied logic, and Roo and Clara were happy to be part of the fight against it. They arrived at the conference center in Lee's Summit, Missouri, on Friday and attended several sessions. Roo's talk expressed the point of view that he'd honed over the last few years. The dogs, he explained, needed to speak for themselves. There was no better way to respond to someone quoting all the negative incidents involving pit bulls and arguing that the breed itself was somehow hardwired toward violence and incapable of living among the rest of us than to point at Wallace and say, "My pit bull is a world champion, he's traveled all over the country, been to dozens of events packed with people and dogs, and never caused a problem." Wallace was living proof that many of the pit bull myths were just that.

Later, after one of the sessions, Roo went to the grand hall, where a crowd had gathered. He hopped on a small stage, where he was presented a special achievement award for all he'd done to help change the perception of pit bulls. The award came from the Animal Farm Foundation, a rescue and advocacy organization in Amenia, New York, that worked on behalf of and supported pit bull causes. Besides the certificate, the award came with a $1,000 check.

Upon receiving the money Roo offered to donate it back to the group, figuring a nonprofit rescue needed the cash more than he did. They wouldn't accept. The group's executive director explained that part of the foundation's mission was giving grants to groups or people doing exactly the kind of work Roo and Wallace were doing. Roo accepted and then had a conversation with Clara. They liked what Animal Farm stood for and how the foundation operated.

They made a decision—they would donate the money from Wallace's collector discs to Animal Farm.

Four days later, after a brief return to Minnesota, they hooked up with Josh and Jen and headed for Georgia. In southern Illinois they stopped off in Metropolis, a small town named after the city Superman had lived in. On their first trip to Atlanta in '05, Roo and Josh had seen the highway sign and stopped off. The town, anything but a metropolis, had been declared Superman's hometown by DC Comics in 1972, and it now had a large downtown statue of the superhero, a small Superman museum, and an annual Superman festival.

On that first visit, Team Wallace didn't hit any of those sites, though. They simply gassed up at a station on the outskirts. But in the parking lot next to the station stood a life-size wooden cutout that allowed anyone who stopped by to put his or her head on Superman's body. Josh and Roo had snapped a few pictures with Wallace's big blocky noggin on the Man of Steel's likeness. Over the years they'd Photoshopped a W on the chest in place of the S and used the picture on Wallace's website, T-shirts, and discs.

Now they wanted to update the photo. The old gas station had been rebuilt, but the cutout remained, and they snapped a few shots. This time, though, they decided to head into town, too. They saw the statue and stopped off in a few small Superman-themed shops. Roo took Wallace for a walk. As they passed by a storefront, Roo stopped for a moment and looked at a Superman statuette on display. A plaque below the figure trumpeted the hero's motto: "Truth, justice, and the American way." Roo read it, the legislative conference fresh in his mind. He looked at Wallace. "Maybe one day for you, buddy," he said. "Maybe one day."

Disc doggers call it jammin'. It happens when person and dog have been playing together for so long and are so in sync that they don't need a routine, don't even need a plan. They can simply walk onto the field and make something fascinating happen. On Friday afternoon in Atlanta Roo planned to jam.

Despite all their success, Roo and Wallace had still never won a Skyhoundz world title, and Roo wanted one because he knew from experience it would help Wallace's Superman mission—he'd seen the impact firsthand. This year, for the first time, Wallace would have three cracks at a title, as he'd qualified in singles freestyle, distance-and-accuracy, and pairs freestyle. Roo was particularly excited for the singles, since in two trips to the finals he'd never competed on Saturday before. He also figured it gave them the best chance to win; distance-and-accuracy was so hit-or-miss, and he, Josh, and Wallace hadn't played a second of pairs together since the final round of the Skyhoundz regional back in May.

But while the triple-header increased the odds of success, it also meant that Wallace could potentially need to perform six rounds in twenty-four hours. Roo needed to save the dog's energy and protect that old shoulder injury. So on Friday afternoon he entered the qualifier simply to loosen up after the long drive. He had no intention of working on his routine or making the cut. He was just having fun. Jammin'.

As they rolled through some of their standard tricks, Wallace came charging back at Roo with a disc. Roo went into his dive roll, popped up, and started into the running air bounce, but halfway into the move an idea came into his head. Instead of simply running forward, he leapt into the air, spun 360 degrees, and then threw the disc as he descended. The throw came off perfectly, and Wallace tracked down the disc. An audible *whoa* came from the crowd.

Roo wasn't done. He spun a disc on his finger and lowered it down, passing under his leg onto his other hand. As he brought the disc back up, he lifted his arm quickly and the spinning disc popped into the air in front of him. It hung there for a second then started to descend, like a UFO landing in a cornfield. As it came down, Roo leapt into the air and kicked at the side of the disc. He knew if he caught it just right, the disc would remain parallel to the ground and shoot off across the field, where Wallace could get it. Unfortunately, he missed his mark and the disc wobbled forward and fell to the ground. Still, the effort drew a *wow* from those watching.

Roo was feeling it, and another idea popped into his head, but he had the sense he'd already done too much. The last thing he wanted to do was make the cut in the qualifier and have to perform again. He eased up, and they coasted to the finish before packing it in for the day.

———

The wind was a problem. Roo and Wallace's opening round of freestyle had gone okay, not spectacular but solid. It left them tied for sixth, but only a point and a half behind the leader. As always, the distance-and-accuracy portion of the freestyle competition would be critical. Roo knew he could do better in the next freestyle round, but he had to keep it close in D & A.

The wind made it tough. It blew diagonally across the field. Competitors were allowed to stand at any point along the start line, so they had some latitude to get a better angle. Unfortunately, the best angle for this wind required a throw that went downwind toward the spectator area. Already today the wind had gotten under a disc and carried it right into a section of onlookers.

Roo couldn't let that happen. Solving the pit bull problem meant changing perceptions and fighting back against unfair laws, but another part of it was responsible ownership—making sure a dog didn't get into a situation in which something bad might happen. If one of Roo's throws sailed into the crowd and Wallace went after it with his single-minded abandon, any number of things could go wrong.

Roo hated to give up, to basically throw the competition, but he had no choice. Reluctantly, he set up at the opposite end of the line than virtually every other competitor had. In this direction, throwing into the wind, he couldn't even heave the disc forty yards. Roo and Wallace gave it their best, but when the time had elapsed they'd earned eleven points. Fifteen other teams did better, and Roo and Wallace dropped into a tie for eleventh overall.

Roo tried to shrug it off. After last year, when he and Josh had gotten too serious during their pairs rounds, he made sure to lighten up. Plus, he'd been working so hard for most of the year that these competitions had become vacations for him—they were the only time he took off—and he wanted to have fun on his vacation. He knew they couldn't win, so he decided that in his final round, he'd simply rear back and let it rip, like he had on Friday afternoon.

It worked. Roo and Wallace nailed the 360 air bounce. Roo tried the jump kick again and this time he got it right. Wallace had never seen the trick as Roo had envisioned it and had never successfully practiced it, but he picked right up on what Roo was doing and chased the disc down. Roo tried another new trick, a leaping, under-the-leg skip throw, in which he jumped into the air, kicked one leg up, and threw the disc under his leg so that it would skip off the ground like a stone off the water. He used a cue for a similar trick to give Wallace a clue about what was coming, and the dog followed along. It came off perfectly except for the throw, which didn't come up off the ground high enough for Wallace to catch.

When they were done they had scored the highest single round of the event. The performance jumped them into a tie for fourth. Chuck Middleton, who was once again judging, approached him after the round. "When you did the jump kick, my eyes were this wide," he said, holding his hands in front of his face with his thumb and forefinger a few inches apart. "You must have been three feet off the ground!"

To Roo, the tie for fourth felt like a win. Roo looked over at Wallace, who lay sprawled on his back in the crate, feet in the air, tongue hanging out. Roo had finally learned the lesson Wallace had been teaching him all along: It didn't pay to get bogged down in the standards and judgments of others; it only mattered that you put your total being into what you were doing.

On some level Roo knew this. He'd certainly practiced it many times with Wallace in the park. All those nights when it had simply been the two of them, out in the field, running, jumping, throwing, catching. No judges or fans. Wallace was not a spurned breed or a dog that no one wanted; Roo was not a man saddled with debts and marital trouble. They were similar in their single-minded determination and tireless drive, and that effort led them to a state in which there was no thinking, no trying, no worrying—they simply were. Man and dog locked together in pursuit of a single goal. Doing, being, sharing. That, thought Roo, was the definition of a lot of things: success, happiness, life.

He felt renewed. The talk around the field had turned to the next day's pairs showdown. Could anyone beat Frank, Shannon, and Shiloh, who were going for three in a row? Roo had come into the weekend thinking it impossible; now he said simply, "We'll see."

———

It all came down to Wallace. Four months had passed since Roo, Wallace, and Josh had last competed in pairs. They hadn't practiced at all. Roo and Josh stood under their canopy going over the routine. Could Wallace remember all the cues and sequences? Roo didn't know. He didn't think many dogs could, and he realized the three of them might just end up providing comic relief.

To make matters worse, Roo and Josh were considering a new trick. Josh would get down on one knee with the other leg bent in front of him. Wallace would charge underneath the leg and as he did Josh would flip a disc that the dog would chase down. That would be familiar; they'd done it before. But this time, Roo would come running right behind Wallace. Josh would lean forward and Roo would jump, put a foot on Josh's back, and launch himself in the air. He'd then catch a disc from Josh and quickly throw it past Josh's original flip. Wallace would have to drop the first disc and continue to get the second one. In most cases the dog did the vault, but in this stunt Roo did it. They dubbed it the Man Vault.

Adding the new trick increased the risk of something going wrong, but they knew it was necessary. They were amazed by how much the pairs competition had advanced in the two years since it had been introduced. The tricks had grown more sophisticated, the routines were more polished, and the number of teams competing had doubled. Pretty good wasn't good enough anymore.

Roo and Josh took the field with a shoulder shrug and hoped for the best. They got it. Wallace amazed. He remembered everything, adapted to the new material, and stuck almost every catch. When the first-round scores came up, Team Wallace stood at the top of the leaderboard. In second, only a half point behind, was Shiloh. The second round would settle the matter.

Roo, Josh, and Wallace had another good performance, maybe not as electric as their first round but good. Frank, Shannon, and Shiloh were better. Their second-round score was a point and a half better than Wallace's, and they won their third straight pairs title. Roo didn't feel bad about it. The year before, he and Josh had the title in hand but threw it away because they tried too hard. This year they hadn't blown it, they'd just been beaten, and Roo was okay with that.

For the weekend he and Wallace would take home a tie for fourth, an eighth (in distance-and-accuracy), and a second. Not what Roo had hoped for, but after his revelation about seeing life through Wallace's eyes, he was happy.

Roo couldn't know it, but he'd accomplished another goal. Danny Venegas had been watching him carefully all weekend. Venegas had won the Incredible Dog Challenge the year before and he was getting set to defend his title. Venegas knew that at the IDC there would be no distance-and-accuracy competition, the only thing that had held Roo and Wallace back. It would be one round of freestyle, winner take all. After one of Roo's particularly successful rounds, filled with jumps and spins, Venegas called a friend and training partner back home in Florida.

"This kid is off the map," Danny said.

"The guy with the pit bull?" his friend responded.

"Yeah," Danny said. "I don't know if I can beat him."

7

Roo felt out of sorts, for two reasons. For the first time, he was at a major disc competition without Josh, who had been unable to get out of work. Instead, Roo had driven down to Purina Farms in Gray Summit, Missouri, with his parents and Clara. When they arrived on Thursday night a giant blow-up dog had met them at the entrance to the grounds, which rolled over three hundred acres of wooded hills and had a barnyard area with cows and goats, a show hall, and a visitor's center. IDC banners flew everywhere.

Roo had spent Friday taping video with the production crew and getting in a practice round on the field, which had been set up similarly to the field at regionals, with stands on three sides and a large tent for competitors and VIPs. Except bigger. Friday night Purina hosted a dinner on an outdoor patio lined with ivy-covered trellises, a waterfall, and a koi pond. Every sight—the banners, the stadium, the patio dinner—got Roo more excited. That was good; he thrived on that energy and competitiveness, as long as he didn't allow himself to get too amped up.

That was reason two for his discomfort. It was the Saturday morning of a competition and he had nothing to do. Usually, he was up at dawn and off to the site to get a prime spot at the field. But things didn't work that way at Purina Farms. Competitors had reserved VIP parking near the field. The large competitors' tent eliminated the need for Team Wallace to haul out and set up their own camp. All Roo had to do was show up. And of all the competitions taking place—dock diving, fly-ball, agility, etc.—flying disc was last.

The spare time allowed unsettling thoughts to rise in Roo's head. Wallace had become such an icon in the pit bull world that Roo felt pressure to deliver. On the forums and in e-mails supporters celebrated Wallace's wins, but they didn't usually hear much about the seventh and eighth places, the bad throws, and the dropped catches. They didn't know how stiff the competition was, and this year it would be even tougher—because of a quirk in the qualifying process, there would be six teams competing instead of five. And every other dog was faster, more agile, and twenty to twenty-five pounds lighter than Wallace. Still, the message-board posters and Wallace supporters expected him to win every time.

Wallace's success fed legal arguments and water-cooler conversations. The competitions had always meant something for Roo and Wallace—and those meanings were converging—but now they meant something else entirely. And the more Roo pondered the implications of this particular competition, the more he grew nervous.

It didn't help that the night before, as he stood talking with the other flying-disc competitors, one of them had made a troubling comment. "Well," she said, looking at Roo, "this is in the bag as long as you don't mess up." That might have been a compliment to their skills, but the tone said something different. It implied that the person thought Purina wanted Wallace to win because of his backstory. It implied that as long as Roo and Wallace made a decent showing, the judges would swing things in their favor.

Roo said nothing, but inside he fumed. Now he didn't feel as though he and Wallace could simply win. They needed to win so decisively that no one could question them.

————

Roo and Wallace were up first. Purina had drawn the names out of a hat to decide the order of competition and Wallace had come up at the top. Roo hated going first, felt it was a competitive disadvantage, but he didn't dwell on it. The competitors' tent proved a bit of a ghost town, so the Yoris set up camp in their car, a short walk away. They were parked in the shade of a large tree, and they had a few chairs and a cooler with drinks. They played the radio. From time to time they would walk over to the field and check out the other events.

Wallace sat on his leash among them. He paced around. He slept. He rolled in the grass. When the other competitions began, he heard the *oohs* and *aahs* of the crowd and stared in the direction of the arena. At one point he walked over to Roo and nudged him with his nose, as if to say, "Hey, aren't we getting in on that?"

"Not yet, buddy, not yet," Roo said, scratching the dog's ears and patting him on the side. The afternoon inched forward, until, at last, it was time.

Roo jogged onto the field with Wallace. He looked at the crowd. As with regionals, the crowds were there for no reason except to watch the show, and they were into it. Roo hoped to tap into their energy. The music began, and he let it rip.

They started out on a roll and Wallace seemed to be feeling good. They hit the 360 air bounce. During practice Roo had noticed the field was firm, the grass thick and bouncy, which makes it difficult to skip a disc off the turf, but he decided to try anyway. He rose and attempted the under-the-leg skip throw, but the disc stuck on a clump of grass and never rose off the ground. Worse, the miscue threw off the timing of the next few moves. Roo couldn't take any more chances, so he bailed on the jump kick.

They had been very good, with a few stellar moments, but the error definitely hurt. Roo came off the field and watched the video board. Their score flashed up: 87. A fair number, Roo thought. He hoped it was enough to at least get them on the podium, which would guarantee some airtime in the final TV show. He felt bad about his errant throw, though. He knew that if he'd hit it, they would have been contenders and likely winners. Now everything hung in question.

Clara took Wallace back to the car to rest, then rejoined Roo and his parents in the competitors' tent, where they watched and waited. Roo's old friend Ron Watson came up next. He, too, struggled, missing some throws. Roo hated the helplessness of the situation, but even more he hated that he found himself half wishing for the others to mess up. That wasn't the way he wanted to succeed. Still, when Ron's score came up, an 84, Roo exhaled. One down.

Next came Becky Mueller and Flygirl. They stumbled badly and scored a 75.5. Two down. There were six total competitors, so if the next player didn't beat Wallace's score, he and Roo were guaranteed at least third place. Penny Mahon and Spinner took the field. They were solid, but they too had a few wobbly moments. Score: 86.5.

Nerves seemed to be getting the best of everyone. Roo thought his score had a chance, but he knew all the competitors were capable of besting it. That none of them had yet was something of a shock. Theresa Muisi and Ciela Azule went out next and looked like they would jump into first, but they stumbled on a few of their tricks toward the end of their routine and got an 81.5.

Only one team remained: Danny Venegas and Oreo. The defending champs, who had also won the Skyhoundz World Championship the week before. Danny went into his routine. To Roo's left Clara stood with his parents. On his right stood a man who vacationed in Atlanta every year to watch the Skyhoundz finals. He and his wife were big Wallace fans, and Roo had become friendly with them. This year they'd extended their trip and gone from Atlanta to Missouri to see Wallace go for the IDC.

They stood in silence as the crowd cheered and shouted around them. Danny and Oreo were doing well. The best so far in Roo's mind. There were a few drops, but they moved well and showed good form. When they were done Roo knew it would be close, but he thought Danny might win. They waited. "Come on, come on," Clara said, hands in front of her face, fingers interlocked. Roo remained stoic, arms folded across his chest. The muscles of his jaw flexed and bulged.

At last, the number appeared: 86.5.

It was over. They had won.

Roo bent over for a second, hands on knees. When he stood up the man from Atlanta was right in front of him. "You did it!" he shouted. "You did it!" And he and Roo wrapped each other in a giant embrace. Next to him Roo could hear Clara screaming. He turned toward his family, and they all came together in one giant hug. Roo felt overwhelmed. He started to cry. They were all crying.

The cameramen appeared, equipment rolling, and the roving reporter came right behind them. "We want to get you out on the field for your interview," the reporter said. Clara volunteered to fetch Wallace from the car. As she ran across the grounds she overheard two people talking: "Hey, the pit bull won the disc competition," one of them said. As she zoomed past, Clara yelled behind her, "That's my dog. My dog just won the national championship!"

By the time she returned and Roo took the field for his interview, he had regained his composure—mostly. "You guys are disproving all kinds of stereotypes today. This is an emotional one for you," said the interviewer.

"Yep," Roo answered, swallowing to hold back the tidal wave. "It is. I'll probably start crying. Just knowing where he came from and what we've been shooting for, it's . . ." He searched for a word. "I just can't believe it."

"He's a bigger, stockier dog. Some people would say, 'He can't be out there doing flying disc.' You proved them wrong, too."

"Yep. He's an amazing dog. Every time we come out here he gives me all he has, and I love him for it."

"Well, all your work paid off big-time," the interviewer said. "You've got a champion dog!"

Roo laughed. "Thank you," he said. "Thank you."

Afterward, Roo ran into Danny Venegas, who congratulated him. Roo felt self-conscious about the comment made the night before. "I think you might have really won," Roo said.

"Thanks for saying that, man," Danny replied, "but you guys are a great team and Wallace is awesome. You deserve it." On the podium Danny leaned over from the number two spot and gave Wallace a kiss on the head. Wallace looked at Danny and covered him from chin to eyebrow with one giant lick. Danny grabbed Roo's arm and lifted it in the air.

Chapter 7

Going Home, Again

———◆———

Everything looks cooler in slow motion.

Roo Yori

1

The plane rose into the afternoon sky. More than a month had passed since the Incredible Dog victory and Roo and Wallace hadn't really come down. Since getting home they'd been featured on the local ABC news station, in *The American Dog, The Bark,* and *Rochester* magazines, and in a few other publications.

After their *Letterman* experience Roo had promised not to fly with Wallace, but he couldn't get enough time off to make the three-day drive out to Arizona for the AWI finals and Cynosport Games. Plus, he had won free plane tickets, so Roo decided to try again. Josh flew with them, while Roo's parents, who didn't like flying, drove with all the gear.

At the Phoenix airport, Roo had to find a porter to retrieve Wallace from the baggage area. The man returned with the crate on his hand truck. Roo could see that Wallace was stressed—eyes dilated, ears back, tail down. He could also see that while the porter tried to be brave, the man was petrified of Wallace. Roo opened the crate to let the dog out and the man took a few steps back. "I always heard about those dogs," he said.

Roo started telling the man about Wallace and why he was there. Roo could see that getting out of the crate had helped relax Wallace. "Go ahead and pet him," Roo said.

"No, thanks," the man said.

"He won't do anything," Roo promised. The man stepped

forward tentatively and petted Wallace. He smiled and continued to stroke Wallace's head.

"Well," he said. "He's a nice dog. I'll keep an eye out to see what happens to you fellas. Good luck out there." It was a sincere wish, but their luck had already begun to change.

————

Roo stood in the middle of the field with the microphone in his hand, Wallace lying on the ground at his feet. For the first time, Roo had volunteered to sing the national anthem before the start of the games, and he led into it with a little speech. "During both world wars pit bulls were considered great dogs and chosen as a symbol of our country on recruiting and morale posters. It's kind of sad how they're treated now. I hope our presence today can bring us back to those times a little." He began to sing, and Wallace, as if posing for effect, laid his head on the ground.

When Roo finished, Alex Stein, the man who started it all with Ashley Whippet, came out and threw the first disc. Then the games began. As soon as he and Wallace started to warm up, Roo could tell they were in trouble. Wallace was doing his best, but as with the *Letterman* fiasco, something was off. On long throws he had trouble timing his jumps. His fatigue made him impatient, and he couldn't wait for the disc to descend far enough. He'd also lost a little spring, so he couldn't jump quite as high. Roo's throws needed to be perfect or they had no chance. Roo felt bad for Wallace, but he knew there was nothing seriously wrong with the dog so he tried to make the best of it.

By Sunday, they had qualified for the finals of the AWI, making the top ten, but they were too far behind in the standings to win. The Lander Cup was gone, but they still had a chance to repeat as FDDO champion and overall Cynosport champion. Once again, the result would come down to the speed-disc competition. If they caught a disc in all three zones faster than any other team, just as they had the year before, they'd be champs.

As he had the year before, Roo made the first throw to the ten-yard zone, then the twenty-yarder, and finally the thirty. All three throws hit their mark, but Wallace dropped them all. Out on the field Wallace looked lost, as if he couldn't even see the discs, never mind catch them. Roo was puzzled. After the round he went out to collect Wallace and pick up the discs, and as he did so he looked back toward the starting line, where he had stood tossing the discs. He squinted. The setting sun sat right above the mountaintops, casting a blinding glare. *Ugh,* Roo thought. If he'd only realized beforehand.

Despite their difficulties they ended up second overall. Roo started to shake his head, but then he looked at Wallace, who sat wagging his tail as if he was ready to try again. Roo laughed. He was proud of the dog for doing as well as he had even though he wasn't himself. He realized that they officially had nothing left to prove—they had ambitions, yes, but no one could question their place in the sport.

Because of that, Roo didn't mind the finish nearly as much as he hated having to crate Wallace up and put him on the plane again. It was the last time Wallace would ever fly. As the pilot announced they were passing over Denver, Roo looked out the window and said to himself, "Ha, you can't get us up here."

At least, he thought, they were headed home to better things. Roo was on the verge of selling his ninth house of the year, which would officially put him and Clara into the black. He had another client lined up, and he expected to complete that transaction soon. Roo had made a deal with Clara back at the beginning of the year: If he got them out of debt, he could buy himself a motorcycle, an idea she didn't like but would now have to go along with. He was excited to start looking.

Things with Clara had gotten much better, too. All through the fall she had traveled with him, tending to Wallace during events. Much of the old tension had dissipated and although she still drifted away at times, they were more of a team than they had been in years.

Roo couldn't wait to get back to Minnesota and enjoy some peace after so many days on the road. But almost as soon as he arrived home, Clara got a call: Her mom had taken a turn for the worse. Sally didn't have much time left. Roo and Clara made the forty-five-minute drive up to Red Wing. It had been almost a month since Roo had seen Sally, and at that point she had begun to lose weight and break down physically. She had taken up residence in a spare bedroom, freshly painted with inspirational quotes on the walls. She spent most of her days there, and a hospice-care worker came and went. When Roo walked in, he could see Sally had deteriorated since his last visit. Her cheeks had pulled into her face, her eyes had sunk, her color had waned.

Clara remained in Red Wing, while Roo returned home, working and tending to the dogs. He found a motorcycle he liked in the want ads and bought it. When Clara came home and found it she was angry, but she didn't have the strength to fight. They leaned on each other. They pulled closer.

Clara's sister, Gretchen, came up from Chicago and stayed at her parents' house. She called Clara one day: "It could be any time. You better get up here." Clara headed for Red Wing that afternoon. Roo arrived that night after work. Clara, Gretchen, their dad, and their grandmother gathered in the room with Sally. They shared memories and told stories. Sally lay on the bed, eyes closed, almost motionless, but when Roo walked in she opened her eyes for a moment and took him in. Roo had brought food and a few minutes later the family filed out to eat. But Gretchen had little appetite and returned to sit with her mother. As she did, she noticed that Sally's breathing had grown erratic. She called out to the others, and as the family ran back to Sally's room, she let out one final sigh, then slipped away.

Clara was strong through the service, helping others and putting on a brave face, but Roo knew that she was devastated. She began to sink back down, disappearing into herself again. Roo tried to stay close while also giving her the space she needed to grieve. They had come so far and he didn't want everything to fall apart again.

2

Wallace stepped into the water and grabbed the binky. He was at a canine rehabilitation center that had opened near Rochester. Other than a trip to defend their IDC title in September, Roo and Wallace didn't plan to compete in 2008. Roo felt that they had done all they had set out to: They'd justified sparing Wallace, proved they were as good as anyone else at flying disc, and spread a positive pit bull image far and wide.

After three years, Wallace's body needed a break. The travel had become difficult and expensive. And Wallace still had that incredible prey drive. It was part of what made him great, but Roo worried that if something went wrong, if some other dog ran on the field during one of Wallace's routines, the negative publicity would undo all they had achieved. DISC CHAMPION ATTACKS FELLOW COMPETITOR was a headline he wasn't willing to risk. Roo figured they would still play together in the park and around the house, but it would be less intense than their competitive prep of previous years, and it would come after an entire winter off.

Still, Wallace, being Wallace, needed to stay active. He needed exercise and distractions. Roo couldn't play disc with him outside during the winter because the dog's feet would bleed. He couldn't take Wallace running because long distances seemed to aggravate the shoulder problem. Instead, Roo and Clara found the rehab center, which had an underwater treadmill that allowed a dog to get a great workout without putting a lot of strain on its body.

Problem was, Wallace didn't love it. Roo and Clara could only get him in the water and running by giving him a large squeeze toy that looked something like a bowling pin and that Clara called a binky. So all through the winter Wallace chewed the binky while making waves on the treadmill.

He needed to stay in shape for his star moment. In January ABC aired the finals of the Incredible Dog Challenge. The show came on during the afternoon, but Roo and Clara had arranged for a friend to record it and burn it to a disc for them. That night a group of about fifteen friends and family were coming over and they would all watch together.

Meanwhile, Roo went to the gym. While he was there, Josh put the telecast on a few of the TVs, and everyone watched as they worked out. At one point Roo found himself standing next to a man he did not know. The guy turned to Roo and motioned toward that set. "That's pretty cool," the guy said.

"That's me," Roo responded. The guy looked at the TV, looked at Roo, and looked at the TV again.

"Whoa!" he said. "Pretty cool."

That night at the house everyone gathered around the set, even Wallace, who tried to eat from a bowl of chips on the table and nose-punched at least three guests. With the slick production and professional announcers, Roo thought the whole thing looked great. He was anxious, though, as the end approached. He knew they'd talked about disproving pit bull myths in his interview, but he feared the producers might cut it. He'd been down that road before.

Purina had a motto for the IDC: Any dog with the proper training and nutrition can be incredible. Roo hoped that "any dog" included pit bulls and that the company would let his comments speak for themselves. The moment came, and the words flowed out of the screen unchanged. Everyone in the room cheered, and Roo pumped a fist in the air, then got up and gave high fives and hugs to everyone. The segment ended with a slow-motion shot of the dive roll into the over-the-shoulder air bounce. "Man," Roo said, "everything looks cooler in slow motion."

Later, Roo found himself alone with Josh. "You know what the best part of that video was?" he asked. "Watching it back again, I can see that we were the best team out there that day. That makes me feel better."

"You should," Josh said. "I'm thinking about a new instructional video. It's called *How to Win the National Championship on Seven Hours of Practice*."

Roo laughed. "Interesting idea, but I wouldn't recommend it."

———

When the weather broke Roo and Wallace took to the yard and the park. With the travel reduced and the financial pressure eased, Roo had more time to simply play. He maintained both jobs, but he slowed the pace. As the weeks went by, Wallace proved that he still had the drive and the moves, even if he wasn't quite the ball of fire he used to be. The pair began to pile up an array of new tricks, and Roo felt good about their chances to defend their IDC title.

As the summer progressed, he wondered, though, if they needed a tune-up before the big show. He entered a UFO event in Colorado at the end of August so they could get the feel of performing under pressure again. Roo took the trip out to Colorado as an excuse to sneak in some time with the guys. Josh and three other buddies came along, and although the weather was unseasonably cold, they did some hiking and whitewater rafting. At the event, even after nine months away, Wallace coasted to a third-place finish. Roo felt reassured, since the only thing that had kept them from winning had once again been distance and accuracy, an aspect of competition that wouldn't affect them at the IDC, which was only a month away.

During the next few weeks, Roo and Wallace worked particularly hard honing the new material. Roo also tried to make sure Wallace was in peak condition. He enlisted Clara to take the dog for a few more sessions on the underwater treadmill. The effort seemed to help, and as the competition approached Wallace looked as fit as he'd been when he was competing regularly.

Five days before the IDC, Clara brought Wallace in for one last training session. For some reason Wallace wouldn't get in the pool. Even the promise of the binky could not lure him into the water. The attendant suggested another approach that had worked with other dogs. She took out a large baking spatula and covered the end with cheese. Dogs, she noted, would be lured on by the smell, and once they climbed into the water she would let them lick the cheese off the spatula. It sounded good to Clara.

The cheese smelled delicious to Wallace. Too delicious. Sure enough, he was motivated to get in the pool, but when the attendant held the spatula out for him to lick, he misunderstood. He clamped down and pulled the end right off the handle and swallowed the whole thing down in one gulp.

When she realized what happened the attendant immediately stopped the treadmill, and Clara pulled Wallace out of the water. They tried to induce vomiting, but the spatula would not come up. They rushed him back to the veterinary office, where one of the vets tried to help. Again, no luck.

Clara called Roo at work. She was crying as she explained what had happened. The vets at the rehab center had said that the doctors at U of M had better tools and might have a better chance of extracting the spatula. If not, Wallace would have to have surgery.

Clara rushed Wallace into the car and took off for the university. The vets put Wallace under, snaked an endoscope down his throat and attempted to extract the large piece of plastic. The spatula would not come out. The vets laid out the options.

They could wait. It was four days until the competition and there was a chance the object would not work its way through his system that quickly, but that was risky. Dogs were known to sometimes swallow large pieces of rawhide that punctured their intestines and killed them almost instantly. The same could happen with the spatula.

Of course, surgery wasn't a picnic either. The doctors didn't expect any problems, but any time a dog went under general anesthesia and had its body cut open there was a risk of death. No one could give Roo and Clara a percentage, but any chance was scary.

Roo and Clara knew this might be Wallace's last shot to win a major event. They also knew that withdrawing meant he'd miss the chance at more TV time and positive publicity for pit bulls. The producers had even arranged for a writer to do a newspaper feature on Wallace. That too would have to be canceled. The lost opportunities accumulated, and they flashed through Roo and Clara's deliberations for an instant, but in truth nothing mattered to them except Wallace's health. They gave the doctors the go-ahead, and the surgery began minutes later.

Roo called Purina to give them the news. The company was sorry to hear about Wallace, but they still wanted to do a story about him. It would just have a different slant.

Wallace came out of surgery a few hours later, twenty-five staples holding his abdomen together and a giant plastic Queen Elizabeth collar driving him batty. Clara asked for the spatula as a memento. They couldn't believe the size of it, maybe two inches by three inches. Purina wrote a story about Wallace, which came out the next day, one day before the IDC. The Associated Press picked up the piece, and it ran in dozens of publications around the country, most often under the headline KITCHEN SPATULA COMES BETWEEN PIT BULL AND FRISBEE EVENT.

Roo laughed. The spatula incident got more publicity than any of Wallace's victories, and his renown only grew. Somehow, Wallace had turned his outsize appetite and bad manners into a positive. Again.

3

Clara had put on a brave face through her mother's last days, but after the funeral her own condition worsened. Besides the lethargy and sadness, she started having heart palpitations. At times her heart raced. At other moments it beat erratically. The episodes varied in duration, but they scared her. She tried to talk herself through it, to tell herself that the flutterings were temporary and harmless, but they would not subside. Finally, terrified, she called the doctor.

The initial appointment led to a series of tests and visits to specialists. All the while Roo did what he could to comfort her and help. The results seemed to take forever. Finally, they heard.

Clara's heart was fine, showing no inherent damage or problems. The flutters she felt were likely a result of stress. The tests, however, did not come up completely blank. Clara had hypothyroidism, meaning that her thyroid gland was not producing enough of the three essential hormones it secreted. She began to tear up as the doctor rattled off the major symptoms associated with the condition: depression, fatigue, weakness, unexplained weight gain.

Suddenly it all made sense. The sadness, the apathy, the extra pounds. Her mother's struggle had played a part, no doubt, but more than anything a physical problem had been causing her mental struggles. The worst part of it: The condition was eminently treatable. Clara began taking synthetic hormones, and her life changed almost immediately. She was happier. She had more energy. She felt better. She felt more like her old self.

The tests revealed something else, too. Clara had a gluten allergy. She switched to a gluten-free diet. With the new diet and the thyroid medication her weight began to drop, she regained even more energy, and the old Clara began to emerge physically as well. Within a few months she had lost thirty pounds.

The stunning thing to her was the shift in perspective. Until she began to feel better, she hadn't realized how bad she'd felt for so long. The degree of her unhappiness and the state of her lethargy had been almost invisible to her while she was experiencing them, but looking back on that time from a healthy place shocked her. Only in retrospect was she aware of how much she had been suffering.

She started running again, cooking healthy meals, and going to the gym with Roo. Wallace and playing disc had kept them connected at the darkest times, and her mother's death had pushed her to the doctor's office, saving everything.

Roo felt incredible relief. He was so happy for Clara. He'd never lost sight of who she was and what she could be, and seeing her robbed of her abilities and drive—of her entire personality, really—had been difficult and troubling. His marriage had wavered over the open field and he had refused to give up on it. And now that he'd recaptured it, he wasn't letting go.

————

In the spring of 2008 Roo and Clara had adopted a sixth dog, Hector, a survivor of Bad Newz Kennels, NFL star Michael Vick's dog-fighting operation. Roo began to make appearances with Hector, who bore scars up and down his chest, not only at local events but on several national TV shows. With his steady demeanor and welcoming personality, despite what had clearly been a horrific previous life, Hector became an even more prominent figure in the pit bull struggle than Wallace.

Wallace was not forgotten, though. Roo and Wallace had never competed in a U.S. Disc Dog Nationals event—the only one of the major circuits they'd missed—and Roo felt it was a box they needed to check. One weekend in May, Roo and a buddy put Wallace into the car and hauled out to Ohio for a USDDN event.

Roo and Wallace won. Check.

Back at home, Roo threw the disc to Wallace when he could, but they had definitely settled into some sort of semiretirement. Wallace had begun to slow down. Or at least slow for Wallace, which was still high energy compared to most dogs. He continued to struggle with his allergies, and he started to accumulate other assorted injuries—a strained hamstring, dental issues.

Roo had seen other guys starting to incorporate more athletic moves, much like his, into their routines. He saw spinning air bounces and jump-skip throws. He also noticed that more pit bulls were turning up on the disc-dog circuits—Karma, Bella, Echo, and Big Mamma Jubilee were taking what he and Wallace had started and running with it.

For Roo this was the most satisfying development. He'd spent the previous years fighting to prove that Wallace and all the pit bull–type breeds were worthy and capable dogs in spite of their tendencies and attributes. Now, though, he'd seen enough other dogs to know that no one trait is specific to one type of dog. All breeds produce individual dogs that are highly driven and may have issues with other dogs. More than once Roo saw other handlers on the podium shielding their dog to keep it away from the one next to it, or restraining them in the warm-up area. Wallace hadn't succeeded because or in spite of his breed; he'd succeeded and struggled because of his individual personality. Roo could already see that the next group of disc-catching pit bulls wouldn't be viewed as such oddities, that they'd be seen simply as dogs. He hoped that one day soon that would be true everywhere—in parks, at shelters, in courts. Problem dogs were problem dogs, regardless of breed, and good ones were good, despite what they looked like.

Roo took the arrival of this new generation as a sign that he and Wallace had accomplished enough and it was probably best for them to ride off into the sunset. Until he got a call from Josh. The AWI had been having sponsorship problems and as a result had held virtually no events in all of 2009. To make up for it the organizers were having a one-time, everyone-is-welcome competition for the world championship. It was a chance to grab one of the biggest titles in the game and get Wallace's name inscribed on the Lander Cup without slogging through qualifying. One day, two rounds of free-style and a toss-and-catch session. Roo couldn't resist.

In the two weeks leading up to Naperville, Roo tried to squeeze in some practice time with Wallace. Something didn't feel right, though. When they got on the field, almost nothing worked, and what did lacked fluidity and precision. Roo pushed harder, but the more he tried, the worse they seemed to get.

"I don't know," he told Clara, "maybe the injuries are catching up to him. It just doesn't feel like we have it anymore."

"He'll come around," she said. "It's worth a try." Inside, she didn't know if it was. She, too, worried about Wallace's health. The last thing she wanted to see was another injury.

On Labor Day weekend, he and Clara loaded up the dogs and took off. When they reached Illinois Roo took Wallace out for another practice, and it felt as if they had gotten worse. Josh and Jen showed up later that day. Roo asked for help, and Josh watched Roo and Wallace practice.

"What's the rush?" he asked when they were done. "Finish a move. Take a breath. Set up the next move."

"That's it?" Roo asked.

Josh shrugged.

Roo once again sang the national anthem to kick off the festivities. He took Wallace onto the field and tried to remember what
Josh had told him. He made the first toss and took a breath. He
moved to the next throw. He slowed everything down and the routine just clicked. Roo was excellent; Wallace was astounding. On
the sidelines, as Josh filmed the action Clara came up and hugged
him from behind. She realized how much she missed him and Jen,
especially now that she was in a better place to enjoy their company.

When the first round ended, Roo and Wallace were tied for
third. The toss-and-catch round started immediately, and the pair
did great. They hit their first four throws and as Wallace sped down
the field for the fifth he launched into the air. He caught the disc:
five for five with a bonus point. As Wallace raced back to Roo the
announcer counted down the seconds. "Nine, eight, seven, six . . ."
If Roo could get another throw off before time ran out, it would
count. He clapped and encouraged Wallace, who sped on despite
his weariness.

"Five, four, three . . ." Wallace gobbled up the final few yards.
Roo grabbed the disc from his mouth and flicked it up the field. He
didn't want to throw it too far because he knew Wallace first had to
stop his momentum, then accelerate again in the other direction,
not the easiest move for the big guy. Roo also tried to get the disc
high in the air to give Wallace time, but in his haste the throw came
off his hand oddly and the disc flew lower than he wanted.

Wallace shot after it and as the disc fluttered down he ran with
desperation, lowering his head and lunging. He was too late. The
disc hit the ground and Wallace pounced on top of it. Roo threw
his arms up. A good catch would have given them an extra few
points, which didn't seem like much, but by the time the toss and
catch ended, only a few tenths of a point separated the top three
teams. Roo and Wallace were number three. Danny and Guinan
were number two.

Before the final round Roo sat with Clara under the tent. Should he try the jumping brush kick? The under-the-leg skip throw? They were high risk.

"What did you tell that ESPN interviewer after the IDC about playing with Wallace?" Clara asked.

Roo cocked an eyebrow, rolled his head to the side. "That he leaves it all out there, every time, you know?" Clara looked over at Wallace, who sat in his crate.

"He's not getting any younger," Clara said.

Roo nodded. "Yep," he said, looking over at the crate. "Yep, yep."

In the final round Roo emptied his bag of tricks. He tried everything—the jumps, the skips, the kicks, the rolls. Some of the attempts came off beautifully, some of them were beautiful disasters, but when they were done, they were done. They'd given their all.

It wasn't enough to win. They passed Danny and Guinan, but they finished second. Roo thought for a moment about the final throw of the toss-and-catch round. A completion there would have won the cup. They had been that close, but he refused to allow himself even a moment of sadness over it.

4

The move came as a surprise. In the fall, Animal Farm Foundation had offered Roo a job as its director of enrichment, a position that would allow him to do as much community outreach as he could and work with dogs every day. It was a dream opportunity. The catch? The Yoris would have to move to upstate New York.

Roo and Clara talked about it long into the night. It would be hard to leave Minnesota, but in a way, they felt as though they were starting over, as if they were remaking the life they had once dreamed of and almost lost. Maybe a change of location would reinforce all the progress they'd made. Clean break, fresh start. Roo accepted.

In November, he and Wallace left for New York and got settled. Clara closed down operations in Minnesota, then she and the rest of the dogs went east in April. The adjustment was difficult. Outside of Roo's coworkers, they knew no one. They missed their friends and family. More than ever, they were thankful to have each other. And the dogs. They bought an old ambulance—the big boxy type—dubbed it the Dogulance and took road trips as often as possible.

Roo liked the job and Clara once again found work as a barista, but it wasn't the same. When June rolled around they reminisced wistfully about Rochesterfest. The stroll down memory lane led to a decision: When the weekend came, they packed the dogs into the Dogulance and set off for Minnesota.

They spent the next two days visiting with friends and soaking up the town. Roo, of course, entered Wallace in the flying-disc contest. Wallace won. When the weekend ended, the ride back to New York seemed like the longest haul of their lives. They felt like they were leaving behind everything they loved.

Roo, though, knew it wouldn't be long before they were back in the Midwest, at least temporarily. Wallace's latest win qualified them for the AWI finals. Roo figured one more trip back to Naperville for one last shot at the Lander Cup would be perfect. If Wallace finally won the prize in his last competition, no screenwriter could script a better ending.

Roo and Wallace were able to practice a bit over the summer, and they had developed a few new moves. Roo thought the stuff was pretty good, enough so that when Labor Day arrived and they fired up the Dogulance, he felt optimistic about their chances, but they knew it could be Wallace's final run.

As usual, they didn't dwell on the topic, but it came up. "This could be it for him," Clara said on the way out.

"I know," Roo said. "I know."

Josh and Jen met the New Yorkers at the event and the four quickly fell into their familiar routines. The women talked; the guys plotted Wallace's grand finale. "You guys want to be alone for a few minutes?" Jen teased. Clara mimicked a little kissing noise. Roo went to get Wallace out of the car. As Roo lifted Wallace out of the crate, the dog gave a sharp yelp. Roo quickly released Wallace. The dog stood awkwardly and moved gingerly. He tried to shake himself but couldn't.

Roo couldn't believe it. He didn't know what had happened or even if he had caused the problem. It could have been a preexisting injury that he somehow aggravated, but from the way Wallace stood, Roo guessed it was a back problem, though he couldn't be sure. A river ran along the side of the park and Roo took Wallace down to the banks. He thought that maybe if Wallace relaxed a little and walked around, whatever was bothering him would loosen up. But within minutes it was clear Wallace wouldn't be able to compete. The dream was over. As carefully as he could, Roo picked Wallace up and started back for the Dogulance. Clara had come to check on him and as she walked up, she looked at Wallace and saw the expression on Roo's face and instantly teared up.

Roo and Clara got Wallace back in the car, and Roo started back toward the tent to tell the others. But as he began to think about what he would say, as the very words formed in his head, he felt something rising within himself. He thought at first he could ignore it, or maybe control it, but as it bubbled up it grew stronger, until he knew he could not stop it. Instead of going to the tent, Roo turned and went directly to the cab of the Dogulance. He slammed the door and everything inside of him burst out. He cried like he hadn't cried since he was a child.

It wasn't sadness coming out of him really. It was something else—pride, appreciation, astonishment. He thought of where Wallace had come from and everywhere he'd gone. The pit bull that no one wanted, bouncing off the walls at Paws & Claws. The outsider on the disc-dog circuit, from the wrong side of the tracks, with the wrong pedigree, unproven and distrusted. The surprise champion, changing hearts and minds with every catch. Finally, the established veteran, paving the way for others. Everything, all the accomplishments and accolades, was a result of Wallace's intelligence and drive, his willingness to pour himself completely into the task at hand, and his unrelenting desire.

Personally, Roo couldn't help but feel that Wallace had kept him and Clara together. At those moments when their connection to each other was strained, their commitment to Wallace and to the larger cause he embodied bridged the gap. They could always talk about him. Even during their most tenuous times, they came together while competing with him and treating his various ailments.

Now it was all over. That reality hit Roo hard and suddenly. The win in Rochester back in June would be Wallace's final competition, and that seemed right: one last moment of glory in front of the hometown crowd.

———

Another ending loomed for Roo and Clara. Life in New York, though nice, wasn't for them. They missed Minnesota. They belonged in Minnesota. Early in 2011, Roo left Animal Farm, packed up the dogs, and drove back home. They bounced around for a few months before landing, once again, in Rochester. Roo got a job at Mayo. He renewed his real estate license, too. Clara returned to Dunn Bros. Their new house had room for all the dogs and a large fenced-in yard.

Wallace continued to be plagued by his allergies. Back in New York he'd started a new medication regimen. He broke out in sores and developed patches of calluses on his body. Eventually, a new vet realized the medicine was causing the problem and made a change. Clara and Roo put Wallace on a raw-food diet, and those two things seemed to help. Still, in New York he had developed a problem with his front left leg that made it hard for him to walk. The new vet put the leg in a metal brace, which relieved the strain, and preached patience. The Yoris, between jobs at the time and cash-poor from the move, held an online auction of Wallace and Hector memorabilia to raise money for the vet bills.

Wallace convalesced throughout the winter and eventually resumed walking normally without the brace. Roo worked with him on a conditioning plan meant to build him back up and ward off any relapses as much as he could, but his responsibilities were many and his time limited.

Then the first warm day of spring, Roo led Wallace out to the car and drove to Quarry Hill Park, where they had spent so many hours working out their routine. As he climbed out of the car, Roo thought about the houses he had to sell and the projects waiting for him in his own home. He worried too about Wallace's health and how much the dog's body could take. But when he opened the back door and Wallace saw the discs in his hand all other thoughts left his head.

Wallace bounded from the car and romped onto the grass, moving in a way Roo hadn't seen in more than a year. The disc, red and unmarked, cut an arc across the sky. Wallace's tail went stiff, his ears pinned back, and his feet tore at the ground. "Go," Roo yelled. "Go!" He had forsaken everything for one more day in the park, playing disc with his dog.

Acknowledgments

Roo and Clara Yori
Josh and Jen Grenell
Patti Evans
Amy Schoenwetter
Sue Stanek
Christina Curtis
Sheronne Mulry
Amy King
Ron and Lynda Yori

Bill Shinker
Lisa Johnson
Jessica Sindler
Lauren Marino
Lindsay Gordon
Matthew Carnicelli
Maura Fritz

Grace Gorant
Alex Gorant
Karin Henderson Gorant

For more information about pit bulls and breed-specific legislation, check out the following sites:

Animal Farm Foundation	animalfarmfoundation.org
Animal Legal and Historical Center	animallaw.info
ASPCA	aspca.org
BAD RAP (Bay Area Dog Lovers Responsible About Pit Bulls)	badrap.org
Best Friends Animal Society	bestfriends.org

About the Author

JIM GORANT is a senior editor at *Sports Illustrated* and has written for *GQ*, *Men's Health*, and many other magazines. He is the author of the *New York Times* bestseller *The Lost Dogs* and a twenty-year magazine veteran. He lives in New Jersey.